HMS *Ramillies*: Vital Statisti

1917

Length: 620.5ft
Beam: 101.5ft (bulged)
Draught: 33ft 7ins deep
Displacement: 33,570 tons deep
Armament: 8 x 15in; 14 x 6in; 2 x 3in AA; 4 x 3pdr;
   5 machine guns; 10 Lewis guns; 4 x 21in torpedo tubes
Armour: belt 13in; turrets 13in; decks 1–4in
Machinery: turbines driving 4 screws; 40,000shp for 23 knots;
   18 Babcock & Wilcox oil-fired boilers
Complement: 936
Cost: £3,295,810

From: R A Burt, *British Battleships of World War One*, Seaforth Publishing 2012

1945

Length: 620.5ft
Beam: 102.5ft
Draught: 33ft 7in deep
Displacement: 35,385 tons deep
Armament: 8 x 15in; 8 x 6in; 8 x 4in twin AA; 24 x 2pdr AA;
   23 x 20mm AA
Armour: belt 13in; turrets 13in; decks 1–4in
Machinery: turbines driving 4 screws; 40,000shp for 21 knots

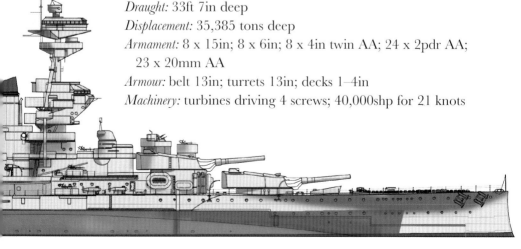

Battleship Ramillies

Battleship Ramillies

THE FINAL SALVO

Ian Johnston *with* Mick French
Foreword by HRH The Duke of Edinburgh

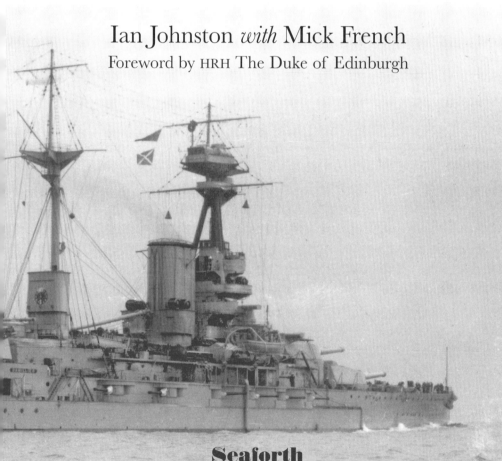

Seaforth
PUBLISHING

Previous page: *Ramillies* c1923. (Author's collection)
Following pages: *Ramillies* alongside at Liverpool May 1926.

Copyright © 2014 Ian Johnston

First published in Great Britain in 2014 by
Seaforth Publishing,
Pen & Sword Books Ltd,
47 Church Street,
Barnsley S70 2AS

www.seaforthpublishing.com

British Library Cataloguing in Publication Data
A catalogue record for this book is available from the British Library

ISBN 978 1 84832 211 0

Typeset and designed by Mousemat Design
Printed and bound in Great Britain by CPI Group (UK) Ltd, Croydon, CR0 4YY

This book is dedicated to the memory of
Eric and Dorothy Marks
who founded the HMS *Ramillies* Association

Contents

HRH Duke of Edinburgh

BUCKINGHAM PALACE

HMS 'Ramillies' was my first ship, and that is an appointment no-one forgets. I completed my Cadet training at Dartmouth at the end of 1939, and in January 1940 I set off to join the first world war battleship in Colombo. I barely had time to find my way to the Midshipman's Chest Flat, with any confidence, before we were off to Australia. After visiting Fremantle, Adelaide, Melbourne, Sydney and Darwin, we took up our duties as escort to the convoy carrying the Australian Expeditionary Force on its way to the Middle East. Meanwhile the Australians could not have been more hospitable.

The war had not yet reached the Indian Ocean, so daily life on board must have been very like the normal peace-time routine of the Royal Navy. Her Ship's Company was composed, almost entirely, of men who had joined before the outbreak of war. Among the other vestiges of the inter-war peace-time Royal Navy, she carried steam-driven picket-boats among her ship's boats. These were 'commanded' by us Midshipmen, although very much under the supervision of their Chief Petty Officer Coxswains. I certainly never witnessed life anything quite like that during the rest of my service career.

I think it was a brilliant idea of the HMS Ramillies Association to put this book together. It is a worthy tribute to all who served in her, particularly during WW2, and an invaluable record for future historians, of life in what is already an extinct form of warship.

Philip

Acknowledgements

The editors would like to thank the members of the HMS *Ramillies* Association for their assistance in the production of this book together with the relatives of former members or members deceased who provided stories left to them by their husbands or fathers. Thanks are due to Andrew Cliff and Brian Newman for proofreading the manuscript.

The photographs are those in the possession of Association members either taken or collected during their period on board or collected subsequently.

However, the collection of Ken D Williams requires special mention and it is by the courtesy of his son, Keith Williams, that we have been able to use them.

Copyright has not knowingly been infringed but should there be any questions please contact the secretary of the HMS *Ramillies* Association, Mick French, at www.hmsramillies.co.uk/default.aspx.

Introduction

In April 2011, the Association dedicated to the memory of HMS *Ramillies* met in Portsmouth to participate in remembrance and social activities. This Association, which was formed in 1978, numbers thirty in total, of whom twelve are former crew members, the remainder being wives, widows or sons of former crew members. Additionally, there is the President of the Association, John Taylor, three honorary members in New Zealand, and other members in Australia and Canada. To all of these persons *Ramillies* is an important ship. Associations such as this are necessarily few in number and one day will face the inevitable consequence of passing time. On this occasion, however, the *Ramillies* Association were hale and hearty, gathered at the Sailors' Home on Queen Street, and ready to celebrate the great ship.

Although the Association has met annually since its inception, it was the view that in this particular year it would be worth recording the memories of former crew members, together with those of others with a connection to the battleship and a tale to tell. This book is based largely on these recollections, supplemented by narratives previously written by members either deceased or unable to attend this meeting. Collectively, these memories, together with photographs of the battleship throughout its long operational history, form what might be considered as a last salvo from HMS *Ramillies*, at least in written form.

To those who served, the Royal Navy was perhaps perceived differently from the Royal Navy of today. For the first two decades of the twentieth century the Royal Navy was indisputably the largest navy in the world, and from then until World War Two, second equal to that of the United States. The Navy was seen as the guarantor of national security, the Service that had endeared itself to the country through an often illustrious history. The Fleet was an impressive sight wherever it was assembled, and of the individual ship types, none more so than the battleship. This sense of awe in their ship and respect for the Navy and its traditions is deeply embedded in those members of the *Ramillies* Association who served.

It goes without saying that a great debt of gratitude is owed by all Britons to ships like *Ramillies* and their crews, which formed the backbone of the Royal Navy in the two great conflicts of the twentieth century, and to them and the members of the *Ramillies* Association this book is dedicated.

Ian Johnston, October 2011

CHAPTER 1

HMS *Ramillies*: A Brief History

The design, fighting characteristics and operational histories of British battleships have been the subject of a large number of books and shows no sign of abating. As this book is primarily concerned with the experiences and reminiscences of those who served on board, only the briefest outline of her activities are given here, although many events are described later in subsequent chapters.

HMS *Ramillies* was one of five *Royal Sovereign*-class battleships and was laid down in November 1913 and completed in 1917. She was built by William Beardmore & Co Ltd at their Naval Construction Works at Dalmuir on the River Clyde. Because of delays in the manufacture of her main armament, the construction of *Ramillies* was held back while she lay on the stocks at Dalmuir and the opportunity was taken to fit her with anti-torpedo bulges. The delay meant that she was the last British battleship to be completed and serve during the First World War, as well as the first to be fitted with bulges.

When *Ramillies* was launched on 12 June 1916, such was the weight of her hull that her stern hit the riverbed, damaging her rudders. As she was not in danger of sinking, she was taken to the fitting-out basin for completion and in September 1917, with no dry dock on the Clyde large enough to take her, she sailed with great difficulty to Liverpool where the damage to her stern was repaired. The difficulty of taking her from the Clyde to Liverpool with non-functioning rudders, and some of her subsequent career in the Grand Fleet at Scapa Flow, are mentioned in Frederick Rollinson's story on page 19.

During the twenty years of the interwar period, *Ramillies* served with the Atlantic, Mediterranean and Home Fleets. She was refitted on four occasions from June–September 1924, September 1926–February 1927, February 1933–March 1934 and July 1938–February 1939. The appearance of the *Royal Sovereign*-class battleships was not altered radically, as was the case with other battleships, and the *Ramillies* of the Second World War, despite additional bridgework, numerous AA guns and later a clinker screen on her funnel, was still recognisable as the ship that joined the Fleet in 1917.

Had it not been for the 'battleship-building holiday' brought about by the Washington Treaty in 1922, *Ramillies* would most likely have been withdrawn from service and scrapped before the Second World War started. However, when battleship construction recommenced in 1936, the Royal Navy was able to build just six new battleships in the period before and during the War, and was obliged to keep its older battleships in service, including *Ramillies*. There are no accounts of this period in this publication, although photographs in the 1917–39 gallery give some idea of locations, conditions and crew activities.

During the Second World War, *Ramillies* served mostly in the capacity of convoy escort, able to bring her big guns to bear should enemy raiders attack. At the start of the War, *Ramillies* was with the Home Fleet, but was transferred briefly to the Mediterranean Fleet in October, and then again to the East Indies in November. From this station *Ramillies* sailed for the first time to the Far East. Service with the Eastern Fleet, the Home Fleet off the coast of Normandy, and bombardment duties off the south coast of France in August 1944 saw the fighting career of *Ramillies* brought to a close.

Many of these momentous events are described here through the eyes and minds of those who were there, including the brief period after the war in the Reserve Fleet at Portsmouth, prior to her final trip in 1948 to the ship breakers in Scotland.

HMS *Ramillies* Association

In common with many other warships of Second World War vintage and after, a crew association for Ramillies *was established, primarily to enable former comrades to meet and discuss old times. The present Secretary of the* Ramillies *Association, Mick French, tells the story of the Association and his own interest in the battleship* Ramillies.

The Association was started by Dorothy and Eric Marks, twenty-one years ago. Eric served on *Ramillies* as a chef. He put an advert in the *Navy News* to see if anyone would be interested in starting up a group, and I think about 120 responses overwhelmed him. The reunions began, and it just grew and grew. More and more members came into it but obviously, over the years, a lot of members fell by the wayside because age was catching up on them.

I could have gone to the very first meeting, but I did not think at the time that it was my sort of thing, and I never went until about nine years ago, when I finally plucked up the courage and went along. My interest in *Ramillies* is because my father served on her as a Royal Marine, and was on board her for about six months around the time when D-Day took place. He never said much about things like that, but if he did talk about anything concerning the war, then it was always the *Ramillies*.

Although a large number of Associations have disbanded, we have kept going, because the members that are left want to keep going, and I think they have put it down to me to keep it going. I do it with pride because they are a wonderful group of people: they are friends rather than associates, and we keep in touch all the year round; I really enjoy meeting up with them and now wish I had joined the Association long before I did.

Royal Marine Ken French, who served on *Ramillies* in 1944, father of Mick French.

Ramillies was always known as a happy ship, and lifelong friendships have been formed because of this ship – it just goes on from there. I can't say much about my dad; as I said, he never talked about it, although I know he saw some horrible sights. He also went to Israel when that was set up, although that has nothing to do with the *Ramillies*, as he was on HMS *Phoebe* and on HMS *Coventry*. HMS *Coventry* sank shortly after he came off it, so he thinks he was a lucky man himself. He served in the Mediterranean, he saw some sights there that he never wanted to see again, and I don't think that he ever did.

There is a story of a grass skirt called a *piupiu*. *Ramillies* was the first capital ship to visit New Zealand when she went to the Antipodes to pick up the first echelon of New Zealand and Australian troops who were en route to the war. While they were in New Zealand, they had a concert party on board which was performed by the Maoris. While they did this performance and dance the Maoris wore these *piupiu* skirts. At the end of the performance, the chief Maori presented the captain of the *Ramillies* with a grass skirt and gave it a legend; I cannot read the legend, but it was something along the lines of 'whoever wears this grass skirt into battle will come to no harm'. This was taken to mean the ship, as well as the captain.

Her crew certainly believed this story, because when they went to D-Day the ship had three torpedoes fired at it which went down either side and the *Ramillies* was actually manoeuvring. She went hard astern and she was going to one side: if she had not been manoeuvring, those torpedoes would have hit her and undoubtedly sunk her. At the end of the day they passed the *Ramillies*, and a couple of the crew members actually saw the trails of the torpedoes going past and they hit, I think, a Norwegian warship behind called the *Svenner*; she immediately blew up, broke in half, and sank within minutes – that could have been the *Ramillies*. Unfortunately, because of the action they were not allowed to pick up any survivors, because they did not know at that time if there was going to be anything else, so they had to steam past the survivors.

Anyway, the *piupiu* grass skirt was also worn in the South of France, and again no ill came to the crew or the ship. It was also worn on what was called Operation Ironclad, which was where Royal Marine commandos and other people went into Diego Suarez at Madagascar, which was governed by the Free French at the time; they were enemies of Britain, and I think within a few hours the French had surrendered. Again no harm came to the crew on shore, but the ship was actually torpedoed by a Japanese submarine. It was a miniature submarine; they caught the two members from the sub the same day. They were killed one way or another; their grave is still marked over there. Apparently, they did sink another ship, an Esso tanker, which was subsequently raised and was taken over to Bikini Atoll to be destroyed during the first atom bomb testing.

There are all sorts of rumours about the *Ramillies*. Although she was holed, she did not sink, there were no great injuries to the crew, and there are stories that she was steamed sternwards all the way to Durban for repairs. We have it on authority that she was repaired in situ and then steamed slowly to Durban, where she had temporary repairs, and then she was sent back to Devonport for final repairs. Again the *piupiu* did its job. They had great faith in it. We don't know what happened to the original *piupiu*, and at one of our meetings a member from New Zealand was asked to see if he could get a replacement *piupiu*, which he did, and it was sent over via him from the son of the actual chief who presented the first one. So we now have the replica which is kept in the Royal Marines Museum in Portsmouth, and every two years when we hold our meeting we get it from the museum and bring it in, and it takes pride of place in our display of memorabilia.

Another thing to mention is that when the Maori Ngati'poneke tribe were performing on board the ship their song, although I can't say the Maori version, the English version is called 'Now is the Hour', and that was adopted as the ship's song. It is still sung at our reunions to this day, and everyone still sings it with pride.

I am so pleased that Ian Johnston had the idea of recording our members and suggested turning these memories into a book. It is a very fitting tribute to the men of the *Ramillies* and their comrades in the Royal Navy of the Second World War.

I will keep the society going as long as the members want it to keep going and am proud to do so; I just can't do enough for them. If I can organise the reunions to their satisfaction, then I am pleased to do so for as long as I am able.

CHAPTER 2

Early Days

Frederick Rollinson: serving on *Ramillies* 1917–1919

Preparing to join the Fleet

My name is Frederick Rollinson. I am ninety-three years old. In 1916 I was working for the Great Northern Railway Company in my home town of Ilkeston in Derbyshire. I was in a reserved occupation and wore a khaki armband indicating that I had been 'attested' for the army, but shortly after my nineteenth birthday I decided to volunteer for the Royal Navy. Three days after signing up, in the first week of November 1916, I reported for preliminary training at Crystal Palace, which had been taken over for the duration.

After three months' training I was sent to Devonport, initially to an old battleship lying in harbour, HMS *Vengeance*, being used as a dormitory ship since the barracks were full. After a week or two, we were transferred to the RN camp at Torpoint in Cornwall where a crew was being mustered for a new battleship, which we learned was to be HMS *Ramillies*.

On 5 May 1917 we arrived at Clydebank in Glasgow to join *Ramillies*, lying at the side of Beardmore's yard from where she had been launched on 12 September 1916. She was still being fitted out, but a major problem was the damage caused to her rudder during the launch. This could only be repaired in dry dock and so, after a short time, we set off for Liverpool. On the way, at Greenock, arrangements were made for her to steam the measured mile. As she could only be steered by the propellers, she went aground twice and had to wait for the tide to float her off.

The journey to Liverpool was accomplished by having four tugs ahead and two at the stern as well as a destroyer escort. At the end of May we arrived at Gladstone Dock where the ship was to remain for three months, swarming with dockyard mateys while her rudder was repaired and fitting out completed. She was also painted in jazzy camouflage colours. During that time we had lots of field training and drill ashore and also plenty of leave – I went home on leave three times.

At the end of August 1917 we left Liverpool for Scapa Flow to join the Grand Fleet. We were rather a motley crew under Captain Grant[1], an Australian, and his second-in-command, Commander Round-Turner.[2] Half of the crew of about a thousand men were (like me) Hostilities Only (HO) men and the remainder of the Navy personnel were regulars or RFR, RNR, RNVR. There were also about a hundred Marines – Royal Marine Light Infantry and big fellows from the Royal Marine Artillery. The Marines manned the two after turrets. We also carried a number of gunnery experts from HMS *Excellent* at Portsmouth whose purpose was to test the main armaments – the eight 15in and the fourteen 6in guns. *Ramillies* also had two 3pdrs, two ack-ack guns and four torpedo tubes.

The Grand Fleet

We arrived in Scapa Flow in the dark and, lit up by the searchlights, our colourful appearance caused some surprise. However, we were not to go on patrol with the Fleet for some time. Several times the signal flags indicated 'Fleet get ready for sea. Speed 20 knots. Negative *Ramillies*', and we would stay behind to carry out gunnery practice in the Pentland Firth. After several weeks, around the end of October, we were allowed to join the Grand Fleet. *Ramillies*, together with her sister ships *Royal Sovereign*, *Royal Oak*, *Revenge* and *Resolution*, formed the first division of the first battle squadron. The second division of the first squadron was formed by the older *Benbow* class – *Iron Duke*, *Empress of India*, *Marlborough* and *Benbow* with HMS *Canada*.

There were two other squadrons in the main body of the Grand Fleet formed by the battleships *Agincourt*, *Collingwood*, *Centurion*, *Conqueror*, *Thunderer*, *Bellerophon*, *Colossus*, *Monarch*, *Indomitable*, *Inflexible*, *Australia* and *New Zealand*, the latter two being manned by nations of those countries. In the centre of the Fleet was Admiral of the Fleet Lord Beatty in a light cruiser. Ahead of the Fleet was the battlecruiser squadron, including *Queen Elizabeth*, *Warspite*, *Barham*, *Malaya*, *Valiant*, *Furious*, *Courageous*, *Glorious*, *Repulse* and *Renown*. Bringing up the rear was a squadron of US Navy ships including *New York*, *Arkansas* and *Delaware*. There were, of course, the usual escorting destroyers and other ships. The whole Fleet formed quite a spectacle and must have been intimidating to the Germans for we were to spend the rest of the war patrolling the North Sea and calling in at Rosyth or Scapa Flow, but without seeing any action.

Life on board

I considered living conditions to be quite good. We sat on forms at tables, one end of which was hinged to the bulkhead and the other end supported by iron rods hung from the deck above. I had no problem sleeping in a hammock, in spite of the limited space allowed. The air-conditioning was effective. We bathed in tin baths. The food was plentiful and we could supplement it by using the canteen on board which was manned by Navy and Army canteen personnel who, nevertheless, were allocated action stations. The chaplain doubled as the ship's censor. When we were in Scapa Flow we could go on shore parties to the island of Flotta where there were such facilities as a YMCA and a football pitch. They also organised religious services which I sometimes attended, having been a Salvation Army bandsman. We always had to row ourselves back to the ship.

On board I met a fellow musician, a storekeeper who played the drums – to such effect that he, a sailor, was sometimes included in the Marines' band, even marching with the band on shore. One day the band was short of a cornet player and I was asked to help out. However, the sight of two sailors marching with the Marines was considered too unconventional and neither of us was asked again.

After a time I upgraded from ordinary seaman to torpedoman with an increase in pay from one shilling (5p) a day to one shilling and threepence,[3] plus a small allowance in lieu of my rum ration. My duties not only involved dealing with torpedoes, including recovering practice torpedoes by boat, but also general help with electrical jobs. I committed one small misdemeanour. I was told to man a telephone exchange and, being new to the job, I put the plug in the wrong socket and consequently buzzed the wrong officer. As a punishment, he ordered me to 'touch the trunk' of the mainmast. Being nimble (then!), I soon shinned up the ladders and, in an act of bravado, with one hand on the top of the mast and one foot on a rung, I held the other arm and leg out in space to the amusement of the hands on deck as well as the officer concerned, Lt Cdr (later Admiral) Wake-Walker,[4] who, fortunately, had a sense of humour. However, as a result of this incident, I was thereafter often chosen for tasks aloft.

The Ramillies aeroplane

Both *Ramillies* and *Queen Elizabeth* carried observation balloons, winched up and down from the quarterdeck. They were not completely successful; our observer managed to fall in the sea on one occasion. During 1918, *Ramillies* was supplied with an aeroplane – a small biplane (Sopwith Pup?). A runway formed of detachable plates was fitted in harbour across the top of 'B' turret and extended above the guns on supports attached to the barrels. The total length of the runway was probably no more than 60ft. The plane could only take off with the ship steaming full ahead into the wind. There was, of course, no question of the aircraft returning to the ship to land. In fact, it took off twice. The first time it landed somewhere in Scotland and it was returned to us on a supply ship. After its second flight we did not see it again. We were told that it had crashed on landing, but we never learned of the fate of the pilot.

Another innovation fitted to *Ramillies* was that of anti-torpedo bulges or 'blisters', forming a second skin on each side of the ship. These must have appreciably reduced her maximum speed. One of the blisters came adrift and we had to put into Invergordon, where there was a dry dock in which repairs could be carried out.

End of the war

In November 1918, immediately following the Armistice, we put into Rosyth where the country-wide flu epidemic hit the Fleet. More than half of the *Ramillies*' crew were laid up in their hammocks. All of the Marines' boy buglers were affected and so for a week I acted as ship's bugler, a full-time job giving the various calls in all parts of the ship (and ducking flying shoes I shouted reveille!). Restrictions were lifted and we were able to go ashore quite often and visit Edinburgh, Dunfermline and other towns in the area. In April 1919 we were lying at Invergordon, and from there I was demobbed. Because of my railway knowledge, I helped in arranging the routeing of a special train heading south, taking those of us who were being demobbed. After a journey of nineteen hours I reached Ilkeston, and did not see *Ramillies* again, although I have always retained my affection for her.

William Beardmore & Co, builder of *Ramillies*, had a large shipyard at Dalmuir on the Clyde, and an equally large steel and ordnance works at Parkhead in Glasgow.

Photo Gallery: Launch to 1939

Ramillies under the shipbuilding gantry on the day of her launch, 16 October 1916. At least part of the reason why the ship hit the riverbed during her launch is because of the extra weight worked into her hull while she lay on the stocks waiting for her main armament, as there was no point in launching her to take up valuable space in the fitting-out basin. The opportunity was taken to fit her with bulges, which meant that much of her side armour had to be fitted first, bringing her launch weight to 18,750 tons, compared to the 9,000–12,000 tons of her class.

Ramillies, almost completed, in the fitting-out basin at Dalmuir.

Watched by shipyard workers, *Ramillies* leaves Dalmuir on the Clyde to begin what would be a difficult journey to Liverpool because of her damaged rudders. She was repaired in Liverpool by Cammell Laird.

Ramillies with her dazzle camouflage in Scapa Flow. (Imperial War Museum)

Above and lower right: *Ramillies* sporting the dazzle camouflage she wore from shortly after completion until March 1918. The colours included pink, blue, black, white and grey. Unfortunately, no photographic image showing the starboard side was found.

Another R-class, *Royal Sovereign*, during exercises with the Grand Fleet in the North Sea in early 1918. (Author's collection)

The quarterdeck of *Ramillies* in early 1918, with *Resolution* and *Royal Sovereign* astern.
(Author's collection)

Ramillies with an Iron Duke battleship and the battlecruiser *Tiger* off the starboard bow. The searchlight platform on the foremast, which served to identify *Ramillies* from the rest of her class, has been removed.

Hoisting a Sopwith Pup on board from a pontoon. Note the deflection scales painted on 'B' turret.

A photographic postcard of two young men on board *Ramillies*. On the reverse side it says 'Me & my chum, taken on starb'd side boat deck by B turret. HMS *Ramillies*, Grand Fleet 8 October 1917.'

On 20 January 1921, the steam-driven submarine *K5*, having given the signal to dive, failed to resurface for reasons unknown. All fifty-seven members of her crew perished. RN ships held services when they passed over the area where *K5* sank. In this photograph taken two months later on 20 March, the crew of HMS *Ramillies* are assembled on the battleship's quarterdeck, where a memorial service for the men of *K5* is underway. Note the white ensign at half mast.

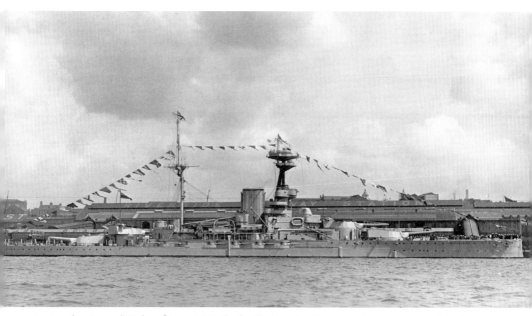

During the General Strike of May 1926, the battleships *Ramillies* and *Barham* were sent to the Mersey to deliver food supplies, although others interpreted this as a more sinister development. Here *Ramillies* is seen at the Princess landing stage at Liverpool dressed overall and attracting the attention of many Liverpudlians.

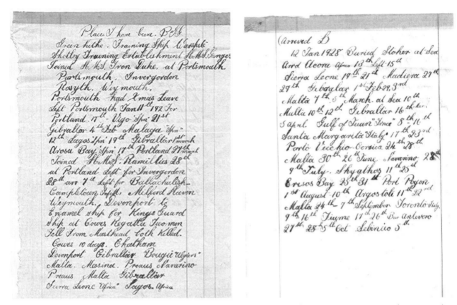

Ramillies on her travels: extracts from a diary setting out the ship's movements at this period.

A sketch made by stoker B Goodenough of the Mediterranean Fleet as it was in March 1928: *Queen Elizabeth, Valiant, Warspite, Resolution, Ramillies, Royal Oak* and *Eagle*. (Mrs E Jarvis)

A snapshot of life on board *Ramillies* in 1928.

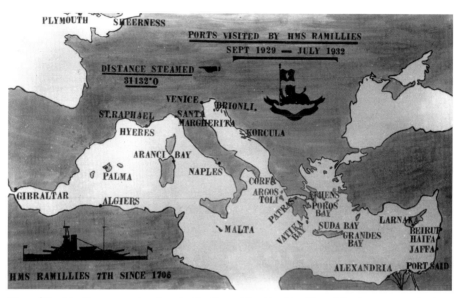

Map of the Mediterranean showing destinations visited by *Ramillies* while she was attached to the Mediterranean Fleet during the twenty-three-month period, September 1929 to July 1932. Some of the photographs that follow were taken during this period.

'Some of the boys'.

Dated December 1929, the caption simply states 'My friend the Count'.

Dated 4 October 1929, the caption written on the back says 'Lowering the cutter during watch evolution'.

Aground! In January 1930, *Ramillies* ran aground at Fort St Angelo Point, at the centre of Grand Harbour, Malta. She is seen here with her forefoot firmly stuck as the rest of the ship fell with the tide.

Ramillies, Malta, 1929: The V&W-class destroyer *Viceroy* can be seen in the background.

Malta, 1929: *Ramillies* with two other R-class behind, *Resolution* with the funnel screen. A *Queen Elizabeth*-class battleship as at right.

The forecastle, forward 15in guns and bridge structure of *Ramillies* in 1929.

Ramillies, photographed in French Creek, Malta, in 1929.

On the passage from Port Said to Malta in December 1929, the ship ran into heavy weather. The booms lying on the forecastle deck have been lifted off their cradle.

The ship's chapel at Christmas 1929.

A cutter has been displaced during heavy weather on the passage from Port Said to Malta in December 1929.

A cable reel has been knocked off its mountings in the storm on the way from Port Said to Malta in December 1929.

In May 1930, Amy Johnson became the first woman to fly solo in a Gypsy Moth from Britain (Croydon) to Australia (Darwin), completing the 11,000-mile journey in nineteen days. On her return journey by sea in the P&O liner *Naldera*, she stopped at Port Said on 28 July 1930, where *Ramillies* was berthed. She is seen here being welcomed on board by Captain Richard William Tilley, officers, and crew, before sailing to Cairo from where she flew home to London.

Amy Johnson posed with the captain and officers of *Ramillies*.

This informal picture shows the obvious interest the crew took in the flyer's presence on board. She is seen here passing the engineers' shop.

Ramillies at her berth in Port Said in July 1930.

Three photographs taken of crew members relaxing at the beach in Malta in July 1930.

Undated picture of the crew of *Ramillies*, probably taken in 1930.

September 1930. A makeshift boxing ring rigged on the quarterdeck complete with lights. The red corner is to the left.

A Fairey Flycatcher on the flying-off platform on top of 'B' turret during flying-off trials, probably about 1924. HMS *Hood* is off the battleship's port quarter.

The Fairey Flycatcher takes to the air. Note what appears to be a smoke marker that has been fired off the starboard bow to indicate wind.

A practice shoot with main and secondary armament off Gibraltar in the 1930s.

Ramillies making smoke.

The ship at Torbay in the 1930s.

Tell England is a film about the First World War Gallipoli campaign, based on a novel written by Ernest Raymond. *Ramillies* and *Royal Sovereign*, serving with the Mediterranean Fleet, were filmed off Malta in 1930 in scenes recreating the fighting in the Dardanelles Straits.

A cartoon drawn by Jack Kettle, who drew cartoons of Royal Navy subjects in the 1920s and '30s.

A view forward from the quarterdeck as *Ramillies* prepares to pass under the Forth Bridge in the mid 1920s.

Looking aft from the forecastle in March 1939 at Malta.

This photograph from March 1939 was captioned 'Our Popeye'.

The port side pom-pom abreast the funnel preparing to fire, May 1939.

The port side pom-pom firing, May 1939. Note the floatplane visible in this shot.

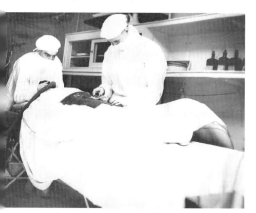

The ship's operating theatre in this, presumably posed, photograph taken in May 1939.

A detachment of sailors from *Ramillies*, taking part in the King's Birthday Parade at Gibraltar on 8 June 1938.

July 1939 and the ship is practising abandon ship at St Raphäel on the Côte d'Azur.

Royal Marines from *Ramillies*, taking part in the King's Birthday Parade at Gibraltar on 8 June 1938.

Serving on *Ramillies*: A Bird's Eye View

Harry Staff: A Bird's Eye View

On 11 January 1943, with five other ratings, I reported to HMS *Vernon* (Electrical Division) Portsmouth after a week's leave, prior to completing a Seaman Torpedoman's (S/T) Course at HMS *St Vincent*, Gosport. The six of us had met at Waterloo station, arriving about midday. Imagine our surprise when being allocated chief and petty officer's (C/PO) messman duties. However, the Wren in the drafting office intimated we would not be around very long.

Having collected our kit, found our headquarters and had a meal, we were permitted to use the CPO and POs' lounge. At approximately 1500 hours, the SRE came to life. One of our party, who was playing snooker, was summoned to the drafting office. He returned looking glum-submarine; from then on, over the next two hours, four more of us made swift exits in the order of submarine, minesweeper, submarine, and myself to a battleship, HMS *Ramillies*. It was not until December that I found out how the sixth member, A/B Harper, S/T, had fared. I was leaning over the guard-rail in Mombasa, East Africa, watching a submarine entering harbour. About six ratings were lined up for'ard. As she passed one of them shouted out, 'Up your fat ar**, Staff!' It was now Leading Seaman Harper.

Fortunately, most of my gear was still in my kitbag, so with case packed, hammock under my arm, and kitbag over my shoulder, I proceeded to the despatching area. After a long period of waiting, I was transported to Royal Naval barracks (RNB) *Victory*. Here my kit was left at the heavy gun battery, and I was joined by other members of the draft. At this point the memory fades, but the next I remember was lining up prior to boarding a train for Devonport in a group mustered by L/SG Lunne, LTO. The party numbered about 150. We were each given a bag containing bread, cheese, a large Cornish pasty (tiddy oggy) and, I believe, an apple.

We travelled through the night, arriving on a cold, damp, 12 January morning at Devonport station, completing our journey to the dockyard by truck. The dockyard was a hive of activity, lorries were flying about, riveting and chipping hammers were kicking up a racket, and ratings in overalls were performing all manner of chores. Various craft were in the basin and dry dock.

The old cruiser HMS *Colombo* was undergoing a major refit. Two destroyers showed signs of damage.

The dockyard and surrounding towns of Devonport and Plymouth had sustained extensive air-raid damage. It was amazing how normal life carried on. Stores like Woolworth's, Marks & Spencer, and all manner of shops were under canvas. In Plymouth, the rubble around Drake Circus had been piled up on the island where the church had once stood. Standing there one day waiting for a bus, a woman's purse rolled out onto the pavement. It contained money, and we handed it in at a warden's post.

The *Ramillies* had been torpedoed after the Madagascar landings (Operation Ironclad) in Diego Suarez. My first sight of her was beyond belief … she looked like a rusting hulk. The aged *Marshall Sault* in Portsmouth dockyard looked in far better condition! *Ramillies'* 15in guns were at all angles; ropes, wires, boxes, welding equipment, cables, barrels, and all manner of items cluttered the decks and companionways. The odious 'dockyard mateys' were everywhere. They are a species most hated by the 'matelots' – the biggest scroungers you ever came across. It is often said that the seven-year apprentice-ship consists of three years to make a box and four years sitting on it!

Apart from a small working party, we were the advance contingent, with approximately one thousand more to come. On getting aboard, the state below was even worse. Everywhere was covered in dust and dirt – discarded packs of sandwiches, cigarette ends, old newspapers, and empty tins were littered about. Paint had been spilt with no effort to mop it up. The gods must have smiled on me and my future messmates – the torpedomen's mess was in excellent condition, situated on the starboard side for'ard of the CPO and POs' mess. Incidentally, this mess was originally a 6in gun casemate. Considering what I saw later of the rest of the ship, our mess was a palace!

Parts of the ship had been opened up to give access to new and replacement machinery (a new dynamo no. 6 had been installed). None of these apertures had been sealed. Tarpaulins were draped over the holes, these flapped about in the wind, resulting in draughty passageways and mess decks. The ship was cold, with no steam or water. We were plugged into the shore power supply for lighting only. Cooking was done aboard a floating galley. By the time we got the food it was stone cold! Washing and toilet facilities were also ashore.

The mess deck consisted of six messes, each with about fifteen ratings, including at least one leading seaman. We also had two QO ratings (gunnery), A/B Milson, an alcoholic who was beached in Mombasa, and A/B White. He went out of his mind as will be explained later. Gerry Lunne was the leading seaman (killick). Gerry was a very soured man when talking about the Navy. Being a timeserving rating, he only had one month left to complete his twelve years' service, plus boy's time, when hostilities broke out. I was with this man for over two years. One could not wish for a more considerate and efficient colleague. He had a wonderful sense of humour – especially when drunk. However, he did not suffer fools kindly.

The next morning we fell in on the upper deck and met our petty officers; CPO Godwin was the torpedo gunner's mate (TGM). Our Lieutenant Tel's name was also Godwin – but no relation. Again, I must emphasise that they were first-class for their fairness, efficiency and humour. This was contrary to my previous experience. We were allocated temporary duties, I was assigned to PO Charlie Bert, a crusty old codger with very fixed ideas about one's social status in the Navy, ie A/Bs with A/Bs, killicks with killicks, etc. At times he was a real 'pain in the bum' but, having said that, I learnt a great deal whilst working with him, and he never gave me a hard time.

During working hours, my duties consisted of servicing the large and small supply and exhaust fans. Being an old ship, many of the wiring diagrams were out of date or missing. Many hours were spent locating and checking distribution, junction, and section boxes. The latter gave me the horrors when pulling a fuse. After working hours when [on] duty aboard, working from the

Posed official photos of the crew carrying gear on to *Ramillies* at Liverpool.

LTOs' workshop situated near the galley, I performed rota duties consisting of lighting, telephone and later heating faults.

The *Ramillies* was an R-class battleship. Her sister ships were *Revenge*, *Resolution*, *Royal Sovereign*, and the ill-fated *Royal Oak*, sunk at Scapa Flow. My father had served aboard her at Jutland. *Ramillies* was built on the Clyde and commissioned in 1917. At 29,000 tons, she was originally planned for coal, but changed to oil. Hence the number of store and bathrooms. In 1943 her armament consisted of eight 15in guns housed in four twin turrets – 'A', 'B', 'X' and 'Y'. She had eight 6in guns, four on either side, four sets of multiple pom-poms (Chicago pianos), and many Oerlikons. She also had four sets of twin AAs, 4.5s, which were on the boat deck. She carried two large motor boats, two whalers, two cutters, a skim dish, and the captain's motor boat.

Slowly the ship began to take shape as more of the crew arrived, and the dockyard personnel and their equipment became less. Cleaning parties from Stonehouse Barracks were drafted in to assist. The painting parties seemed to leave with more on themselves! One morning we were treated to the arrival of our Marines, accompanied by their band. The CSM was Pony Moore, then the tallest man in the Royal Marines. It was said that he slept in two hammocks stitched together. They occupied the after mess deck. Many performed 'flunkies' duties and they manned 'X' turret.

The day dawned when we dispensed with the floating galley and the shore power supply. Our stokers were now manning our turbines to run the generators. Two of our party took over switchboard watch-keeping duties. Both were old shellbacks [long-serving men]. One was a real three-badge reprobate! Walter Leonard Bashford, A/B, S/T – the nearest to Fagin you could get – a real bug*** in drink! With heating, washing and cooking facilities back on board, our lot improved immensely.

Close companionships soon developed. Gerry Lunne became father-figure. My close associates were Bob Cliff, L/S, LTO; Harry Goldsmith, A/B, LTO; Ginger Styler, A/B, ST (hockey goalminder for Worcestershire); Harry Chown, A/B, ST; Charlie Chase, A/B, LTO; Ted Moss, A/B, ST; Sid Drew, A/B, ST; and Ron Jones, A/B, wireman (who was the captain of Bognor Regis football team). There were many characters, one in particular was a crusty old three-badge, A/B LTO Cliff Mitchell. At some time, I suppose when drunk, he had an eye tattooed on either cheek of his backside. Down in the bathroom one day I asked him why. 'So I can keep an eye on dirty bug***s like you!' was the reply!

We soon settled down to life on board, taking advantage of the limited shore leave to play football and hockey at HMS *Raleigh*, Saltash, and visiting many of the outlying towns such as Plymouth, Plymstock, Dawlish, Plympton and Seaton. One afternoon a party of us were playing table tennis in the church hall at Plympton. Before leaving, we asked the vicar to give us a guided tour of the church. In our little party was John Stebbing, A/B, ST, a native of Norfolk. John was a likeable chap, but from time to time suffered brainstorms. As we came to the end of the tour John, spying the clock, asked the old vicar if it was showing the correct time. When the vicar replied in the affirmative, he turned and with all to hear, said, 'Come on lads, its time we ****** off,' and promptly marched away, leaving us behind, horrified, with a very stunned vicar. From then on we were very wary of his company.

One weekend we mustered enough cash to stay at one of the hotels on Plymouth Hoe. The party included Bob, Harry, Ron and Ginger. After Sunday breakfast we walked through the gardens past Drake's statue and along the Hoe. It was very cold and damp, but at least it was different. By now, our complement of officers was nearing completion. Captain Keble-White[5], Commander M Dolphin[6], Commander E Steele, Captain Royal Marines T K West, Lt Com (Nav) Moore, DSC, and numerous others, including an Aussie Lt Com cable officer, a real 'B'.

When Commander Dolphin came aboard, his first act was to increase shore leave, allowing all night for local ratings ('up homers'). The last of the crew to

Posed official photos of the crew carrying gear on to *Ramillies* at Liverpool.

arrive were about fifteen boy seamen, and twenty-five prisoners from various 'glasshouses'. These latter arrived handcuffed in pairs wearing coarse duck suits (number 5's) with no blue collar. Commander Dolphin had their handcuffs removed, and when the kit was aboard, he mustered them to the quarterdeck, and informed them he was fully aware of their records, but from that moment they were dismissed they would become normal crew members. However, he also informed them, in ripe lower-deck language, that if they put one foot out of place, their life would become a misery! Not one of these men defaulted. Some had lost the rate: in most cases it was reinstated (leading seaman).

Activity aboard became more and more urgent as all manner of stores began to arrive. All available crewmen were pressed into service. Long lines of ratings could be seen with anything from cases of food to sides of bacon, walking up the brow to the quarterdeck. All the starboard derricks were in operation. I worked SI, bringing in nets full of frozen lambs. The last of our needs was ammunition. For this we had to be moved across the basin, as our crane was on the port side. During the manoeuvre, a wire hawser parted, resulting in two dockyard men sustaining broken legs.

With the ammunition barges alongside, another long hard day commenced! P/1 derrick was used for 'A' and 'B' turrets and the crane was used for 'X' and 'Y'. An incident occurred right at the beginning of the operation. I had been detailed to operate P/1 derrick during the forenoon. A seaman, when rigging the derrick, had attached the snatch block to the wrong deck eyebolt, resulting in the wire over-running the drum on the first lift! The shell fell 15ft. I was able to brake in time to prevent it crashing into the barge. I had a big fright, but the rating in the barge must have died a thousand deaths. I am convinced that he broke the world high jump record! The commissioned gunner directing the operation, called me everything – demanding I be removed. It was fortunate that our Lt Tel Godwin was on the scene, he observed the situation almost immediately, and subsequently had the gunner removed.

Another incident occurred that evening, more laughable than serious, concerning cordite being brought inboard. It is packed (two quarter charges) in tubular paxillin containers, approximately 5ft 6in x 2ft 6in. Charlie Chase was manning the crane, lifting about six of these containers at a time, down a hatch on the quarterdeck where a RNVR lieutenant, with a working party from barracks, were in attendance. They are lifted inboard fastened with a timber hatch. One of the lifts was insecure – as it arrived over the hatch the contents cascaded down. To a man, the ratings disappeared in a wink, expecting an explosion. The officer, after drying his eyes, explained the nature of cordite: exposed it is slow to ignite, burns a sickly yellow smoke; when confined it is a very different medium!

One day we were mustered on the quarterdeck for the commissioning ceremony and service. The articles of war were read out and the 'sin bo'sun'[7] said his piece. As our departure drew nigh, seven days' leave was granted to the ship's company. At about this time, Captain Keble-White was found to be suffering from tuberculosis. His sudden departure elevated Commander Dolphin to acting captain.

Tugs towed us from the dockyard, past Drake's Island to M1 buoy in the Sound. The day was biting cold with a heavy swell running. Securing to the buoy involves a delicate manoeuvre: a cutter is put over the side, and rowed to the buoy, conveying a wire rope that is being paid out from the fo'c'sle. Arriving at the buoy, the 'buoy jumper' fastens the wire, enabling the ship to manoeuvre and shackle on the mooring cable. What did happen, due to the rough conditions, was that the cutter was double-banked. The crew wore corked lifebelts over watch coats and leather sea boots (rubber was at a premium in those days). The fo'c'sle party paying out the wire failed to compensate when the cutter went down a trough, resulting in the boat being snatched up in the air, depositing the crew into the drink. The launch was quickly on the scene, a rope was passed to each man, and they were towed back to the ship, where the crane lifted each man out. Back on board they were each given a double tot of rum, and no doubt got their heads down! When the operation was finally completed, anti-torpedo netting was put round the ship.

We were now in possession of our duties (part of ship card). I was in

Work proceeding on Carley floats by 'B' or 'X' barbette.

starboard watch, assigned to 'A' turret (turret monkey), responsible for lighting, heating, fans, firing circuits, telephones, and batteries in the gun house, magazine and shell room. Duty watch as before. My abandon ship station was the starboard floater net (one's first job was to see how quick you could get there – day or night) I was also special sea dutyman, manning the fo'c'sle telephone, a duty I detested until we got rid of Aussie Lt Com (Cable Officer) at Cape Town. Bennet from *The Cruel Sea* fits the bill[8] – but I knew nothing of his love life!

There were four degrees of readiness. We closed up at night, sleeping in the turret (night defence stations), action stations was sounded at dusk and dawn, the most vulnerable time for a submarine attack. We were stood down at sun-up and sunset.

After so many months in dockyard hands, we discarded our anti-torpedo nets, and sailed back into service, leaving the southern waters for the next fourteen months. We sailed with a destroyer escort up the west coast into the Clyde, passing the *Queen Mary* and the *Queen Elizabeth*, painted a drab grey, anchored off Gourock, finally mooring off Greenock. Gun crews were constantly training, and we were learning all about the ship. In 'A' turret, it was like a mad-house, I soon knew all the drill. They became imprinted on my mind, I can still rattle them off (ie right gun cannot load the gun loading cage with the tell-tale showing ready but the pedal not pressed, pedal-to).

The turret cleaner was an old shellback, Jim Withers, A/B, a very fastidious man who took immense pride in his work. The turret was a showpiece. The brasswork gleamed. He burnished all the metal, including the deck, which he dressed with shale oil. Being the only non-gunnery rating, I soon fell foul of him. However, things soon improved when I volunteered to look after part of the deck. In fact, we became the best of friends.

At Greenock we were kept busy going out on training exercises under the watchful eye of the training commodore. Daily we sailed off the west coast in the vicinity of Ailsa Craig (the Onion Island), performing speed and slewing trials. Our boilers were tested above normal pressure. We exercised damage control, action stations, and boat drill was also carried out.

The day dawned for a practice 15in and 6in shoot. The guns in 'A' turret were named 'Lorna' (port) and 'Lilian' (stbd). Each had its own crew. The gunnery officer was Lt Dunne, RN, the gunner's mate was PO McLaughlin, RN. Both these men were very popular! Having closed up, each man calls his position. The breech is worked, the cage is raised and lowered, the rammer tested, the air-line and water squirt checked (for damping and blowing out burning residue). Each crew had two boy seamen (range followers); they sat at the front of the turret, close to where the gun leaves the gun house. I must admit I was very apprehensive and hoped I did not look like them.

The order 'Load! Load! Load!' was given. The breech worker at Lilian,

Jim Withers, opened the breech (hydraulically) and inserted the firing tube into the vent, which I had previously tested. The cage was then raised and loaded with a practice projectile and two half-charges. The shell weighs one ton and it has a copper driving band around the base. When the rammer rams it into the breech, the driving band embeds itself into the rifling.

Further 15in shoots took place and, for reasons of economy, a sub-calibre gun is fitted into the breech. This enables a much smaller shell to be fired, at the same time preserving the rifling, and giving firing training.

One day we were in the vicinity of Ailsa Craig, and tragedy befell us. We had been practising firing our AA armament, when somehow we managed to stray into the fall of shot of some motor gunboats firing at drogues, resulting in live Oerlikon shells falling on our boat deck where the 4.5in AA gun crews were closed up. Members of one crew sustained minor shrapnel wounds. One rating had a calf muscle torn out. At this point in time, apart from an alcoholic surgeon commander and two sick-bay ratings, we had no competent doctor on board. To make matters worse, the hospital ship requested failed to find us. On arrival at Greenock, Acting Captain Dolphin nearly tossed the surgeon commander over the side when he staggered over the patient on the stretcher as he was being transferred to a fast launch. Feelings were running high on board, particularly when news was received that night that the rating had died. A blood transfusion would have saved his life.

From Greenock we sailed to Scapa Flow, anchoring off the isle of Flotta, which we used for recreational purposes – football, mainly, although I did some cross-country training with A/B Manley, S/T. Many ships were also using that island, including the American cruiser *Wichita*. Their liberty men played baseball. All one seemed to hear was, 'Let's go! Let's go!' They were a happy crowd and mixed well. Apart from a few crofts, Flotta boasted one pub called The Fox. It looked like a small farmhouse. There was always a long line outside waiting to be served. The beer came in buckets, probably brewed from the stream nearby!

Each morning between 0600 and 0700 hours, we performed evolutions (exercises), for example, working the main derricks to hoist our motor boats aboard. This entailed using No. 1–5 dynamos or 6 on its own – raising the anchor by capstan bars, rigging sheer legs, abandon ship stations and damage control. My division was responsible for running emergency cables should the ring main be severed. Each division had its own set exercises: they were not popular.

One morning the sea temperature was deemed warm enough for swimming. 'Close the port chute' was piped and then, fifteen minutes later, 'Hands to bathe portside'. John Stebbing decided to go in. We told him he was crazy but to no avail. He came out blue with cold. Next day he was sent to hospital with a collapsed lung. He never returned. I wonder if the old vicar at Plympton had anything to do with it!

At 0200 hours one morning, 'Clear lower deck' was piped. The captain's message was short and sharp, 'Prepare for sea in two hours.' The *Tirpitz* was out! The ship became a hive of activity. 'X' and 'Y' doors were closed, hatches were battened down, and all unnecessary equipment was stowed away. It was during this scramble that our second fatality occurred. L/S Harvey was in charge of a party supplying 6in shells to the casemates. A hoist situated near the port battery brought them up from the shell room, where they are transferred to the guns on manual overhead tramways. L/S Harvey, on arriving at his action station, found the hoist not working. It appeared that he got no response from the alarm bell, so he put his head inside the hoist to alert the shell-room crew, just as the hoist was activated. He sustained a broken neck, and within an hour the 'Stand down' was piped.

From Scapa Flow, we returned to Greenock, where a three-badge man L/S Hardy, LTO, joined us. He was a pleasant but very nervous man, and he had cause to be. He was a survivor from HMS *Royal Oak*. He hated sleeping below decks, and always carried a knife on his lanyard around his waist, even when sleeping.

We had many passengers come aboard, consisting of submarine ratings, RAF and army personnel. Our destination was unknown, but an unsigned notice appeared on the ship's board stating that it was an offence to get sunburnt.

We sailed back down the Clyde with a three-destroyer escort (names have faded) and an oceangoing tug. Along the way we collected five auxiliary aircraft carriers (banana boats) *Biter*, *Boxer*, *Battler* and two others. Our destination was Gibraltar. All was pleasant sailing until we came to the Bay of Biscay – then all hell broke loose. The wind became gale force and the sea mountainous. We were to ride out the storm for three days. The '*Millie*' did not like to ride a wave, she ploughed underneath. We were awash on most decks and the storm caused havoc on board. The for'ard hatch (weighing about one ton) was torn off and water poured down fan trunkings. A paravane trolley near the starboard for'ard screen door broke loose, causing much damage before going over the side and taking a section of the guard-rail with it. The noise below was thunderous. Our heads (toilets) were right for'ard. Using them was an art, one had to climb two steps to a cubicle and hang on. The rise and fall was about 30ft. Many of our passengers had been billeted in the 6in casemates. The water simply poured in the gun ports and what with wet gear and most of them seasick, theirs was a miserable lot.

On my twenty-first birthday my parents had bought me a very modern camera. On the first night of the storm three of us went to a degaussing compartment, Charlie Bert's (Cabush), to help rescue his gear. We waded knee-deep along a narrow corridor with the aid of torches. What with the groaning of the ship and the phosphorus glowing in the water it was very scary. On returning to the mess deck I found my locker awash and my camera ruined.

I estimated at least a quarter of the crew suffered with seasickness. Some of the cases were pitiful. Those that were able to took on various charges. I had four men situated on the boat deck near the beef screen and low-power battery room. They wore duffel coats, balaclavas and sea boots, with a tarpaulin cover. Each had a bucket, towel, water and dried bread. I visited them regularly day and night, cleaning them and making them as comfortable as possible. One of these ratings was from our mess deck – a replacement for John Stebbing. He was a wireman who had been in the Andrew (naval slang for the Royal Navy) for about four months. His father had been in the Navy and consequently he knew it all. He could not be told anything and had a voice like a foghorn. There he was, in the scupper whispering, 'Oh, Harry, I wish I could die. Please let me die.' I would clean him up, pop a barley sugar in his mouth and try to convince him that the storm was abating. By the time we reached calmer water he was back to his old self. Cliff Mitchell cursed me like hell for not granting him his wish!

15in cordite cases being brought onboard. Note the temporary runway made from planks to run the cases along.

As was practice, we arrived at Gibraltar during the night with only two of our carriers. The others had turned back due to storm damage. We stayed long enough to land some passengers, and smell the spice aroma. At dawn next day we were out of sight of land, with HMS *Quickmatch* and HMS *Roebuck*, our destroyer screen.

Shortly after we left Gibraltar, my mother at home listened to Lord Haw-Haw, the German propaganda minister. He stated that an R-class battleship called at Gibraltar, and had been sunk in the Mediterranean. This caused her sixteen weeks of worry before my mail arrived.

Each morning when hands are piped, we were informed of any relevant information, the day, date. And the dress of the day. That morning it was tropical rig (whites). We still wore overalls in working parties. The other information given was that we were bound for Casablanca and the time-change factor. On entering harbour, one immediately observed the destruction rent on units of the French fleet, by our Navy – wrecks were everywhere. Two freighters lying on their sides had been blown onto the quay. The Frogs had built a roadway over them. The battleship *Jean Bart* sat on the bottom with a list to starboard. Her decks had been built up to compensate the list. Part, if not all, of her crew were living on board.

After mooring fore and aft, leave was piped for the starboard watch. However, before proceeding ashore, the skipper gave the first of many lectures of the pitfalls to beware of. He strongly emphasised the need to beware of certain drinks. One, I recall, was called 'snake eyes', a crude brandy that could cause blindness. He also reminded us that we were the first battleship to visit the port since the occupation, and to be on our best behaviour. Alas, the morons failed to heed his request.

With Ron, Harry, and Ginger, I was on the first liberty boat. Bob had been detailed to patrol duty. Ashore he experienced confrontation with the US Provost Marshal, because his PO refused to carry revolvers. Their detail was to prevent any of our crew from entering the US officers' brothel! Armed with a few francs, wearing white shorts, shirt, cap, and black shoes and stockings, the three of us set forth to see the town. We were most surprised once outside the dockyard, for, despite the destruction inside, there was no damage whatsoever. The large blocks of flats outside had not been touched. The temperature was 90° Fahrenheit[9], and the place reeked of camel urine and was infested by flies. We proceeded to explore, walking along the avenues of medium-sized trees, climbing to the higher parts of the city, where we sat in a shaded square, and sampled the local muscatel, a raisin wine. It was here that I purchased some postcards (of the cleaner variety).

The city was predominately Arabic, marshalled then by American and French troops. Many French matelots were promenading about, dressed and acting like prima donnas. Making our way back, we passed a large *estaminet*, and, spotting Gerry, Cliff, and a few others, we joined them for a beer. Sitting at a table near me, a Froggy matelot made a point of informing me that he disliked the British, and preferred Germans. I asked him why, after giving up his country without any resistance, he should get it back? He sneered and replied in French, 'C'est la vie.'

The wine and spirits began to take their toll. Many of our crew were hopelessly drunk. They became aggressive, singing bawdy songs – and then the place erupted. It was like a scene from Errol Flynn's film *Dodge City*. Tables and chairs were smashed, and bottles and glasses were flying about. The small orchestra decided to call it a day and having played the French national anthem, they tried to leave the stage, only to be confronted by Walter Leonard Bashford, out of his mind with drink, with a broken chair in his hand, demanding that they play 'God Save the King' before leaving. The poor beggars, not able to understand, were trembling. At this point, a swift exit was called for and, on reflection, perhaps the cocky French matelot had a point.

Patrols were everywhere. The Americans stood no nonsense. The riot was soon brought under control, and our libertymen were herded back to the dockyard and despatched on any craft available. The four of us were put aboard an oiling barge with about fifty others (imagine the state of our whites). Trouble flared up coming alongside and the command, 'Silence in the boat!' caused derisory remarks. Some of the drunken idiots decided to go for a swim, two in six suits, with their collars flapping up and down, were babbling, 'It's cooler in here!' A party of cooks were forcing a duck to swallow grapes. Claude (the demon barber) had a puppy, the Regulating PO (Crusher) Moody (by name and nature), ordered both to be thrown over the side. This caused a storm and the duck had its neck wrung and was thrown up onto the signal deck, where someone bent a rope round its neck and hauled it aloft. After much wrangling, the puppy was allowed aboard, but it died after a few days. As a result of this escapade, many of the crew handed in their station cards and punishment duly followed. The affair became a diplomatic incident involving the British, American and French, and we were given six hours to leave port, putting paid to repairing our storm damage. We prepared for sea, much to the annoyance of the port watch.

With two destroyers and a couple of freighters, we sailed to Freetown, in Sierra Leone, West Africa ('white man's grave'). It was here that the replacement for Captain Keble-White joined us. He was Captain G B Middleton, CBE,[10] and he had transferred from HMS *Royal Sovereign*, which was loaned to the Russians for the duration. He was an approachable man with a sense of humour, but like most of his breed he was ambitious: in his wardrobe hung a rear admiral's uniform. On his arrival the lower deck was cleared and the hands fell in on the quarterdeck, where he introduced himself and lay out his expectations. Prior to being dismissed, we filed past, saluting him and

The forward turrets and bridge with officers and men assembled. Somewhere in the Mediterranean.

calling out our name. Later, he mingled with ratings who had previously served with him and they all spoke well of him.

My first encounter with him was almost immediately. Gerry Lunne, the duty TTO, told me to report to the admiral's stateroom. On arrival he pointed to two electric bowl fires situated on a bulkhead. Alas, it was my first encounter

with wiring 'in series', and not being able to fathom out the problem, I took them down, with the intention of returning them to the LTO's workshop.

The skipper asked what I was doing, and I replied it was a dirty job and did not want to make a mess. 'Don't worry, Torps,' he said, 'It could soon be cleaned up,' adding that he wasn't fussy. By now I was praying for action stations to be sounded! After a while, I said that the repairs would have to be carried out in the workshop. With a broad grin on his face, he enquired as to how long I had been an S/T. After I replied, he said, 'Torps, you are trying to bluff me.'

I said, 'Yes, sir,' and explained my predicament. He told me to take it away, and informed [me] the next time he saw me, he wanted to know 'what, why, and how.' He never did ask me, and on returning to the workshop, Gerry told me that [the captain] once was an electrical officer.

On arrival at Freetown, we found the facilities very minimal. It boasted a depot ship and a few shacks on the waterfront, and inland was a small army barracks and a hospital. The verandas were covered with mosquito netting, and there were monkeys everywhere. We moored in the stream, and in next to no time we were surrounded by bumboat-men. Some were bartering their wares and others were entertainers, begging for coins. Some were young lads diving for coins, and some were pimps, soliciting on behalf of their sisters. The tide on the ebb is very dangerous as it runs at about 8 knots. As soon as it turns these fellows disappear as if by magic.

We were forbidden to trade with them, but despite the efforts of Moody, fruit and all manner of curios managed to come on board. Moody was involved in an incident where he caught a coconut that had been thrown on board. He threw it back, shouting to all that no bartering was allowed, but unfortunately it hit a native on the head. He paddled away furiously shaking his fist, and no doubt cursing the RPO. The natives managed to pick up a smattering of English, as many a troopship passed through the port; unfortunately, most of it was the worst kind. Freetown was notorious for malaria, yellow fever and many other nasty diseases and because of this we were given regular doses of quinine. This made our hair fall out and our teeth turn yellow. Coconut oil helped with the hair problem, but made it grow faster.

After dire warnings from Commander Dolphin, and his advice on wine and women, the port watch went ashore and they returned without any problem. Next day it was the turn of the starboard watch; armed with some local currency and two McEwans beer tickets (quinine-based), a party of us set out to walk over one mile to King Tom's canteen. The beer was horrible, but it did not go to waste as some soaks in our party were only too pleased to finish it off, and gratefully accept the rest of the beer tickets. On the return journey, passing one of the native huts, a young girl was grinding mealies by pummelling the seed with a pole into a hollowed-out log. Seeing that she had attracted an audience, she started throwing the pole up into the air and clapping her hands, not realising the onlookers were more interested in her bare breasts than her artistic prowess. However, her exhibition gained its reward with a generous supply of cigarettes.

We remained in Freetown for about seven days. During that time we made good some of our storm damage. I spent many hours fishing – sport was excellent, we soon found out not to fish the bottom, as 'eel snakes', up to six feet in length, grabbed the bait immediately. One of the best fish caught there were said to be called 'gazels' (my spelling); they were about 8lbs, had red flesh and were very tasty. We had to serenade the cooks: a couple were awkward, but removing the fuses from their fans worked wonders!

Our departure from Freetown was not without incident. Whilst slipping the buoy, a link in our mooring cable broke. It is standard procedure that a court martial has to take place; this was subsequently held in Durban some months later. The cable officer was none other than the 'White Abbo' – what a pity he was exonerated.

Whilst in Freetown, two canvas pools had been rigged; they were about 15ft x 15ft x 4ft and seawater was pumped in and out during daylight hours. They were used for cooling as swimming was forbidden. With an additional destroyer, HMS *Nizam*, three freighters and one troopship carrying West Africans, we left the tropic of Cancer behind, making our way to the tropic of Capricorn, in the South Atlantic; our destination was Cape Town, but first we had to cross the equator.

Entertainments aboard were encouraged: not everyone had hobbies, boredom for some was a problem. Whenever possible, competitions were arranged. The advent of crossing 'the Line' stirred the various entertainment committees to life, for King Neptune insisted that all novices entering his domain are initiated! The cast was as follows:

King Neptune – A/B Milsom; Lady Amphitrite – Mne Copeland; Lady-in-Waiting – Mne Page; Clerk of the Court – Lt Clover, RNVR; Dolphinus – Sgt Maj Moore; Court Equerry – Sub Lt Taylor; Court Jester – A/B Needham; Doctors – A/B Husslebee, A/B Bashford; Chief of Police – Sgt Maj Moore; Barber No. 1 – L/S Mahoney, LTO; his Assistants – A/B Butler, A/B T Moore; Barber No. 2 – PO Mclaughlin; his Assistants – A/B Bennet, A/B Ritson.

The Police – O/A Parker, O/A Peel, Cpl Adamson, Mne Pullen, Mne Shepherd, Mne Churcher, Mne Ladley, Mne Garlick, Mne Lewis, PO Kelsey, Sto Langford, Sto Starkey, Sto Lucas, Sto Waterhouse, Sto Hedgecock, Sto Shepherd.

The Bears, Bath No. 1, Group 1 – Mne McLean, Sto Hampson, A/B Dores, A/B Hughs; Group 2 – Men Young, L/Sto Hadnum, A/B Morrison, A/B Evans; Group 3 – Men Hickman, O/A Marshall, Sto Richards, A/B Murphy.

Bath No. 2, Group 1 – Men Moffat, Sto Ormroyde, L/S Cliff, LTO, A/B

Goldsmith, LTO; Group 2 – Men Hall, L/Sto Ravine, A/B Humphries, A/B Donkin; Group 3 –Mne Bennison, Mne Tomlinson, O/A Tolly, A/B Brown.

Order of the Bath (Superintendents) – Sgt Henry, RM, Sgt Gill, RM, Sgt Simmonds, RM, CPO Joyce.

The Committee – Lt Cdr Morrissey, RN, Lt Clover, RNVR, Colour Sgt A Moore, CPO W Joyce, CPO R J A Hardy, Ch Spwt Parslow, A/B Husslebee, A/B Milson.

A booklet of the event was written by Sgt G S Penn, RM, an artist aboard drew an ornate scroll: these were printed some months later in Durban. Everybody aboard received copies signed by the Clerk of Court.

On the morning of 27 August 1943, I recalled leaving 'A' turret, the weather being overcast and on the cool side, thinking to myself, it was not a good day to be playing about with water; spray was whispering over the fo'c'sle. Not long after breakfast the festivities commenced: at 0900 hours, King Neptune and his retinue came aboard, the side was piped and the guards presented arms, the band played a few bars of 'Colonel Bogey', then the guard sloped and ordered arms. King

A Crossing the Line ceremony underway.

Neptune was received by Captain Middleton and escorted to his throne, situated on the quarterdeck. From here he issued the following orders to the police to round up every knave for shaving and to let the 'bears' loose.

> Shave him and bash him,
> Duck him and splash him,
> Torture and smash him,
> Don't let him go.

We crossed the Line on the 27th. In latitude 07° about 750 of us were subjected to a lathering with a floury paste, shaved, then a smelly substance was rubbed in our hair; the brush, razor and comb used were about 2ft in length. After the Barber came the Doctor, who examined our mouth and administered a soapy pill; we were then tipped into the bath where the Bears gave us a hard time!

What a day! The festivities went on until mid-afternoon, various games were played including giant 'Uckers' (Ludo): the dice were about 18in square on a large canvas board. Not an enemy in sight; however, full security was maintained, AA guns crews and lookouts were on full alert. Before departing, King Neptune gave the following speech:

> Hark all ye infants enrolled as my freemen!
> Before I return to my rock-covered shore,
> See you stand by the kinship of all worthy seamen,
> And hold fast to the faith of the sea and her laws.

One of the good things about our skipper was his concern for our destroyer escorts; at sea for any length of time, even more so during hot weather, they soon ran out of bread and vegetables. He would have them come close enough to pass their requirements over by line.

Slowly, we made our way into the South Atlantic. As we did so the temperature rose; with this our fresh water became rationed. Being an old ship, the distillation plant could not cope for all our needs; the hydraulics, mainly for our 15in guns took priority. Many of the crew developed 'foot-rot', a soreness between the toes which made walking very painful. Another nasty complaint was 'prickly heat': the skin became covered in blisters on the back. And under the arms, these would itch then weep, and again became very painful; perspiration, dobeying[11] and washing in saltwater was the main problem. In the old days, mariners were issued with limes to combat scurvy; we were issued with lime juice, hence the Americans calling us 'limeys'.

All members of the crew qualified for tropical money, I also qualified for climatical pay, as my duties entailed working in the shell room and magazine.

It was during this trip that we lost the third member of our crew. The rating had developed a bad abscess on the jaw; our dentist, who was a commander, extracted the tooth. Complications followed: the bleeding could not be stopped, arrangements were made for us to call into Walvis Bay where a Catalina flying-boat flew him to Cape Town. On arrival we received news of his death ... blood poisoning. The captain, with a Marine funeral firing party, and some crew members attended the funeral. Nobody went near the dentist after that!

Walvis Bay was then in Damarland Protectorate of South Africa; it had been an old German whaling station. It appeared that all the unwanted remains of the whale were just dumped back into the bay. On leaving, when our anchor broke surface, it was covered in black slime which took ages to clean off; the smell was revolting.

Sleeping at night-defence stations in this area was uncomfortable, to say the least. With the sun beating down on the turret during the day, the inside became a furnace. I had purloined as many portable fans as I could get my hands on; they made little effect. Our guns were trained at 5 degrees, known as the lookout bearing. There was no muzzle covers (tompions) in, this allowing the breech to be opened for a welcome through draught. One morning, about

King Neptune presiding over Crossing the Line ceremonies by the pool erected on the quarterdeck.

one hundred miles from Cape Town, cloud formation could be seen above the toe of Africa.

We arrived at Cape Town in the forenoon. An earlier briefing had warned us to observe the noon minute silence, for what, I never found out: the maroon went off as we came alongside the quay. Elections were in progress at the time of our arrival. The port watch was the first ashore, Commander Dolphin (he had received the award of 'Lord Telephone' at the crossing the line ceremony) reminded the libertymen to conduct themselves whilst ashore, to be aware of Cape brandy and 'snake-eyes' – both were said to cause blindness! The Cape then comprised of many districts, two of which were out of bounds, No. 6 and, I believe, No. 14: these areas were of mixed races. One was Cape Coloureds: these people were only recognisable by the pink moons on their fingers. Another section of the community to beware of were the 'OBs', 'Osna Brogons' (my spelling), a section of the Dutch element who still harboured hatred from the Boer War.

The following day I went ashore with Bob, Harry (Goldie), Ron and Ginger; our first stop was the Red Shield Club,[12] where we enjoyed a slap-up meal with all the trimmings for about ninepence (old money). This was our first meal ashore since leaving Glasgow. Next, we took in the local sights, avoiding the taboo districts: the market, shopping area, Kruger Park, where we were fascinated by the tameness of the different coloured birds. Nearby was the parliament and university buildings.

Bob and Goldie had been to Cape Town before whilst serving in the cruiser HMS *Emerald*; they suggested that we went to Simonstown. We boarded the train at Central Station. The track was small-gauged with overhead electrical cables; the siren sounded about every twenty seconds. We passed through Woodstock, Observer, Rosebank, Newlands, Wynberg, Constancia, and Retreat. At Muizenberge we ran along the coast passing St James, Clovelly, Fish Hoek, Glencairn to Simonstown. The views, particularly along the coast, were breathtaking: the blue sea with the white rollers bursting on to the beautiful golden beaches were straight out of the present-day holiday brochures; numerous bathing parties were seen. We were told later the population of this area was predominately Jewish. We spent a very pleasant afternoon and evening in Simonstown, lazing in deckchairs and later playing table tennis and drinking in the dockyard naval canteen. It was here on one of the rare occasions that Bob mixed his drinks. I say rare: we were not heavy drinkers – in any case we could not afford the luxury, so we quietly nursed him back aboard!

Cape Town is very picturesque – the mountains look down across the city to the sea. Two that come to mind are the Lion's Head and Table Mountain. The latter had a cable car for taking visitors to the top, but clouds appearing from nowhere can make the trip hazardous! Prior to leaving Cape Town, we said goodbye to many of our passengers. Some were relieving the signal station – they had also been great shipmates who had mixed very well.

Much to my relief the 'Odious Aussie' also left. My first encounter with him was on the fo'c'sle leaving harbour in Devonport. 'Are you the phone number?' he snarled.

I replied, 'Yes, sir,' to which he said, 'I want the phone cable increased by another thirty feet immediately,' adding that if I was not back within ten minutes I would have to answer to him! On returning, he said, 'See this arm?' pointing to the left. 'If you stray one yard from it, I'll have your guts for garters.'

He gave all the fo'c'sle party a hard time   I often wondered if he could swim! From the day he departed, entering and leaving harbour was a sheer delight under his replacement, Lt Commander Evans, RNVR.

We left Cape Town with our three destroyers and four troopships (three were of the Strath Line), and four merchantmen bound for Durban, leaving the South Atlantic and entering the Indian Ocean. Leaving the harbour can be hazardous: it appears the heavy ground swells are very common. Immediately, we 'catted' our anchors and stowed the cable, closing all hatches and screen doors.

Now we were in these waters extra vigilance was called for, as Japanese mothercraft were abroad with their midget submarines. The trip to Durban was uneventful. The weather to start with was glorious; however, slowly it changed, the temperature began to fall; by the time we arrived we were back in 'blues'. As we tied up alongside in the dockyard, I saw the amazing spectacle of a tall, stout woman dressed all in white, standing on the dockside singing a welcome to us. She was affectionately known as 'The Lady in White' by many thousands of servicemen and women who passed through the port. The ship's company always presented her with a bouquet of flowers when departing. She died I believe, in 1993; ex-service associations, including the *Ramillies*, have contributed for a memorial to be erected in her honour.

The commander gave his usual lecture, with much emphasis regarding the hospitable local people. They were not to be taken advantage of, their kindness far exceeded any other he had known. Offenders would be severely dealt with! In next to no time the SAWAS (South African Women's Auxiliary Service) were aboard with invitations, handouts, all manner of useful information, and fruit; in fact, we had a case of oranges each. These people were the salt of the earth: many thousands of service personnel who passed through Durban during the war are indebted to them. Ashore they provided bed and feeding facilities at unbelievably low prices – they had taken over empty car showrooms and garages and turned them into dormitories.

Our arrival caused much excitement. At the dockyard gates I was amazed to see the large crowds of people standing there to greet us. There was an endless line of cars along the road: the people offered their services to run us in and give us a conducted tour of the city, which inevitably resulted in being invited to their home. Their main object in being so hospitable was to point out the advantages that South Africa offered, in the hope we would emigrate out there after the war. The ratio between black and white disturbed them, and they were desperate to redress the balance.

I met a family by the name of Klokie; he was German and his wife French. They had married after the First World War and settled there; they had two daughters and one son. The son and son-in-law were serving at the time in the Western Desert. Mr Klokie assured me I would get a good job on the East African Railway, accommodation was also assured. The only condition was that I must learn Swahili or Zulu as to speak to the natives in English was taboo – they considered that you gave the coloureds an advantage.

We soon saw the dark side of this beautiful country: coloureds were treated like lepers. There were signs everywhere saying 'European' and 'Non-European'. Should a white be sitting on a black's bench, he would not sit down until the white left. Two incidents come to mind: one occurred in Smith's Square. Having spent the night ashore with the usual three, we were standing at the bus stop. In front of us stood a very well-dressed coloured girl. When the bus arrived only four seats (non-European) were available. The driver told the girl to stand back and let us board; we told him we had plenty of time and told her to get on. As she did, he slapped her face shouting, 'I told you to stand back.' He only just managed to close the door of the bus in time!

The second incident involved a dockyard electrician; this man had emigrated from the UK just before the war. As the four of us were going ashore, he had offered to give us a lift to town, stopping first at his club for a drink. Sitting in the van opposite me was his coloured assistant. Taking a pack of twenty Woodbines out of my pocket, I offered him one and to the others in turn. When I got to the driver of the van he knocked the packet out of my hand shouting, 'Don't you dare offer him a cigarette before me.' Ron Jones ordered him to stop the van, still in the dockyard, then commenced to tell him what he thought of him, adding he was a typical dockyard scrounger, advising him not to come near our mess deck as the water in the dock was very dirty!

It was now spring; the weather was still variable – we were still in blues. The West Africans we had been escorting were daily exercised in the dockyard. I have a photograph of these troops marching up and down in the rain. They were only allowed ashore escorted in groups of about twenty-five; they were not allowed on the pavement or to speak to anybody. They were inclined to be childish men; I can see them now, standing on the kerb, fascinated at their reflection in the shop windows and mirrors. They were destined for the Burma campaign; I wonder how they fared under fire?

With repairs to be carried out, we were able to visit numerous places of interest outside of Durban: Amanzimtoti, with its beautiful freshwater lagoon

– the swimming was great. It was here we hired a boat and proceeded along a river that necessitated in our female companions (the Klokies) getting out and pulling us through small rapids – the 'tars' stayed in the boat! It was along this river that we came across a restaurant run by a woman who had lived near Bob. We were well looked after and, needless to say, we spent a long time answering questions about home.

Brighton Beach was another favourite venue, but swimming was out for fear of sharks put us off! We also visited the towns of Isipingo, Kingsburgh and Unkomaas. One Sunday we watched the native dancing in the area known as the Valley of the Thousand Hills. It was a very colourful spectacle. Many years later I saw the film *Zulu*, recalling the maidens' dance and the sounds made by the warriors and their mournful song. The Umgani Roadhouse was another favourite venue; here one could dance providing one knew how. I think Ginger was the only one amongst us that could. To get to the Roadhouse, one way was by crossing the Umgani River by a rope bridge. It was a bit nerve-racking – I always thought what might be lurking in the water below!

Invites were always being received from the SAWAS for dances, clubs, outings, etc. I, with a PO and four other ratings, attended a wedding at Cheeka's Corral of a local chief's daughter. Many people attended this function – we sat crossed legged on a large rush mat with some squaddies. There was plenty to eat and drink, but being careful I stuck with fruit. As regards the ceremony, we were far too far back to see what went on. However, it was a nice day out with plenty of laughs.

With our repairs completed and more of our passengers having left us, we sailed with our three destroyers, three troopships, and a captured German freighter, bound for the East African port of Mombasa. Almost immediately on clearing the harbour, our gyro developed a fault and at one stage we were on a collision course with one of the troopers.

As previously stated, the troopships in the convoy were bound for the Burma campaign, and also included were a large contingent of nurses and NAAFI girls. There was plenty of activity aboard, and through our binoculars we could see numerous boxing competitions being held, PT in progress, and the pleasing sight of the girls sunbathing!

Our course took us through the Mozambique Channel, passing Lourenço Marques[13] on our portside, and Madagascar to starboard. The weather was glorious, apart from our fresh water problem, conditions aboard were comfortable; thinking about it today, people pay a lot of money to cruise in these waters. Just after we had cleared the Mozambique Channel, our SRE came to life announcing a typhoon warning (you don't get typhoons in these waters). Immediately, we secured our anchors, cables, boats, closed all screen doors, and battened down the hatches. Within fifteen minutes of the pipe, the blue sky turned to a sickly yellow, the halyards started to sing, and flocks of

Taking it easy on the forecastle.

birds made their way towards the mainland. In thirty minutes all hell broke loose, the *Millie* was sticking her bows deep down, and tossing tons of water on to the foc's'le and *over* the fighting top.

The German freighter with her prize crew aboard had a hard time. One minute her bows were up in the air, the next all you could see was her stern! It was during this spell, while on the boat deck, that I actually saw a waterspout. The mayhem lasted about two hours – it went as quick as it came. Later we were told we were only on the outer fringe: I wonder what the eye had been like! Soon we were back to a calm blue sea, and golden sunshine.

Somewhere in the Indian Ocean, Gerry Lunne and Spike Mahoney celebrated their birthday. The pair of them saved up their tot for a month; Gerry's being two waters and one rum had raisins put in to soak up the water. Came the great day, they added meths and lime juice to the brew and then had a party. All had to wish them a happy birthday, then sample the concoction. It was awful, one sip made our toenails go black! It did not take long before they were out of their minds. They piled up the bread barges and potato boxes at either end of the mess deck, then commenced to bombard each other with potatoes.

Spike was eventually despatched back to the POs' mess and Gerry to the hammock netting, where he was incarcerated for two days. Once he had a drop of water, he would start singing and raving. Toilet was the biggest problem: pliers were a bit harsh to hold his manhood, so I used my long-handled screwdriver to winkle it out and let it hang over the edge.

And so we proceeded slowly towards Mombasa. Passing the islands of Mafia, Zanzibar, and the spice island of Pemba, the old shellbacks said that on certain times of the year the smell of the spices were overpowering one hundred miles downwind! It was a beautiful day we entered the lovely harbour bedecked in palm trees and golden, sandy beaches. It is situated in Kenya colony, adjacent to Tanganyika, and Uganda. I thought this area was the jewel of Africa.

The docks were yet another area developed by the Americans to aid the build-up for the eastern campaign. Numerous naval craft were in the harbour, including our sister ship HMS *Revenge*, the submarine depot ship HMS *Adamant*, and Bob and Goldie's old ship HMS *Emerald*, plus many other craft. It was here that we said goodbye to the last of our passengers; apart from a few RAF chaps, they were mainly submariners. We also beached A/B Milson, QO (King Neptune). He had become a chronic alcoholic, drinking meths, surgical spirit and anything he could get his hands on; his screams some nights were horrific (*The Lost Weekend*[14] came to mind).

Mombasa, with the neighbouring area of Kilindini, in comparison with other African towns was quite modern. Its two main thoroughfares dissect one another; the town boasted the usual bazaars, shops and cafes run mainly by the Indian element. The traffic was directed by tall native policemen: they were all over 6ft 6in, immaculately dressed in khaki, bare feet with their trousers about 6in above their ankles. They were an awe-inspiring sight, standing on a dais, baton in hand, whistle in mouth, wearing a red fez. The baton was no ornament. I saw one young boy with a cycle who disobeyed the officer's instruction beaten to the ground. It was whilst walking along Kilindini Road, passing the cafe that always played the Andrews Sisters records, that I espied two 'bent' merchant seamen: they were dressed in silk blouses and rouged up to the eyebrows. They were sitting near the sidewalk, fanning themselves. As I passed, I heard one say in a ducky voice, 'Oh, these blessed flies.' I told the boys what I had seen and heard. Bob, ambling along with his beloved pipe, came to an immediate halt saying, 'I shall have to see this!' Having witnessed the pair, he uttered his usual remark, 'Strewth, I would never have believed it.' To digress a little, I always suspected Bob never came to terms with the rawness of the Andrew; he always had to be convinced, but when he was, he would giggle and those wicked black eyes would gleam!

We spent the evening in the outdoor 'wet canteen'; when the sun went down, a film was shown. On leaving, two of our stokers [were] chatting the 'bent' ones up – one of the lads said, 'Come on girls, I only want a few minutes of your time.' The reply was, 'Oh, you matelots are bold.'

At the entrance to the harbour stands Fort St Jean, said to have given protection to pirates in years gone by. Many of the old cannons are still there – some had fallen from the walls to the ground below. Lizards were everywhere, and the building was derelict. In 1994 I was in Spain and whilst there I saw a German documentary film on Sky TV, about a voyage by dhow from Zanzibar to Mombasa. Fort St Jean had been renovated, the guns were all back on their trunnions – it had now become a tourist attraction. The upmarket part of the area was Kilindini, where nice houses, estates and the yacht club were situated. The Sultan of Zanzibar had a palace situated nearby in Pele Lisa (my spelling) near the beach we used for changing when swimming.

Outside the town was a large open market where I observed men buying meat. It was wrapped and they carried it tied on the end of a piece of string. They were very polite people: the men always shook hands when meeting and departing. There was excellent playing field facilities for football and hockey, there were tennis courts but for camp personnel only. There were two camps 'Ganjoni' and 'Tarlna' (my spelling). They housed Wrens and ratings: they were a snobbish crowd, they behaved like the 'yacht club brigade'.

Whilst here, divisional competitions were held in football, hockey, water polo and deck hockey. The latter was played on the quarterdeck, with walking sticks and wooden pucks. Before playing we had to cut up [make] about thirty pucks because most of them finished up over the side. It was playing one of the soccer ties against the Royal Marines that their centre back had his leg broken. I was playing in goal that day, and from where I stood I heard the crack!

One afternoon the usual crowd set out to explore. Following a well-used track we came across fertile fields of maize and pineapple, then, in the middle of nowhere, a Red Shield club. Needless to say, we were royally treated.

Shore leave was about noon until 2200 hours. We generally finished up in the canteen watching a film. At the boundary end was a line of trees: the natives climbed the trees to watch the film, their cigarettes glow[ing] like fireflies in the dark. We also had films aboard shown in the 'Recs' space in cold weather, and on the foc's'le when warm; the natives would secure their boats around our mooring buoy to watch the show.

On one of our swimming trips I lost my pay-book; it was found later, in the toilet, and subsequently returned. Next morning I was on commander's report. Cdr Dolphin commiserated with me, stating that the pockets in the supplied tropical clothing were unsuitable, however, AFOs had to be complied with. I was given fourteen days' stoppage of leave and with a wry grin he added, 'We will be at sea all that time!'

That night we slipped our mooring and set sail with our destroyers for Durban. The trip was uneventful, and as a man under punishment, I mustered daily with the group lighting party, which kept me away from extra working duties.

Back in Durban we visited our old haunts, the cinema (Bio-Scope) with the sliding roof, another where the admission charges included a meal served at your seat. One of the films I saw there was Victor Mature in *2000 Years BC*. An excursion one day took me to Verulam. The only thing I recall about this trip was the swarm of locusts descending on the area. I was standing on the station platform when they arrived – it was frightening so I took refuge in the waiting room. To this day I can still hear the dreadful droning noise.

Another caper we used to get up to ashore was to line up a few rickshaws outside the dockyard gates, with two of us in each, and race to Smith's Square; the winning boy was given a bonus by the losers. The lads enjoyed the race; all of them, in addition to their fee, were given plenty of cigarettes.

Whilst out one day we encountered a very large Zulu dressed in full feathered regalia. 'Rickshaw, Bwana?' he called.

Goldie said, 'Where to?' With a huge grin on his face he replied, 'Cape Town.' Seeing we had enjoyed his joke, he asked for a cigarette. Bob, shrugging his shoulders pointed to his pipe, where upon the beggar opened his box and produced a large calabash. Needless to say, Bob obliged.

It was during this visit to Durban that we were given seven days' leave and many of the crew, through the SAWAS, were given invites to various places. Ron and Goldie went to Johannesburg; Bob, Ginger and I stayed at a boarding house near Brighton Beach. If my memory serves me well, three women resided in the place; with respect, they were a bit long in the tooth, and they had the nasty habit of eyeing us all the time. Poor old Bob, having taken a bath and in the process of drying himself, had a visitor, who inspected his credentials and quietly closed the door.

Since our last visit, Durban had changed dramatically. Servicemen now passing through were behaving like hooligans, fighting, stealing, drunken brawls and causing wilful damage. Bars that once were open until 2300 hours now closed at 1700 hours. Where we were known, we could still go to our regular haunts. Access was by a side door – in our case it was the Tudor Bar, not far from the Esplanade. One night, having spent a pleasant evening in the Hollywood Restaurant, we observed Durban railway station being taken apart by a group of commandos. One of them was actually staggering out with a chocolate machine on a trolley. Because of these 'cretins', the city came to a halt after dark. Many of the smaller bars and restaurants closed permanently.

The rickshaw boys by law had to be off the streets by 1800 hours [and] were strictly controlled, performing this work for a maximum of eighteen months, as the work was considered strenuous on the heart. They mainly came from up-country; when they went home they were expected to have saved enough for a smallholding. The local bus service stopped at 1800 hours and taxis were at a premium – their fees were out of our range and that was provided you could get one – so we walked along the Esplanade back to the ship. One of the fascinating sides of Durban at night was no blackout. This was quite a novelty, considering we had been subjected to this in the UK since 1939!

Walking along the front one night we came across Cliff Mitchell. He had been out on a bender with Gerry Lunne and, to our horror, he told us the last he had seen of Gerry was climbing the railings into the snake park. We finally found him on the other side of the park, suspended upside down with one foot caught in the railings. Whether he had crossed the park we never knew; however, if he had been bitten, with the amount of alcohol inside him it would have killed the snake!

We left Durban for the last time at the height of summer 1943. With our faithful greyhounds and some troopers we made steady passage in pleasant weather to Mombasa, where on arrival we moored fore and aft with our portside to the jungle. One of the reasons we were here was because of the high tide. Japanese submarines were capable of landing troops in the area and penetrating the harbour. For about a week our 'Royals' patrolled the jungle during the night and our searchlight and gun crews were on standby. The harbour had no boom defence, resulting in ships in port supplying a patrol consisting of a motorboat plying backward and forward through the night, crossing the harbour and dropping charges every so often. With Spike Mahoney, PO, LTO, I went ashore to collect the requirements for this coming operation, ie Bickfords safety matches, fuses and charges. At the supply depot, the PO tried to give us Cortex fuses. Bearing in mind I had used this medium in Southampton, I warned Spike of the danger. The supply PO was very sheepish after he had been given a 'broadside'. Back on board, Spike gave me a 'sipper' of neaters![15]

That night I found myself in the boom patrol boat, which turned out to be a very uncomfortable night. Shortly after leaving the ship, I developed 'the runs'. This continued throughout most of the watch, during that time I was sitting on a bucket, applying a safety match to a length of fuse attached to a charge, squeezing it with pliers to ignite it, throwing it over the side and shouting, 'Rev it up, coxswain!'

One day we sailed for the usual firing practice. With us went a party of about six dignitaries bedecked in white suits; included in the party was a woman. Being the showpiece they came into 'A' turret. Everything went according to plan up to the loading and firing, then Jim Withers opened the breech of Lilian and out spewed a dirty yellow cloud of smoke: the air blast had failed. All were consumed with coughing and our whites and paintwork went black. Our guests looked a sad and sorry sight!

From Mombasa, with our escorts and the old cruiser HMS *Frobisher*, we sailed to Manza Bay, situated about five degrees from the equator. We were puzzled to learn we were here to carry out bombarding exercises. When in harbour the temperature was scorching. We worked from 0500 to 1100 hours.

It was here that I discovered that the 15in shell room wiring was faulty and with A/B Johnny Bowker, S/T, the 'B' turret monkey, we set about the task. The humidity was such we could only work below for about twenty minutes at a time. Dressed in a pair of flimsy shorts, and a sweatband round our heads, we laboured with perspiration streaming off us like a river into the shell bays. Our arms became leaded; by the time the job was completed we had lost a considerable amount of weight. Daily we carried out the required exercises with HMS *Frobisher*, firing both our 6in and 15in armaments. The night firing was very spectacular, huge tongues of flame spurted many yards across the water. Little did both ships know we were preparing for Normandy !

Our anchorage off Manza Bay offered no shore leave as such, however, sailing was permitted. It was on one of these trips a party of us set off with a supply of lime juice and strict instructions not to visit the nearby small town because of a smallpox outbreak. After a while we came across a small village, there appeared to be no sign of life, but canoes were parked under the sloping palm trees. Being not sure of the tide, we decided to drop our small anchor and swim ashore, leaving two non-swimmers in the boat. The water was warm – when we got into the surf it was boiling; the sand was like a furnace. Our clothing consisted of a shirt, money belt, trunks, but no shoes. Being that the sand was too hot to walk on, we took off our shirt and trunks, and walked on them up the beach. From the water's edge to the trees was about thirty yards, what a sight to behold, about a dozen 'hairy a****' matelots groping their way up the beach with just a money belt on! Having got to the point of no return we were aware we being watched – in fact, the whole village appeared from the trees giggling like a load of monkeys. They were very hospitable, giving us fruit and beer, they even made our return to the boat more dignified. On leaving them we left them with some East African money.

Christmas 1943 was celebrated back in Mombasa. It was strange, dressed in tropical kit, absolutely roasting below deck, and eating turkey that we had brought aboard in Devonport. The mess deck was decorated with palm leaves, coloured lamps were hung, adding to the heat, even condoms were inflated in the place of balloons. In the harbour was the hospital ship, and on Christmas Eve we witnessed a most moving sight aboard her, the medical staff, including nurses in their red capes, walking from deck to deck carrying lanterns and singing carols.

In ninety degrees of heat we sat down to a traditional Christmas dinner and in the afternoon most of us went swimming, later to have another meal in the Rex Hotel. I can still see my chicken leg arriving floating in oil! That evening we spent in the canteen; here we met Bonsa. He was delighted to see us and seemed content. He was billeted in a hut next to an army major who suffered with the same complaint; now speaking in a squeaky voice, his only concern was walking back to his billet on windy days. Coconuts had a tendency to arrive unannounced. Thinking about him these days, he reminded me of Ben Gunn in *Treasure Island*.

Prior to leaving Mombasa we were stunned to learn that the ship's company was to be reduced. The ratings selected were mainly men with the least service time. To our dismay, Ginger was one of them; another on our mess deck was the wireman with the foghorn voice. In most cases they were drafted to the Far East.

Now the next port of call was to be Aden. There is a matelot's song that begins like that, but my granddaughters will no doubt read this narrative. It was on this trip that we lost our fourth member of crew, A/B White, Q/O. He was a time-serving man billeted on our mess deck. He had become moody and depressed – some days he would be vacant, on others aggressive. One morning he was missing after dawn action stations, it was assumed that he had thrown himself over the side.

On arrival at Aden, no shore leave was granted as bubonic plague was rife in Quator Town. We moored at the old coaling station which was alive with ragged birds the size of a rook. They had light brown and white feathers. One of the comforts we had looked forward to was fresh water, just the thought of having a bath out of a bucket, and rinsing off with a bucket of fresh water was good! Instead, what was pumped inboard was almost brine. Having washed my hair it stood up like a load of spikes; come to think of it, I must have been the forerunner of punk rockers!

From Aden we sailed through the Red Sea to Suez Bay; the weather had turned cold especially during the night. As we crept our way toward our anchorage, I with the fo'c'sle party was dressed in tropical kit. Lt Cdr Evans, seeing our plight, made a request to the bridge for permission to change into blues. The White Abbo would have seen us freeze first. As the sun began to rise, the sky and surrounding hills became deep red, turning lighter as it gained height, then, when we dropped our anchor, thousands and thousands of flamingos took to the air – what a sight, never to be forgotten!

Once again bubonic plague was about, this time in Suez Town; however, shore leave was piped for the port watch in Port Tufic. During the afternoon a launch came alongside and a searchlight was hoisted on to the foc's'le and secured for'ard, then a boat with two traders was lifted onto our boat deck. We had been advised to be wary of who and where we purchased our souvenirs – the two chaps aboard were registered traders supplying leather goods, trinkets, fruit and confectionery. I purchased two handbags, two boxes of Turkish Delight and some photographs.

It was here we said a fond farewell to our destroyers – no doubt they went off to nurse another charge. That night with the assistance of tugs, our searchlight on, all screen doors and hatches firmly closed (given a chance, the Arabs would steal the shirt off your back), we entered the Suez Canal. Next morning as dawn broke we saw the wonder of this phenomenon, a waterway that passes through the desert.

During the day we passed the canal service stations and working parties of Italian prisoners, guarded by French Foreign Legionnaires wearing their traditional kepi.

Aden: 15in shells being made ready for lowering down into the shell room.

At the Bitter Lakes we released our tow, and proceeded through on our own steam. It was here we saw numerous Italian naval ships that had recently surrendered at anchor. On re-entering the canal, our tugs again took over and it was along this stretch we encountered two wrecks, victims of the magnetic mine. Slowly, we edged our way past, on one we scraped our port blister. An RAF Wellington with an anti-magnetic coil attached patrolled the area.

On arrival at Port Said, we tied up near Government Building: it was surrounded with barbed wire and sandbags. There were plenty of well-laundered army sentries and Red Caps[16] about. One of the imposing sights of the canal were the statues of the canal builder Ferdinand de Lesseps. Sadly, they were destroyed during the Suez Crisis.

I recall little of Port Said: I found it very crowded and smelly, servicemen were everywhere. It was here for the first time we saw the troops wearing their medal ribbon, much to the consternation of our American 'sin bo'sun', who complained why ours had not been issued. Whilst we were here numerous naval traffic passed through the canal, including the battlecruiser HMS *Renown* and an aircraft carrier. No doubt they were en route for the Eastern Fleet.

For some months a PO's and L/S's course had been in progress. Bob was keen to participate and urged me to join him. Although I agreed, I had no intention of taking the exam, for should I have passed and only being an S/T, it would have meant me leaving the torpedo party, and going to another part of the ship. I recall on one occasion sitting in some obscure compartment with a made-up Aldis lamp, sending out Morse to about six potential candidates. Bob eventually passed, not bad for a hostilities-only man, and there was more to come!

From Port Said, well escorted, we sailed to Algiers and from the outset we immediately went to the second degree of readiness. Even at that period of the war nobody was prepared to take chances in the Mediterranean. The voyage was uneventful, reports were received of enemy aircraft, but they came to nothing.

On arrival at Algiers, we tied up stern to wall, large catamarans from the quarterdeck gangway to an elevated brow gave access ashore, blue group lighting was rigged for night passage. It was here I saw large beetles between the 'cats' timbers – they had black and yellow striped backs and were the size of a small terrapin!

Like Casablanca, Algiers had suffered from our naval bombardment. Wrecks were scattered about the harbour, but again there was no damage ashore. On my first trip ashore I encountered the sight of what could have been alcoholics sleeping in various places in the dockyard, their eyes covered in a mass of flies. Algiers is a tiered city, then governed by the French. The buildings were predominately white, the avenues were narrow and lined with medium-sized trees – in some cases access from one to the other was via alleys with very steep steps. Whilst there I visited the Casbah: this was only possible under American escort in a jeep. The area was mainly Arab: it looked very seedy; all the bars, etc, were out of bounds. Ashore one day with Charlie Chase and Sid Drew, we visited a large store. It was here I purchased wool for my mother. The language problem was soon overcome by signs. I pointed to an assistant about the size of my mum, then to the wool I required, resulting in much laughter. I still have the photograph of the three of us, with the package of wool under my arm.

It was here that one of our mooring wires parted: it was called a 'ganger'. It was the largest wire in the ship and was housed roved around 'Y' turret. As previously stated, I had worked in the rigging shop while in Port Edgar, my father having taught me some years before. This resulted in the instructor on the training course assigning me the task of showing the class the art of splicing a 'soft eye'. I must admit, it was like handling a lively conger eel!

With our destroyers, whose names I have forgotten, we sailed to Gibraltar, arriving this time in daylight and anchoring in the bay. The harbour had been vastly improved, again I believe thanks to the Americans. As you would expect, the place is very Spanish, but it seemed strange to see British Bobbies[17] and our red pillar boxes. Most of the bars boasted guitar-playing señors, flamenco dancers and women wearing mantillas and large combs in their hair. Those days the 'Rock' practised a two-price system, up when any large ship or ships came in, and down when they went out. At the time the place was crawling with matelots.

Assuming that we were on our way home, what money I had went on presents, a small bottle of scent for my mum and a leather wallet for Dad. I also purchased a large hand of green bananas. On our last day at Gib, Bob, Ron and Goldie and I were making our way back to the ship, having visited Alameda Gardens, when we came across A/B Armstrong, the gun layer from 'A' turret. 'Armie' was a three-badge man who had spent a period on the Rock before the war. He had been visiting an acquaintance and he was carrying, among other things, an extra-large bottle of what we never found out, except it was very potent. Not being able to take liquor aboard we hailed a 'Garry' and disposed of the contents in comfort back to the docks. The effects did not take long to show; aboard the liberty boat, Bob's unsteady actions gave us cause for concern. Being a L/Seaman he was required to fall in separately to us. Fortunately, we were in tropical rig, so we untied his killick's badge and propped him up in the rear rank between a couple of us. Within minutes of reaching the mess deck, the four of us were spark out. When I came to, we were at sea. One of the lads had covered my fo'c'sle duty. We suffered no ill effects from this escapade – in fact, we pooled what money we had left and played tombola. It turned out to be a good investment; we won the last full house. How much I cannot remember, except it put us back on the gold standard. So, with our greyhounds and convoy of merchant ships, we set out to cross the Bay of Biscay (it was friendly this time!) up to the Irish Sea, into the Clyde, to moor off Greenock.

On leaving Gibraltar we had changed into blues, the temperature plummeted, the fans I had purloined were stowed away and the heaters came out. Life in the turrets became pretty miserable, condensation dripped from the deckhead, for the lads who slept on the deck on 'corkers' (bed roll) were subjected to water running down the bulkhead. On our arrival at Greenock, we were welcomed with bitterly cold snow showers, a situation we were not conditioned for and many of the crew were soon to succumb to colds.

In next to no time the Customs launch was alongside. It was rumoured they were royally entertained in the wardroom. Shortly after their departure, the mysterious signed notice appeared on the ship's noticeboard stating that we had exactly twenty-eight days to get our 'rabbits' (contraband) ashore. On the twenty-ninth day, the Boys Instructor, a PO, was stopped at the Customs Control, and found to have a carton containing one hundred cigarettes. This cost him the loss of his Long Service Medal, which I believe carried a pension.

Wearing thin Burberrys,[18] the four of us set out to visit Glasgow; en route we visited a pub just outside the dockyard. The place was packed to capacity. Having just secured a drink, I was tapped on the shoulder by a local who enquired if I had got a drink, when I replied, 'Yes,' he then said, 'Get out of the bl**** way, I've not had one yet.' On another visit to this pub we were confronted by a kilted Scot carrying a set of bagpipes, and a sad tale of woe. Having collected generously from the matelots, he explained that by law he had to play outside. After some time had elapsed the question was raised regarding the music. The bartender said he was probably now in the next pub spinning the same yarn, adding that it was more than likely that he could not play the pipes.

The transport to Glasgow was limited, we flagged down a lorry, and the driver allowed us to jump in the back. To our dismay, he was carrying torpedoes – shale oil was everywhere. At Port Glasgow we got off and waited in the rain for a train. We arrived at Glasgow, cold and miserable, a blizzard was raging, and snow had settled to a depth of eight inches. In Glasgow, because of the snow drifts, when crossing one of the roads we were not aware that the kerb was about eighteen inches high, resulting in four unhappy 'tars' lying prostrate. We found solace in the nearest cinema.

Fourteen days' leave was given to the ship's company. Armed with my gifts, plus tinned fruit, jam, butter, and a loaf of white bread (wartime bread was a brownish colour), I set off like a pack-mule for the 'Smoke' (London). The night journey was pretty grim, nearly always one sat or stood in the corridors all the way to King's Cross station. We set out on this journey all spick and span and arrived looking like a 'pull-through'. I experienced a very embarrassing incident while the bus was going to Liverpool Street station. At sea, our bank notes were housed in a contraceptive (should you go over the side they were kept waterproof). For some reason, mine were still stowed in this fashion! I was confronted by the conductress for the fare only to find that I had not got the required loose change.

On arrival home, my parents killed off the fatted calf in the shape of a chicken. My mother was over the moon with her wool, and her handbag. Her Turkish Delights lasted about two years, only having a piece on high days and holy days. Dad's best gift was his two half-pound tins of 'ticklers' (cigarette tobacco). The bananas travelled well; however, it was disappointing that my niece and nephew, having never seen this fruit before, would not touch them.

With leave over, some of our crew left the ship – there were no replace-ments, although we took little notice at this point. Firing practice was carried out in the Ailsa Craig area, with emphasis on damage control. After a while we sailed to Scapa Flow and on arrival found many naval and merchant ships at anchor. Many of these merchant ships were destined to be used as blockships at Normandy. Later the cruiser *Belfast* arrived with King George VI, onboard to review the fleet. When the King arrived onboard, we were lined up in our various parts of ship. He spoke to one of our old shellbacks, having spotted a horned pipe sticking out of his jumper. Having enquired of its origin, laughingly he assured him that he would not be put on a charge for being improperly dressed.

King George VI being welcomed aboard *Ramillies* at Scapa Flow.

It was very noticeable that the King was ill, he looked drawn, and to combat his sallow complexion he was wearing foundation makeup. In our travels along the way we had acquired a bushbaby and the King was most intrigued by its antics whilst taking tea in the admiral's stateroom. He left Scapa Flow aboard *Belfast*, flying the signal, 'Splice the mainbrace.' For all, this was the best part of the day as it meant an extra tot of rum!

While at Scapa Flow it was discovered that some of our AA firing circuits had sustained damage, the result of an engine room uptake being left open, so Rosyth dockyard was our next destination. On entering the Firth of Forth I was back in familiar waters. Seeing the Bass Rock, and Inchkeith lighthouse and the majestic Forth Bridge made me remember my previous shipmates. As we approached the bridge I recall standing on the fo'c'sle listening to the speculation as to whether our aerials would clear. They did, with plenty to spare.

Whilst our repairs were being carried out, I took advantage of reviewing 'the New' (Edinburgh), places like the Usher Hall, the King's Theatre, The Three Tuns, near St Andrew's Square, and Fairley's Dance Hall. My one disappointment was not being able to see Hibernian FC play. We managed to see a couple of films there and for some reason Bob, Ron and I dashed over to Glasgow.

The King inspecting officers on the quarterdeck.

D-Day, 6 June 1944: Operation Neptune through the eyes of a turret monkey

From Rosyth, we sailed through the Pentland Firth to Greenock. It was late May 1944, and buzzes were going round the ship that we still had problems with our firing circuits and that leave was imminent. On arrival at Greenock, more of our crew left us, including our respected Commander Dolphin, who was replaced by Commander Campbell.[19] What we did know was that he had been made captain, but what we did not know was that he was to be one of the beach marshals at Normandy. His day of departure was very nostalgic, and in his last speech he humbly thanked us for everything – except Casablanca! He was piped over the side and climbed aboard the captain's launch, and the whole crew, lining the starboard side, gave him three hearty cheers. The Marine band played 'Sussex by the Sea'. He circled the ship twice, beating time with the music, before departing. Many of the old shellbacks remarked that they had never known a naval officer to be so popular.

Shortly after this, another puzzle presented itself – three foreign naval lieutenants came aboard, one from France, one from America, and one from Russia. The Russian gave his flunkey a hard time, making him scrub out his cabin three times before he was satisfied.

On the evening of 2 June 1944, we sailed down the Clyde. On the foc's'le, as the special sea dutyman, I recall one of our greyhounds racing by with her SRE blaring out 'The March of the Guns'. I remarked to the cable officer that I had never seen so much Aldis lamp activity on leaving harbour before.

After a while, our SRE came to life, announcing the captain would be speaking in fifteen minutes' time. All were convinced that Rosyth was our destination – with a railway warrant at the end of it.

Above and right: Normandy, 6 June 1944. *Ramillies* opens fire.

This is the captain speaking. I am delighted to inform you that we are on our way to participate in history! The second front is about to commence. Landings are to made on the Normandy coast of France on the morning of 5 June 1944. The combined operation is called OVERLORD and the naval operations NEPTUNE. Detailed briefings by divisional officers will be given in due course. Good luck to you all!

An air of doom and gloom descended all around. What was the use of an old tub that could not maintain more than five rounds of 15in per turret before breaking down? This conversation continued from then on and opinions were unanimous – a bloodbath. I sat down to write a letter home, and then tore it up – the post box was closed.

On the morning of 3 June 1944 the briefings were held in the 'Rec' space and the three foreign lieutenants were present aboard as observers. We were told that there [were] to be two task forces: the Western (American) covering the Utah and Omaha Beaches, and the Eastern (British) covering Gold, Juno and Sword Beaches. We were assigned Sword.

Rear Admiral Philip Vian was in charge of the Eastern task force aboard the cruiser HMS *Scylla*, Rear Admiral Arthur Talbot was in charge of Sword aboard the converted passenger vessel HMS *Largs* (HQ). With us was the battleship HMS *Warspite*, the monitor HMS *Roberts*, and cruisers *Dragon*, *Mauritius*, *Frobisher*, *Arethusa*, *Danae*, and eleven destroyers.

For our initial target we had drawn the 6in railway guns at Benerville; *Warspite* had the 16in battery at Villerville, and *Roberts* a battery at Houlgate. The action was scheduled for 0500 hours on 5 June 1944. We were given

details of the landings, the role of paratroopers and gliders. The sinking of blockships in preparation for the construction of the Mulberry harbours and even PLUTO (Pipe Line Under The Ocean) was mentioned. Many other details were also mentioned, including where the hospital ships were situated, and wearing one's lifebelts. We were each given a letter from Supreme Allied Headquarters, Allied Expeditionary Force, signed by Dwight D Eisenhower, Supreme Commander. What was even more horrifying was that once the landings were established, we would anchor fore and aft.

Aboard at this time, two of the crew were incapacitated. A Marine had sustained a broken leg, and A/B Mainsbridge, S/T, had a broken arm – both men were in plaster. The captain was requested to put them ashore, but the request was denied on the grounds of security. Under the circumstances, they would have to take their chances like the rest of the crew should anything untoward happen.

The ship was systematically prepared for action. All utensils on the mess decks were stowed away – in fact, everything that could be moved was secured. The anchors were 'catted' and the cable stowed in the locker below. We were advised to bathe and put on clean clothing, prior to going to action stations. As I recall we fed very well. Whilst in Devonport, the *Millie* had a barrage tower installed, but the equipment was never fitted. On the morning of 4 June 1944, I was instructed to supply a length of asbestos cable, a battery and a firing key, then report to one of these towers, on the starboard side. I was required to wire up a V-shaped ramp that had been erected for firing Window rockets.

Our passage from Greenock had been comfortable, but during the evening of 4 June the weather began to change. At dusk we closed up and remained at night defence stations, later to be told that, due to weather conditions, the operation had been cancelled for twenty-four hours.

During the early hours of the 5 June 1944, I went to the galley for a fanny of cocoa (kai) and was chatting with Lofty, a leading cook (I have since found out that it was Eric Marks). I asked him how he felt about the impending action and he replied that he felt just as apprehensive as everyone else. I could not have agreed more. At dawn, the vastness of the operation became apparent. We were off the Needles at the Isle of Wight, with many, many ships of all shapes and sizes, including the old American battleship USS *Texas*.

On the night of the 5th we again closed up. The armoured door under the turret was winched up and clamped into position and the sliding manhole on the top closed. The only way out now was to climb down a 3ft x 3ft trunking, hand over hand, to the magazine via the 15in shell room. Above the magazine hatch was a brass plate, recording the loss of the magazine crew – the compartment was flooded by the lieutenant when the fire broke out.

During the afternoon a church service was held in the chapel of St George, and no doubt the 'sin bo'sun' prayed for a good result. The last time I had spoken to him he was still upset that our medal ribbons had not been issued.

In 1940 HMS *Ramillies* was in Wellington, New Zealand, and on leaving with a number of Maori troops for Singapore (to escort the first echelon of New Zealand troops to the Middle East, along with a large contingent of Australian troops subsequently picked up from that country), the captain was presented with a *piupiu*, a Maori (male) skirt. This was a very rare gift, said to protect the ship if worn in times of danger. As the ship cast off, a choir sang the Maori farewell, 'Now is the Hour', in Maori and English. Captain Middleton wore the skirt on the morning of 6 June 1944.

As previously stated, the ship's company had been reduced. The seamen of 'A' manned both 'A' and 'B' turrets, as required, and the Royal Marines manned 'X' and 'Y'. When Colours were sounded on the morning of the 6th, we raised two enormous battle flags, the white ensign and the Union Jack. With bated breath we watched the clock creeping nearer to zero hour and at the same time praying that we had not been spotted by the German shore batteries. Suddenly, the order was given, 'With AP and HE shells and a full

Warspite and *Ramillies* off the beach head at Normandy with a Hunt-class destroyer in the foreground.

charge, load! Load! Load!' Instantly the turret was consumed with the noises of breech, cage and rammers, followed by the training engine. Nobody spoke, the interceptor lights glimmered, the only noise now was the gun layers applying the required range. The order of firing was to be HE fractionally before the AP, as the HE fuse was delicate.

Approximately at 0530 hours, the two standby bells sounded. Almost immediately our guns erupted and from then on we were loading and firing as fast as possible. The smell of burning residue crept into the gun house and it became very warm. The lads tied the top half of their overalls around their waists. Due to the constant concussion some of them developed nose bleeding.

Being the least occupied, I went round with a bucket of water, flannel and towel. As the day went on we all developed nausea and headaches. After forty-eight rounds, a walking pipe (hydraulic) valve burst. The gun crew immediately transferred to 'B' turret. During the action, we were kept informed of some of the events to date, the progress of the landing craft, the landing, and later the positioning and sinking of the blockships in preparation for the Mulberry harbours.

Initially, the noise of the guns was deafening and we also felt the shudder of our after turret firing. As time went by we became used to the din; the apprehension, at first very apparent, soon diminished! The guns crew worked like clockwork, their hours of training paid off, there was no shouting other than to make their report. Upon the guns' recoil, one heard the hiss of the hydraulics opening the breech, the air blast, the cage arriving and the next consignment, the rammer, the cage returning, the breech closing, interceptor made, the training engine and the report, 'Gun ready.' Another one-ton shell on its way!

At about 1100 hours the gunner's mate suggested that I go looking for food and drink, also anything else that I could purloin. Down the trunking I went; at the galley, corn beef sandwiches were available. With two potato boxes full and a dixie of tea, I returned to the shell room where they were hauled up into the gun house.

I then went exploring, first having a look from the boat deck – the sight was quite unbelievable. The shoreline was a mass of smoke and flame, the noise from the guns all around was horrendous, everything seemed to be vibrating, everywhere I looked smoke and flames was coming from guns. The sea was a mass of ships of all shapes and sizes, landing craft with troops, tanks, guns and all manner of equipment were heading for the beaches. On our portside, a landing craft full with wounded requested our assistance, but they were directed to the hospital ship.

From the signal deck, with the aid of binoculars, I recall seeing what looked like Bren-gun carriers making their way across a field, with troops crouched down behind. I thought to myself, 'Thank God I am in the Andrew!'

My return to the turret was even more welcome than the food. Passing the regulating officer, I observed that rum was being issued. On being asked which mess I came from, I explained that the 'A' turret gun crew were incarcerated and could not get to their messes. Much to my amazement, I was given a liberal supply.

It was whilst below, again restoring lamps, that I came across our Q/O Tiffy having problems with the sliding tray that transfers the shells to the gun loading cage. I spent some time with a tin of thick grease and a brush, greasing the runners, whilst he attended to another problem. The lads were chalking on the shells all manner of advice to Hitler.

The armoured door under the turret was now released, enabling the gun crew to have a breath of fresh air and a cigarette. At about 1600 hours, whilst we were on the upper deck, the air became black with gliders and their tugs. We watched them released to our right and the tugs returning to our left. Just watching them slowly descending into the unknown was awe-inspiring. I wonder what were the thoughts of these men – I at least knew where, if not when, I would be sleeping that night.

By now the 16in, and all but three of the 6in train guns, had been put out of action by the RAF; the remaining 6in and mobile guns were still causing problems.

The story is now taken up by Bob Cliff, a radar rating now domiciled in Australia. It appeared we had come under fire from the 6in guns, at that point in time Bob, with his party, were in the mess-deck area. They were ordered to lay flat on the deck. Bob has since stated that the old girl, at full astern, was vibrating like hell as she withdrew from the area.

The guns in question remained a problem for some time, even our spotter aircraft had difficulty in pinning them down. Eventually, we destroyed their escape routes and subsequently the guns. During the afternoon I received an urgent call from the shell room, they were nearly in darkness. With my tool bag hanging from my belt, I went below, finding that most of the lamps had broken as a result of the concussion. It was whilst perched up on the side of a shell bay, unscrewing a shade to replace a lamp, that the SRE came to life. 'E-boat attack, E-boat attack! Hard to starboard!'

The *Millie* could almost turn round on a sixpence. It was whilst holding on to a stanchion for grim death, I heard torpedoes race by on either side, followed by a loud thump. It was the Hunt-class destroyer, HMS *Svenner*, with a Norwegian crew. Fifty years later I learnt that one hundred survivors were picked up by HMS *Swift* against orders. She too was sunk some days later.

From the shell room I made a quick trip to the upper deck, seeing HMS *Svenner* in two halves. A Carley raft floated by – a body was underneath with an arm trapped in the netting, a watch was on the wrist! We continued firing throughout the day, eventually running out of 15in ammunition. That evening we sailed for Portsmouth, arriving in the early forenoon. Only the postman was allowed ashore; he returned with the mail and first edition of the local papers.

We had moored near to designated ammunition lighters, one for every ship except us. A member of the ammunition party, having received some verbal abuse, suggested we were expendable. It did not go down very well (fifty years later the newspaper *Navy News* confirms this in many D-Day features). Eventually, our requirements arrived, we ammunitioned at full speed, then proceeded back to the Sword area.

For the next week we were kept pretty busy giving assistance to the fighting ashore. We would get calls from our troops to dislodge areas of resistance. Daily we saw amazing sights, railway engines and cranes on barges, also sections of the Mulberry harbours being towed by tugs; I also saw PLUTO (Pipe Line Under The Ocean) being laid. From time to time the air was filled with the roar of the multi-rocket launchers.

Another amazing sight was four destroyers near the mouth of the river Seine running on to a target in line ahead, firing until their guns would not bear, then going round again. About D-Day +3, HMS *Nelson* joined us; I watched her firing a 6in broadside. Her 16in guns were out of action due to cracked barbettes, the result of previous torpedo and mine damage.

Allied aircraft had strict instructions not to fly over the fleet during the operation. One afternoon an RAF Typhoon came flying over at great speed. It met with extensive AA fire from the fleet, our Oerlikons and Chicago Pianos let loose. I am not sure if he survived. Another occasion when we were called upon to give assistance was when our troops were bogged down by snipers. The American observer in the spotter plane gave us a very fruity commentary describing a large chimney crashing down.

The time came for a direct assault on the town of Caen. A barrage said to be bigger than the one at Alamein was due to commence at 2300 hours. The *Millie*, with *Warspite* and *Roberts*, was anchored line ahead. We had been firing for less than an hour when things became uncomfortable. Bombs began to fall around us and a ceasefire was ordered. Fortunately, the bomb aimers were aiming between the flashes of either ship. After a while we recommenced firing – the barrage was considerable. Eyewitnesses said that the sky glowed and that the huge tongues of flame from the fleet's guns was enormous and the noise horrendous; the assault was a failure.

As result of the constant gunfire from the fleet and batteries ashore, at times we were actually vibrating, with huge shoals of jellyfish all around us. As the action died down, long spells of inactivity prevailed – we were even allowed to play deck hockey on the quarterdeck.

Service personnel and all types of stores and equipment going ashore was non-ending, the scene was out of this world. At the time I never gave thought as to the planning required for the operation. It was not until later years when the story unfolded that the sheer magnitude of the operation sunk in! Our only casualty was the bushbaby, which the King had been so fascinated with at Scapa Flow. It had been put in a supposedly safe place but unfortunately had suffocated!

After about D-Day +12 (18 June), we were withdrawn. At the time we were not aware that it was to prepare for the landing in southern France: Operation Dragoon. That evening, we sailed for Portsmouth looking a sad and sorry sight. The paintwork had been burnt off the 15in guns and the turrets. Some of the deck planking had sprung and sections of the guard-rail [were] missing. Below deck, carnage was everywhere. Overhead channel plating carrying electric cables had come down and mess traps had come away from their bulkhead fittings. The master-at-arms (Jaunty) R/CPO had his cabin next to the sickbay: it was completely flattened. On the fo'c'sle mess deck some broadside mess tables attached to the bulkhead were smashed in half; they measured 15ft x 3ft x 1.5ft. Broken glass littered the deck from deckhead and bulkheads lights, such was the concussion!

There is an interesting point to ponder, it is possible that the *Millie* during the Neptune action became the only ship in the history of the Royal Navy to have fired the most 15in shells in one action! HMS *Warspite* developed problems and was withdrawn.

Our arrival in Portsmouth was royally received and cheering crowds lined the Hard Blockhouse, and HMS *Dolphin*. We docked in the inner harbour and from the fo'c'sle I saw Fred Hiller, now in the Andrew. He was one of the shore mooring party. We had a reunion aboard, and later he left with plenty of duty-frees. Shore leave was given, but only as far as Havant. With a ticket to Havant many of us proceeded to London. For a while we remained on standby, taking advantage of numerous illicit trips home. The all-round trip cost us just sixpence. I would walk the two miles to Chadwell Heath station, meet up with Ted Moss, catching the 0230 hours train to Liverpool Street station, walking to Waterloo station, and catching the Portsmouth/Southampton paper train.

One of these excursions, about thirty of us were put in the wrong half of the train (truck). As with most gatherings of servicemen, the language was pretty raw. As it got light, we were horrified to find a woman amongst us. She had received news that her son had been wounded and was somewhere in the Southampton area. She left us with all manner of goodies, our apologies and best wishes. Our problem was now getting back on board in time. We arrived at Pompey with minutes to spare: running like hares we arrived back on board about seven minutes late. RPO Moody accused us of going to London, which, of course, we vehemently denied!

One day who should walk into the mess deck but Tommy Sullivan: his minesweeper was in the dockyard. Needless to say, we had a fair old time ashore. I finished up aboard his boat and had a good time with his mates; in fact, they suggested staying aboard for the night, but the neaters were flowing thick and fast, and I did not want to get into one of those sessions.

Came the day when we were warped under the giant crane in the dockyard, Operation Neptune had worn our 15in guns out. Ordnance workmen descended upon us, stripping off the roof of the turrets, taking out our old guns, and replacing them with new. We said goodbye to Lorna and Lilian, and hello to their replacements and, when completed, Jim Withers was soon painting, polishing and burnishing.

As a result of the amount of hours firing and a minor incident, a turret's gun-house crew were suffering from poor vision. Consequently, we were sent to Whale Island for an eye test. Those days, HMS *Excellent* was the gunnery school for the world. It was here that we trained the Japanese gunnery officers, prior to 1939, how to knock eight bells out of us later on! With my gun-house colleagues, I duly arrived outside the gates of this feared establishment, not suspecting I was going to be set up by the very men who I had looked after during hot and cold weather, and supplying them with food and drink on 6 June. Across the main gate entrance was a foot-thick white line, this I casually walked across.

Immediately, the air erupted with a most deafening order, 'That man there!' It came from a PO with a mouth like a hippopotamus. 'Come here and double!' he screamed. I hastily obeyed his order and running on the spot he

enquired the purpose of my visit. Explaining the reason, I pointed to my so-called mates who were grinning on the other side of the white line. At the time I was wearing a Burberry, and the bow of the cap ribbon was over my right eye. He instructed me to take my coat off and, on seeing my torpedo badge, further loud abuse followed. I was given a lecture on how to enter a man's establishment, and how to dress correctly. 'Once you put your foot on that white line, you double!' The latter advice I swear could have been heard in Brighton!

Still shaking from the broadside I had received, we proceeded doubling past the parade ground on our left, and what appeared to be trainee 6in gun crews on our right. We were still laughing about the incident, when suddenly I nearly jumped out of my skin – one of the 6in guns fired, followed by another.

The optician was a commander RNVR, a pleasant man who immediately put me at ease. Having completed the preliminaries, he adjusted a metal frame over my eyes in which he placed different lenses. It was whilst doing this and holding a desk lamp I received a sharp pain in my eye. Asking why I kept jumping, I said I was getting an electric shock. He seemed surprised – he was even more so when I stripped the lamp down and found it to be earthing. He was delighted and come to think of it so was I!

The *Millie* soon began to look her old self above and below deck, our blood pressure became normal, although flying bombs were now arriving. As

Ramillies lying off Greenock on the Firth of Clyde towards the end of World War Two.

time went by, news of our successes in France began to come through and with it thoughts of the war coming to an end began to creep into our minds.

It was not long before we were on the move again, alas once again the memory fades, I cannot recall where we sailed to, the testing of our new guns. Did we go back to Gibraltar before going to Algiers? It was now August 1944 and this time we were aware of another landing, unofficially, but where and when would come later. Algiers at the height of summer was a very uncomfortable place; the temperature was over the nineties, our discomfort increased by the sirocco, winds that blew in from the desert. We found breathing very laborious, at night it was difficult to sleep. Ashore, the perspiration dripped off us as we sought respite in the bars, drinking cool beers and wines. To make matters worse, the sea around the port was polluted. This meant no swimming or using our canvas pools.

The time came for us to depart. It was nice to be getting away from the heat, but once again the anxiety of taking part in another landing returned. We left Algiers for the last time, with a destroyer escort; the only one I can recall was HMS *Wessex*.

During the voyage we were again briefed on the plan of action – the operation's code name was 'DRAGOON'. We would be operating in the Marseilles and Toulon areas. Our three Allied officers were still with us, I do not recall all the facts at the briefing, but one point is indelible in my mind. The last two waves of troops to go ashore were American and British, in that order. We were told that our commandos were there to keep the Americans moving! All eyes turned to the American lieutenant, he just nodded in agreement to this amazing remark!

On the morning of 15 August 1944 we opened fire, as at Normandy, one gun crew to man two turrets. The initial bombardment did not last very long and from then we were used as required. The weather for the operation was perfect. The troops aboard the landing craft had a flat calm sea, and a warm mist prevailed, a little different to Neptune. Once again, a considerable Allied naval force was present. It included one of our modern cruisers HMS *Black Prince*, the old battleship *Texas*, and the French cruiser *Gloria*.

During the day an incident occurred regarding a small boat full of German soldiers. They were of the ethnic variety who had been pressed into service by their masters. Things ashore must have been pretty sticky, surrender to them being the better part of valour. They had been picked up by the destroyer USS *Moresby* and transferred to us, as one of our officers could speak German. There [were], if I recall, about fourteen. I have two photographs of them walking on our quarterdeck; they were later returned the same way as they came. During this period a gun battery ashore was causing problems. We had fired many salvoes to no avail, even our spotter plane could not locate the position; however, after the Germans had been interrogated, a few rounds did the trick.

That night we sailed for Corsica, using the most beautiful Bay of Propriano for our night anchorage, returning daily off the French coast and firing as required. This went on for about a week, finally leaving one warm misty night for Propriano. We had not been under way very long, when a string of large red spheres appeared on the starboard side. Commander Campbell, having congratulated the 15in gun crews on their prowess, invited the Oerlikon gunners to sink these objects. Not one of the gunners hit the target from about one hundred yards, much to the annoyance of the AA gunner's mate. With a face like thunder, he strapped himself into a gun, and taking aim hit the target with every burst; he was given a derisive cheer from the turret crew.

At Propriano we lazed and swam, looking forward to going home. As previously stated, the bay was beautiful, with golden sands and no obstructions on the beaches; also many of the naval craft there were old and some leaking oil, resulting in the beaches soon becoming contaminated. There was no urban area nearby, apart from one farmhouse and its grapevines, and no transport to take us inland.

The day dawned when the old *Millie* left the Mediterranean for the last time, sailing to Gibraltar, staying for a few days and buying the usual gifts, not forgetting the bananas, and finally arriving back at Greenock. After seven days' leave, we were towed into the Gareloch; here we remained on standby for some time, using Helensburgh for shore leave.

It was from here [that] I was able to enjoy a couple of weekend leaves with Gerry Lunne and his wife in Glasgow. One of Gerry's old shipmates, now a CPO, had a big house on the outskirts. I was made very welcome but, alas, one of his daughters was going through a rough passage having had news that her husband, a matelot, had been killed.

The biggest problem whilst on standby was boredom. Competitions were held, quizzes were broadcast, and a five-mile road race was organised. Cdr Campbell had a brother stationed in a nearby army barracks, I have forgotten his rank, who organised a route march to keep us fit, led by a kilted piper, for all those that could not get out of it! At one stage alarm prevailed. Buzzes swept round the ship that we were going to the Far East, when all that was on our minds was going home for good. In November, we returned to Portsmouth; here many of the crew left. Bob was now a petty officer; he departed to Roedean, where he qualified as a TGM (torpedo gunner's mate). Captain Middleton was promoted to rear admiral; he went there as commanding officer. Bob became his dry land coxswain (chauffeur). I spent Christmas at home, the first since 1940, it was very austere, but nice to be home.

The *Millie* remained on standby until 14 May 1945; hostilities had ceased in Europe on 7 May, VE Day. One of the most noticeable events was lifting the blackout. The celebrations in Pompey were fantastic – I, with some of the lads, went to the Coppersmith's Arms in Northend.

Now that the war in Europe was over, X-rays became the order of the day, for ratings had spent months in damp and draughty conditions, resulting in many cases of TB coming to light. The day came for me to attend RNB (Royal Naval Barracks). The sickbay tiffy[20] said, 'Stand up close, chest out, and wait for the second click.' I moved on the first. We were told that unless there was a problem, no notification would be given. To my horror, next day I was summoned back to RNB, and told I was to be X-rayed again with no other explanation. This time it was a more sophisticated machine, 'Emmit' would have been proud to have invented it! From the moment I was told I had to go back to RNB, my dynamo went completely off the board, the tiffy could not convince me all was well. He took me up to the doctor, who showed me an X-ray of a rating who had TB, covering the name up. He then put mine on the screen and enquired if I had ever had pneumonia. I replied, 'Yes,' whereupon he pointed to three small scars on my lung, saying, 'There is nothing to worry about.' I had moved in my first X-ray. It was not until the mobile X-ray machines came into being that I really became convinced.

On 15 May 1945, HMS *Ramillies* – *Millie* – was decommissioned. With the old battleship HMS *Malaya* alongside, they became HMS *Vernon*. Work began immediately, in stripping out the 6in guns and converting the casemates and fo'c'sle mess deck into classrooms. The *Malaya* was used as a dormitory. I had now finished with 'A' turret and worked permanently from the LTO's workshop.

Soon, demob notices began to appear, and many from our division began to leave, CPO Godwin, PO Spike Mahoney, L/S Gerry Lunne, L/S Phil Redman, A/B Cliff Mitchell, and A/B Charlie Chase. There were many others. The mess became a ghost town: once it had been a vibrant, happy family, now it was no more. Shortly after Gerry left, he wrote to me saying he was to become a father; the crafty beggar was too shy to announce it before he left!

A/B Leonard, S/T, had now taken over the electrical stores from L/S Redman – one of these stores was the Marines' mess deck. Len was married with one child, and came from Tottenham. One Friday morning, prior to going on a long weekend (we had planned to travel to London together, I was going to Wolverhampton) Len went round closing his various stores. The one on the Marines' mess deck had a one-ton hatch, which was opened and closed by a chain tackle. The hook had to be kept moused all the time. The hatch also had a spring retaining clip. That morning the dockyard man had used the tackle and not re-hooked it to the eyebolt. Len, in closing the hatch, had not seen that the hook was not connected, until he released the spring clip. The hatch crashed down, breaking his left leg and foot in many places. His heel was sliced off and the bone exposed from the knee down. I was called aft at his request, and he asked me to go and see his wife, and explain his non-arrival. I sat there with the doctor for over half an hour holding his leg under the calf muscle. As time went by, he began to rave and the doctor was asked to administer a painkiller. This he would not do, but allowed a tot of rum. When I finally left the scene, I had to shower and dobey my clothes.

On returning from my weekend leave, I visited him in RNH Haslar a few times. He was very bitter, and nothing could console him. He had survived the war, only to be crippled by a thoughtless dockyard matey. When my demob came through, I never had the heart to tell him. I did notify his wife. I often wonder if he really came to terms with it.

One day with A/B Weston, S/T, we were summoned to the torpedo office, and informed that we had been temporarily promoted to L/S, LTOs. Our duties were to re-install the upper-deck lighting. I had been performing this work for some time, when out of the blue I received a drafting to the Tribal-class destroyer HMS *Nubian*, now moored in Deadmans Creek. It appeared my promotion had stirred the drafting office up in RNB (short of time-serving men). Efforts were made to cancel the draft to no avail.

On 4 May 1946, a little under the weather, I unhappily left the *Millie*. I had been aboard her for two years and four months. During that time I lived with some great guys of all ranks. I cannot recall having a cross word with anybody. My only real hate was the 'White Abbo', the Australian cable officer.

CHAPTER 4

'What's the Buzz, Bunts?':
Signalmen on HMS *Ramillies*

Ken D Williams, Yeoman of Signals

The following has been compiled mostly from personal records and photographs.[21] I have tried not to over-elaborate or use too much nautical language, so as to enable our associate members and non-seagoing friends to gain some knowledge of what life at sea in a battleship involved during World War II. This account involves describing some situations from memory in which I have done my best to be accurate, but if I have slipped up on any details, my excuse is that not many who have passed four score years have a perfect memory. I joined HMS *Ramillies* at Devonport in January 1939 as an Acting Leading Signalman, and left her as an Acting Yeoman of Signals, to join the staff of Commodore Durban in June 1942.

Leading Signalman K D Williams, HMS *Ramillies*, Alexandria, November 1939.

Yeoman of Signals K D Williams, NHQ, Durban, June 1943.

Durban 1943: the Carmel Hotel, Old Fort Road. Wrens about to leave to report for duty at Signal Distributing Office, NHQ, Tribune House, Durban. K D Williams at the centre, with Molly Lewis, Audrey Maynard, Wendy Lindsay, Amy MacLachlan, 'Bungy' Williams, Joan Higginson, Betty Taylor, Grace Hale, Jean Pettifer.

1939

12 January

As an Acting Leading Signalman, I joined the main party of the ship's company to recommission HMS *Ramillies*, boarding a special train in the siding at RNB Portsmouth, bound for Devonport. On arrival I soon made myself at home in the communications mess deck, identical to that in *Revenge* in which I served from 1932 to 1934.

16 February

C-in-C Plymouth, Admiral Sir Martin Dunbar-Nasmith, VC, inspected the ship's company. The whole back page of the *Daily Sketch* of 17 February was given to reports and photographs of this event.

22–26 February: Gibraltar

2 March–19 April: Malta

About 0630, whilst rigging the starboard gangway on the quarterdeck in a rough sea, the davit swung round and knocked Sergeant C E Young, RM, overboard. Lieutenant A T Turner, RM, lost his life in a vain rescue attempt. After carrying out a fruitless search, the ship entered Grand Harbour. *Ramillies* proceeded to sea on the morning of 9 March and at 1300 stopped over the spot where the tragedy took place, to hold a memorial service for the two men. The service was conducted by the ship's chaplain, the Rev J Stubbs, BA. The Royal Marines provided the firing party and the buglers, who sounded the Last Post and Reveille. As the Royal Marine Band softly played 'Rock of Ages', the many wreaths laid on the quarterdeck were cast to the waves below by four midshipmen. On conclusion of the ceremony the ship returned to harbour.

Memorial service for Sergeant Young, RM, and Lieutenant Turner, RM, off Gozo, part of the Maltese Archipelago, 9 March 1939.

At the first Sunday Divisions in Malta, I was ordered to stand on the grating over the quarterdeck capstan, when the captain informed those present that he was not satisfied with their appearance, and that I was how a sailor should be dressed. This incident took me a long time to live down!

Malta seemed to be an entirely different place, with the Grand Harbour almost deserted, and the floating dock taking pride of place. We were able to arrange a few inter-divisional soccer matches at Corradina sports grounds, near French Creek, and in the canteen afterwards to quench our thirst with one or more bottles of Blue Label beer, brewed on the island by Simmonds and Farsons.

There was keen competition among the *dghaisa* men, as customers were very scarce with so few ships in harbour. Valletta had not changed and one could reach the central area around Strada Reale either by the Barracca Lift below the Castille or the tedious climb up Step Street.

No tombola evenings were being held at the Vernon or White Ensign clubs, so the normal run ashore was to the cinemas or to Strada Stretta (commonly known as The Gut), where one could imbibe the usual drinks in the many bars and have some good food afterwards with large plates of mixed grill always in demand.

With so few matelots ashore there was no need to go further afield to such places as Sliema, Senglia or Cospicua. One attraction during daylight hours was a visit to the famous Mosta Dome. San Antonio Gardens was always colourful, with a good display of orange blossom in early spring, and occasionally the seedless Maltese oranges were on sale.

The main event in March was the carnival procession, comprising many decorated floats and people dressed in brightly coloured costumes. Another event I had not previously seen, as the Mediterranean Fleet was normally in the Western Mediterranean on the Spring Cruise in March, was the religious processions on Good Friday, in which most of the population seemed to participate. Large crosses bearing figures of Christ were carried, as well as other biblical figures, and those who did not take part lined the streets to witness these events.

22 April–24 May: Gibraltar

As Mussolini had invaded Albania, *Ramillies* was ordered to proceed to Gibraltar to act as guard ship, as most of the ships of the Mediterranean Fleet had moved to Alexandria. Splinter mats positioned around flag deck, etc.

24–30 May: Tangier

A welcome break after a month in Gibraltar. Set up a 'dobeying firm' with two leading telegraphists, which restricted runs ashore.

30 May–26 June: Gibraltar

Returned to South Mole. French battleship *Lorraine* berthed astern, which led to exchange visits during which we received coloured souvenir cap ribbons. A detachment of ratings and Royal Marines took part in the King's birthday parade on 8 June, when the salute was taken by the Governor General Sir Edmund Ironside. Alameda Gardens in full bloom. Time ashore to shop in Main Street and consume a few *café royales* in Universal Bar.

29 June–7 July: Villefranche-sur-Mer

Pleasant runs ashore to Nice, Monte Carlo and Menton. Organised coach trips to inland venues, including Pont-du-Loup, Gourdon and the scent factories at Grasse, after which it took some time to wash out the scent which had been liberally daubed on our collars by the girls at the factory. Many took advantage of the mail order service to send bottles of scent home.

7–14 July: St Raphaël

Anchored near French naval signal station. Exercised 'Abandon ship'. Very good beach and only a short bus ride to Cannes, where there was plenty to see and do.

Ramillies, Villefranche-sur-Mer, July 1939.

16 July: Gibraltar

20 July–7 August: Portsmouth

8–9 August: Weymouth
Reserve Fleet Review.

11–12 August: Rosyth

13–14 August: Invergordon

15 August: Stornoway

16–19 August: Faroe Islands

20–21 August: Wick

21 August–1 September: Scapa Flow
Ships of Home Fleet at anchor. Ship was still in Mediterranean Fleet grey, but during this period was painted dark grey and on 31 August in a day and night exercise, back to Mediterranean Fleet grey. Some communications ratings were transferred to *Royal Oak* am 1 September, just prior to *Ramillies* sailing. Sadly, they were the unlucky ones.

During evening of 2nd at sea received signal from Admiralty stating that a sighting report from a U-boat had been intercepted reporting position, course and speed of *Ramillies*. Speed was increased from 15 to 18 knots. SS *Athenia*, carrying evacuees, was torpedoed in that area late on 3rd.

3–5 September: Portland
Unable to enter harbour at Plymouth as aircraft carrier *Courageous* anchored in harbour and boom was closed. Proceeded to Portland, anchoring about 0300. Observed at daylight that harbour was full of ships, mostly Reserve Fleet. 5 September, proceeded with destroyer screen of *Exmouth* and *Escapade* to

First convoy of war, sailed from the UK 4 September 1939. Taken from *Ramillies*, 800 miles west of Cape Finistère en route to Gibraltar. Ships include HMS *Eclipse*, HMS *Encounter*, *Montcalm*, *Orford*, *Orion*, *Britannic*, *Duchess of Bedford*, *Orcades*, *Scythia*, *Reina del Pacifico*, *Clan Ferguson*, *Durban Castle*, *Strathaird*.

rendezvous with first troop convoy to sail after declaration of war, consisting of eleven troopships and seven destroyers. Route of convoy was set west of the Bay of Biscay. On passing Portland Bill, Captain Lord Louis Mountbatten, working up the new destroyer *Kelly*, signalled, 'The spirit of the 5th DF salutes you.'

One morning during voyage, Witherington (Captain D), carried out a depth-charge attack on a suspected submarine contact. A Kriegsmarine cap and a lot of oranges broke surface, but a definite 'kill' was not confirmed. The commodore of the convoy, Commodore Dowding, RNR, was lost on his return voyage to the UK when SS *Yorkshire* was torpedoed and sunk in Bay of Biscay.

11 September–5 October: Gibraltar
French battleship *Bretagne* at anchor (sunk by British Fleet at Oran, 4 July 1940).

8–15 October: Gibraltar
Orders to proceed to Halifax, NS, cancelled. 14 October special edition of newspaper reporting sinking of *Royal Oak* in Scapa Flow.

20 October–11 November: Alexandria

12 November: Port Said

16 November: Aden

18–21 November: Socotra
Used as secret refuelling base. Rendezvous with *Plumleaf* (Fleet oiler) in company with aircraft carrier *Glorious*. German pocket battleship *Graf Spee* reported to have rounded Cape into Indian Ocean.

28 November: Socotra

2–4 December: Aden

10–11 December: Colombo
Commander Leggatt and most of ship's company started to grow a full set. Crossed Line (equator) at 0200 on 13th; 84° 50′ East, course 139°. Usual CL ceremonies performed later in day. A very attractive Crossing the Line certificate was designed by Lieutenant Knollys showing each port visited during first year of commission, which was later printed and copies issued to each member of ship's company.

20–21 December: Fremantle
Very tasty crayfish on sale from stall at dock entrance at 6d each, to be consumed on walk back to ship. Pubs open until 2100 in Perth. Full sets unpopular with ladies.

25–27 December: Melbourne
Berthed at Princess Pier before noon. Ship lying on mud at low tide (33ft draught). Shore leave pm but city almost deserted; almost everyone had gone to the races! Issued with personal inflatable lifebelts, which were later found to be a much better design than those issued in the UK.

Took onboard several drums of copper cable as used for overhead wires on tramways. This was later coiled around ship, just inside guard-rails, to form a temporary degaussing system as a defence against magnetic mines.

Ramillies entering Wellington harbour, 31 December 1939.

31 December–6 January: Wellington

When entering harbour, ship hoisted a large hessian sheet between foretop and mainmast showing in white, 'Well done, the *Achilles*', a tribute to the NZ light cruiser which had taken part in the Battle of the River Plate on 13 December.

The Centennial Exhibition was in full swing and visitors were presented with a certificate signed by the Governor General, Viscount Galway, confirming attendance. The ship's Royal Marine Band played on stage in the Band Shell for the dance given in the ship's honour. *Ramillies* berthed at Pipitea

Flying the 'Well done, the *Achilles*' banner on entering Wellington harbour.

Marae, where large numbers of people queued every afternoon to come onboard the first battleship to visit New Zealand. Razors came into use again! Maori dancers from Otaki came onboard to give a display and we had a visit from a party of Maori soldiers. A Maori ceremonial skirt, which is called a *piupiu* and is made of flax, was presented to the CO, Captain H T Baillie-Grohman, DSO, RN,[22] at a ceremony onboard, to be worn by the captain whenever the ship was in danger, so that no harm would befall the ship's company. It is interesting to note that although *Ramillies* was involved in later actions such as Operation Neptune (D-Day) and the subsequent bombardment of targets in the Benerville area, followed by the landings in the South of France in August 1944, no fatal casualties were sustained due to enemy action during the whole period of the war. It has been reported that the CO at that time, Captain Middleton, did wear the *piupiu* whilst on the bridge.

The skirt was missing after the war and when Lieutenant Jim Pollok, ex-RNZNVR, attended the *Ramillies* Association reunion in 1993 he was asked to endeavour to obtain a replacement. Due to his efforts Mrs Riria Utiku, one of the original members of the Maori choir who came onboard in 1940, kindly donated her late husband's *piupiu* to the HMS *Ramillies* Association. It was brought to the UK by Lieutenant Pollok and his wife Fay, and duly presented at the April 1994 reunion at Southsea, thus preserving the historical association with the ship. They conveyed a framed photograph of *Ramillies* and other gifts back to New Zealand, which they duly presented to the members of the Ngati'poneke Club at a ceremony in Wellington. (Lieutenant Pollok served as the ship's radar officer from September 1942 to September 1944.)

Trips were organised to places of interest such as Masterton and Wanganui, combined with frequent visits to the Centennial Exhibition, where entry was free to members of the ship's company. The hospitality of the local population tended to be overwhelming and many firm friendships developed.

On the day the 1st Echelon NZEF sailed from Wellington, the Ngati'poneke Young Maori Club, who formed a choir, and about twenty young soldiers who were in training at Trentham military camp were aboard *Ramillies*, when the troopships cast off and Viscount Galway, who was also onboard, asked them to sing the Maori farewell song 'Po Atarau' in Maori, and then to repeat it in English, which was a very emotional scenario and very few of those present were able to avoid shedding a tear. The party disembarked from *Ramillies* to a tug on reaching the harbour entrance.

During the ship's short stay, two scrolls of appreciation were put on display in the port 6in gun battery, with a request that every member of the ship's company should append his signature. One was addressed to the National Patriotic Council and the other to the County Library Service to thank them for their gifts of produce, books and magazines, and the great hospitality extended to them in New Zealand waters. Each scroll was signed by almost 1,300 men.

1940

10 January: Sydney

As soon as the ship passed Sydney Heads to enter harbour, she was met by an armada of yachts and small boats, which kept pace until she anchored to top up with fuel. Quite a number of people in the 'welcome party' were calling out, 'How do you like our harbour?', etc. The only audible response from the hands manning the ship for entering harbour came when one 'wag' repeatedly called, 'How do you like our bridge?' A lone voice from the forecastle called loud and clear, 'When are you going to pay for the b——d?' The captain sent a messenger from the bridge to order the Divisional Officer Lieutenant Commander Hooper to 'Bring that man to me!' I was on the bridge at the time and as far as I am aware the identity of 'that man' was never disclosed. (NB When Sydney Harbour Bridge was built by Dorman Long & Co, it was done with the aid of a huge loan from the British government.)

18–20 January: Fremantle

The ship's company were saddened by the death of Boy 1st Class Herbert Iddon, who died following an accident. A committal service was held approximately three hundred miles northwest of Australia.

Each forenoon during the long passage from Fremantle to Port Suez, via Colombo, *Ramillies* steamed through the columns of ships in the convoy with the band of the Royal Marines on the quarterdeck playing such popular tunes as 'Roll out the Barrel' and 'I Love to Ride a Ferry', in response to waves of cheers from each ship in turn.

New Zealand officer cadets on the flag deck of *Ramillies*, January 1940.

One morning a soldier, who was standing on the guard-rail of one ship, fell overboard and before we could hoist the signal 'Man overboard', the next ship astern, which I believe was *Rangitata*, sounded her siren, hauled out of line, put engines to full astern, stopped to lower a lifeboat and picked him up. This was a remarkable piece of seamanship and I have often wondered if, having been rescued from a shark-infested ocean within minutes, his luck held out long enough for him to return to his native land after taking part in battles in the Western Desert and Crete.

30 January–1 February: Colombo
Midshipman Prince Philip of Greece joined ship.

8–15 February: Aden
Convoy proceeded to Suez. Huge mounds of sea salt on land at northern extremity of harbour.

Arranged football match between communications messes and staff at Aden W/T. When having a drink after the game, I was surprised to be introduced to a leading telegraphist who had attended the same junior school as myself (Gateshead 1920–26), and whom I had not seen since moving in 1928.

20–28 February: Colombo
Crossed Line 1 March. Full calibre 15in practice firing at sea.

8–9 March: Fremantle
At about 1300 one day the ship was yawing heavily in a choppy sea and on the bridge it was noticed that 'Jimmy the One' (first lieutenant) was standing near the 'gash' chute rigged on the port side just abaft the breakwater, when a young rating emptied his mess kettle as the bow plunged down, sending the contents

The first contingent of the AIF end echelon NZEF, Wellington NZ to the Red Sea – 6 January to February 1940. Photograph taken approximately on equator at sunset in the Indian Ocean. Ships include *Rangitata, Dunera, Sobieski, Orcades, Orford, Empress of Canada, Otranto, Empress of Japan, Orion, Strathnaver, Strathaird.*

back inboard and over both of them! Jimmy (Lieutenant Commander Pugh-Cook) promptly threw his cap on the deck and proceeded to stamp on it. The staff on the bridge found it most hilarious, except for the captain who, like Queen Victoria, was not amused. This incident coaxed a laugh from the Navigating Officer Lieutenant Commander Dewar, a dour Scot, who occasionally smiled but from whom a laugh was almost unknown!

15 March–10 April: Sydney

Berthed at Woolloomooloo wharf. The RM band and a battalion from *Ramillies* took part in a naval parade through Sydney to celebrate the arrival of HMAS *Perth* on joining the Australian Squadron. This stay was used as a self-refit period. The Royal Easter Show was held during the third week in March and, although it was primarily an agricultural show, there were log-cutting competitions, steer riding, etc, similar to a rodeo.

We found Sydney to be quite modern in comparison with Victorian Melbourne. It was very easy to get around the city with an underground railway similar to London, and good bus and tram services. Ferries from Circular Quay connected all parts of the harbour. Runs ashore included visits to Bondi, Coogee and Manly beaches and to other well-known places such as the racecourse at Randwick and Taronga Zoo Park, which was home to a number of koala bears.

Above left: Sydney Harbour bridge at night, March 1940.
Above: *Strathnaver* passing under Sydney Harbour bridge, March 1940.
Above right: A turret firing, March 1940.

There were many good places to eat including a restaurant in Elizabeth Street, which reputedly could serve more than forty varieties of fish. Reaching the city centre was quite a pleasant walk starting from the first 'port of call' for many, the Tilbury Arms, then on towards King's Cross and through Hyde Park, which was overlooked by the city's tallest building, the Oddfellows Building. The pubs ceased serving at 1800 and from 1700 until 'time' was called, it was like being in a football crowd and we soon realised it was better to keep clear.

12–15 April: Melbourne
Escort to convoy US.2 (AIF).

21–22 April: Fremantle
Crossed Line 2 May.

3–5 May: Colombo

12 May: Aden

17 May: Port Suez

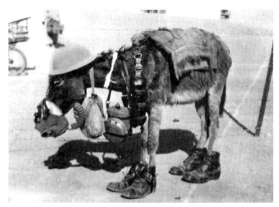
British forces in the Middle East, 1940.

17–23 May: Port Said

25 May–28 June: Alexandria
Entered floating dock for bottom scraping and refit. Undocked before completion of work, because of danger of capsizing in air raids after declaration of war by Italy on 10 June. Camouflage paint system introduced. Prince Philip drafted to a destroyer. To provide cover for eastward convoy.

2–13 July: Alexandria
Each time fleet put to sea, one battleship and one submarine remained in harbour as guardships to prevent French battleship *Lorraine* (our chummy ship of a year previous) and a cruiser squadron from leaving harbour. Guns crews were kept on standby during the whole of this period. Cruiser squadron included *Tourville*, *Duquesne*, *Duguay-Trouin* and *Suffren*, our friend from 'down under' days.

Shot from a shore battery falling astern of *Ramillies* off Bardia, Libya on 17 August 1940.

Their flag officer, Admiral Godfroy, eventually agreed to have the ships demilitarised and to the removal of ammunition and fuel. Crew members wishing to be repatriated were embarked in the French SS *Providence* in early October. *Ramillies* sailed with destroyer screen, *Diamond*, *Havock*, *Imperial* and *Vendetta* to provide cover for slow convoy Malta to Alexandria, being escorted by the light cruisers *Caledon* and *Capetown*.

Gunfire from HMAS *Sydney* straddling the Italian cruiser *Bartolomeo Colleoni* off Crete on 19 July 1940.

15 July–16 August–8 October: Alexandria
There were occasional high-level bombing sorties by the Italians, which were fairly accurate, but most bombs either hit the coal jetty or fell to seaward of the breakwater in the vicinity of Ras-el-Tin lighthouse (the original site of Cleopatra's Needle). In one raid just after sunset, several bombs landed in the swept channels (Boghaz Pass and Great Pass), probably intended for the nearby Shell oil installation. The 'run ashore' area in the vicinity of Mohammed Ali Square remained unscathed.

Bartolomeo on fire with bows blown off after the action.

Battleships *Warspite*, *Malaya* and *Ramillies* with 8in cruiser *Kent* sailed late on 16th and at dawn on 17th carried out a heavy bombardment of Sollum and Bardia, which was fortified with batteries of 9in guns. Broadsides of eight 15in guns and six 6in guns were fired. Using telescopes or binoculars it was possible to see trucks and tanks tumbling over the

Bartolomeo Colleoni before settling down after being hit by torpedoes from HMS *Hyperion* and gunfire from HMAS *Sydney*.

escarpment onto the beach. Large portions of the cliffs disintegrated as the shells exploded. I have some snapshots, taken from the flag deck, of shells exploding and bomb splashes, about two cables astern of the ship. The fleet rarely got very far to sea before being spotted by Italian aircraft, and subsequently had to endure very accurate, heavy high-level bombing.

During our time based at Alexandria I renewed my friendship with the young manager of a photographic shop which began during the nine months

I spent there in the fleet minesweeper *Halcyon* (Captain V A C Crutchley, VC) in 1935–36. His late father had been British vice consul at Port Said. His mother was Greek, and on the occasions I was invited to Sunday tea, she insisted on serving her 'special treat', home-made rose petal jam, which, although perfumed, was quite nice. I am unable to recall coming across the delicacy anywhere else.

I also renewed contact with the Hungarian restaurant proprietor, whose daughter was now engaged to a sergeant in the Royal Engineers based at Ras-el-Tin barracks, and we all sat at the family table to eat. The goulash in particular was very good and appreciated as the food onboard was now not up to the standard we had become used to. Very many tins of camp pie and jugged rabbit from Australia (myxomatosis was unheard of then!) took passage through the portholes, and several bumboats ensured that we did not go aground on them, as most were retrieved before, or soon after, they touched the bottom!

A Fleet Club had been opened by the autumn, but I think the majority of naval personnel preferred to bathe during the afternoons, especially at Rose Bay and Stanley Bay, and to spend the evenings at the Mohammed Ali or Royal cinemas and at their own favourite bars and restaurants. After the introduction of an overall blackout, walking back to the dock gates via side streets was rather risky.

11 October: Malta
Covering east to west convoy to Malta in company with Mediterranean Fleet.

HMS *Liverpool* after being towed stern-first over 200 miles back to Alexandria by HMS *Orion*, photographed from the flag deck of *Ramillies*. *Liverpool* was struck by an Italian aerial torpedo at 1855hrs, 14 October 1940. A petrol tank exploded and the ensuing fire melted the forecastle, killing thirteen men, eighty-three were seriously wounded, some of whom died later. The French battleship *Lorraine* can be seen behind *Liverpool*.

15 October–6 November: Alexandria

At 1510 on 14th, west of the Kaso Channel to the south of Crete, a submarine was spotted surfaced on the port quarter from the spotting top and flag deck. A salvo was fired from the port 6in battery and the submarine dived immediately. There was no further contact. At 1856 HMS *Liverpool* was struck on the starboard side by a torpedo dropped by an aircraft. Although the bow was lost, *Liverpool* was towed astern to Alexandria by HMS *Orion*. Entered Alexandria on 15th.

9–10 November: Malta

Covering convoy. On one of the two trips to Malta the destroyers *Ilex* and *Imperial* were carrying out a stern sweep as *Ramillies* entered Grand Harbour. *Imperial* struck a mine and her stern was badly damaged. She was towed into harbour by one of the two oceangoing tugs based at Malta, *Roysterer* and *Respond*. Italian S/M *Pier Capponi* made an unsuccessful attack on *Ramillies*.

13–23 November: Alexandria

24 November: Suda Bay (Crete)

Cruisers *York* and *Ajax* at anchor (*York* later sunk in harbour). *Ramillies* sailed from Alexandria in company with 8in cruiser *Berwick* and 6in cruiser *Newcastle*, both requiring repairs to boilers, anti-aircraft cruiser *Coventry* with destroyer screen, *Defender*, *Greyhound*, *Griffin* and *Hereward* (designated Force D), under cover of main Mediterranean Fleet to pass through the narrows between Sicily and Tunisia, and pass east to west to Gibraltar. Force D was to rendezvous with Force H south of Sardinia, which was covering a fast convoy of three ships passing west to east, together with four corvettes for Alexandria.

Renown and *Coventry* engaging the Italian fleet off Sardinia on 27 November 1940.

26 November: Malta

Battle of Cape Spartivento (off SE coast of Sardinia)

After sailing, guns crews were closed up at sunset and there was a lot of tension on the bridge as we were aware that we were passing through a very dangerous area. This situation guaranteed the usual response below decks, 'What's the buzz, Bunts?'

About 0030 abortive attack made on Force D by Italian torpedo boat *Sirio*. It became obvious that the situation was becoming more interesting when *Ramillies* intercepted a signal from one of *Ark Royal*'s Swordfish TSR aircraft at 1037 on 27th: 'Bearing and range of seven enemy cruisers from *Ramillies* 311° – 70 miles', followed immediately by another reading 'Six cruiscrs, San Giorgio'.

At 1046 a signal addressed to *Ramillies* was received from SO Force H, Vice Admiral Sir James Somerville, giving position, course and speed of his flagship *Renown*. He then detached *Despatch* and two destroyers to join convoy and signalled *Ramillies* to detach *Coventry* to join convoy, which was at a distance of 28 miles to the south at this time. At 1052 *Ark Royal* was ordered to fly off striking force and attack, but at 1225 another signal from aircraft reported that the enemy had altered course to 010° and, at 1247, still on the same course, speed 27 knots, which was the course for Naples! Force H had opened fire shortly after noon, but were unable to close the two enemy battleships, *Vittorio Veneto* and *Giulio Cesare*, and the defects in *Berwick* and *Newcastle* prevented them from continuing the chase, and they were being straddled by gunfire from the enemy cruisers. *Berwick* was hit on 'Y' turret, which was put out of action, and sustained casualties. *Ramillies* fired two salvoes at extreme elevation but, although she had managed to reach 20.7 knots, the fall of shot was short.

After action was broken off, Force H reformed and, joined by ships of Force D, set course for Gibraltar late in the afternoon. The force was heavily bombed, *Ark Royal*, especially, being very fortunate to survive. The Italians later claimed that a battleship was observed to be stopped and burning furiously which was, in fact, *Ramillies* doing her utmost to keep up! It should be noted that, after the action, Mr Churchill in his usual form ordered an immediate inquiry, headed by Admiral of the Fleet the Earl of Cork and Orrery, to ascertain why Vice Admiral Somerville did not pursue the enemy battleships (steaming towards Naples at well over 30 knots!). The highest reported speed reached by *Renown* in this action was 27.5 knots.

28 November–7 December: Gibraltar

Just before sailing, a signal was received from SO Force H: 'Goodbye and good luck. Proud to have had you in the battle with us. I shall remember your magnificent turn of speed and I still maintain the Italians made more smoke than you did.' Reply: 'Thank you very much. Your signal is much appreciated by all. We were very glad to give you moral support in your victory.'

Escort to UK-bound convoy.

14–15 December: Greenock

17 December–6 January: Devonport
Entered dry dock. Permission had been given to use one HA twin mounting only during air raids whilst the ship was dry-docked for a bottom scrape. After one heavy raid, a signal from the Army GOC was received, complaining about the amount of gunfire emanating from *Ramillies*, and that more than one mounting must have been in use, which was not so. Quite early in the commission the ship's PTI had formed a party of keep-fit enthusiasts, and it had been decided that loading HA guns using practice ammunition was a good bodybuilding exercise, especially for boxers. It was later decided that they should form an authentic guns crew, who were later reputed to be able to load in excess of forty rounds per minute, and a leading seaman was allocated as the gun-layer.

1941
8–12 January: Greenock
New CO Captain Read.[23]

Escort to convoy which included Polish SS *Sobieski* with German POWs, two of whom escaped soon after arrival in Halifax and were spotted by a little girl next morning, hiding at the bottom of the back garden.

22 January: Halifax, Nova Scotia
Having been in the Mediterranean and Indian Ocean for most of the previous

Ramillies entering Halifax, Nova Scotia, January 1941.

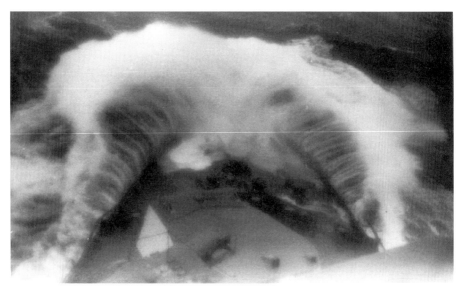

HM Submarine *Ramillies*.

two years, the ship's company found the sub-zero temperatures in Halifax quite a problem, and we were provided with blue windcheaters and woollens by local organisations. Signalling with an Aldis lamp was difficult as the fingers tended to go stiff after a very short time. Using a Heather lamp (a small lamp giving a blue light which was fitted to binoculars for use at close range at sea, at night) was even more difficult.

We were later issued with two pairs of very thick long johns, which were very useful when on watch in an exposed position, but were much too warm to wear below decks, especially with the hot air from a boiler room blowing through a doorway into the mess deck. Washing and drying them was a difficult problem to solve and most were discarded. One HO telegraphist decided that the easiest solution was to live in them, but after a time some ratings complained of the odour and we killicks of the mess decided that the answer was to take him down below in the bathroom and give him a good scrub. No more complaints! I met him later in Durban when he was serving in a destroyer. He was very pleased to see me again and he was wearing the ribbon of the DSM. Whilst in the Mediterranean his ship had depth-charged a submarine and brought it to the surface. He had been 'ordered' to 'volunteer' to retrieve the signal books and codes before she sank! After the war my long johns were taken home and pulled out and then made into a useful rug.

When going ashore there was a good tram service from the docks, which went all the way along the main street (Barrington Street), but standing at a tram stop after leaving a centrally-heated cinema or restaurant was not a pleasant experience. My first introduction to deep apple pie with maple syrup, worth going ashore for!

30 January: Convoy HX106

At dawn on 8 February sighted superstructures of two large German ships. Hauled out of convoy to intercept, but ships immediately altered course and drew away. Later identified as *Scharnhorst* and *Gneisenau*, which were under orders not to engage a superior force!

Exceptionally cold weather made conditions hazardous on upper deck and thick ice formed on upperworks. The intense cold combined with ice caused the wires attached to guard-rails to snap off and before entering harbour a number of seamen were kept hard at work chipping ice from capstans, cable, etc.

17–20 February: Halifax, Nova Scotia

After convoy was taken over by destroyer escort from Londonderry and course set for return leg, very heavy weather was encountered and constant pitching sprang a leak at the for'ard end of the blister on the port side. The amount of water shipped caused a slight list to port and the hole expanded during passage, causing the ship's speed to be reduced.

The regular officers of the watch at sea were Lieutenants Knollys, Dreyer and Portman. Lieutenant Portman founded a 'nutty' club in his watch, whereby a small stock of thick bars of Moir's milk chocolate was kept in a biscuit tin, and it was the leading signalman's duty to inform him when it required replenishment. He provided the necessary few dollars to top up. The use of this 'perk' was confined to the watchkeepers on the bridge and, of course, did not affect the taste of the cocoa made by the middy of the watch.

9–16 March: Halifax, Nova Scotia

17–30 March: St John, New Brunswick

Entered dry dock for repairs. Entering the dry dock was a rather complicated operation as the water level between low and high tides in the Bay of Fundy rose by 35ft, said to be one of the highest tides in the world. The two weeks at St John allowed a lot of minor repair work to be completed, such as reeving new signal halyards and replacing the steel wires on the guard-rails, which had snapped during the very cold weather. There was still plenty of snow at St John, but not at all unpleasant, lots of hospitality was shown by the people there, and a dance was held in honour of the ship's company.

31 March–1 April: Halifax, Nova Scotia

Convoy escort.

14–21 April: Halifax, Nova Scotia

Convoy escort.

24–25 April: Halifax, Nova Scotia
Convoy escort.

7–16 May: Halifax, Nova Scotia
Convoy escort. Rapid change of weather from winter to summer!
24 May am, battlecruiser *Hood* sunk and battleship *Prince of Wales* damaged by German battleship *Bismarck* and heavy cruiser *Prinz Eugen*. Received signal from Admiralty to leave convoy to try to intercept enemy! After having lost track of enemy, *Bismarck* was again sighted and damaged by torpedoes from carrier aircraft of Force H. On the morning of 27th she was brought to action by Home Fleet. At 1045 C-in-C HF signalled to SO Force H, 'Cannot get her to sink with guns.' At 1107 *Dorsetshire* reported to C-in-C HF that she had torpedoed *Bismarck* both sides and that before she sank she had ceased firing, but colours were still flying. *Dorsetshire* began to pick up some of the hundreds of survivors, but left the scene to rejoin the fleet when a suspicious object, believed to be a U-boat, was sighted nearby. *Ramillies* received orders to rendezvous with troopship MV *Britannic* and to escort her to Halifax.

30 May–1 June: Halifax, Nova Scotia
Convoy escort.

14–21 June: Halifax, Nova Scotia
Convoy escort.

Whilst escorting west–east convoys we frequently intercepted SSSS distress signals (indicating attack by submarine) from merchant ships in the convoy a few days ahead or astern, but none of the convoys escorted by *Ramillies* in the North Atlantic were attacked by U-boats.

Above left: A summer evening near Reykjavik, July 1941.
Above right: The Midnight Sun: sunset at 0420 GMT, Iceland, July 1941.

28 June–19 August: Hvalfjordur, Iceland

For duties as guardship. Battleship USS *New York* in harbour. Later visited by battleship USS *Oklahoma*, cruiser *Nashville* and destroyer *Benson*. Exchange visits to *New York* to see their 'soda fountain'. Their signalmen were interested in our mechanical semaphores. Frequent visits by other ships, including HMS *Wolfe* and HMS *Suffolk*. Some spectacular scenery, but otherwise rather boring. Run ashore by ferry to Reykjavik broke the monotony, but very little to do or see. Regularly played soccer against teams from other ships and Pioneer Corps camp, but pitches were like ploughed fields!

On 16 August Mr Churchill paid a visit to the ship, during passage home in *Prince of Wales* from a visit to President Roosevelt in the USA. He was

Mr Churchill returning to HMS *Prince of Wales*.

Winston Churchill followed by Chief of the Imperial Staff, General Sir John Dill and Lieutenant Franklin Roosevelt, Jr, USN, arriving on board *Ramillies*, 16 August 1941.

accompanied by the First Sea Lord, Admiral of the Fleet Sir Dudley Pound, Chief of the General Staff, General Sir John Dill and ADC Lieutenant Roosevelt, USN. In a speech to the ship's company assembled on the quarterdeck, he stated that it had been his personal decision to order *Ramillies* to try to intercept *Bismarck* and *Prinz Eugen*, in spite of the fact that her speed and gun range were much inferior to that of *Bismarck*, because he knew *Ramillies* had a reputation as a good gunnery ship! He had heard about the special AA guns crew and demanded a demonstration of their ability. When he left the ship Captain Read said, 'We now know what happens when politicians take over control of the Navy!' This was the only occasion I can remember during sixteen years' service when a departing VIP was not accorded three cheers.

22 August–20 November: Liverpool
Moved into Gladstone Dry Dock for extensive refit, to include changing 15in guns in 'B' turret. Very slow progress by workmen as Luftwaffe began heavy night air raids especially in late October when oil bombs were used, which caused serious damage in Bootle. Owing to slow progress of refit, the Mayor of Bootle asked C-in-C Western Approaches (Admiral Sir Max Horton) to move ship out of dock to reduce civilian casualties. Ship was towed over to Cammell Laird's yard at Birkenhead to have the replacement guns fitted.

22 November–1 December: Scapa Flow

2–8 December: Greenock

9 December: Milford Haven
Top up with fuel.
Convoys WS12Z and WS14.
    After entering South Atlantic resumed normal procedure of passing through lines of convoy in forenoons with RM band playing on quarterdeck.

21–25 December: Freetown, Sierra Leone
Convoy and escort refuelled, a rather lengthy operation in a poorly-equipped harbour. A very backward area with little to do ashore. Towards the end of the forenoon watch on 25th, US liner *Santa Clara* sailed with many passengers on deck, mostly women and children. A loud explosion was heard some time later, but when *Ramillies* reached the end of the swept channel later there was no sign of wreckage or oil. I have often wondered what happened in this incident. Christmas dinner was served about 1100. Convoy sailed, followed by *Ramillies* in early afternoon.
    Crossed Line on 27 December 27 at 0915, longitude 11° 03° West, course

158° at 13 knots. Traditional Crossing the Line ceremony performed with Ben Milsom once again taking the part of King Neptune, but with a new Queen Amphitrite. Convoy entered harbour in Cape Town on 4 January. *Ramillies* carried out night exercise with ships of SANF and entered harbour am 5th.

1942

5 January: Cape Town

A large sea-cow floating near the ship's berth created much interest and it was assumed that it had been injured, probably by a ship's propeller. However, after two days it swam out to sea and was not seen again.

Decision made to close down dobeying firm as it was difficult to find sufficient drying spaces, but my two partners were both married and wished to explore other possible means of enhancing income. We went ashore and noticed that in the window of the Singer Sewing Machine shop in Adderley Street was a new hand-machine, similar to the one onboard which was used for repairing flags, etc, for sale at £11. We bought it and, after obtaining a supply of pusser's white drill, decided to make haversacks in which to carry the personal inflatable lifebelt, which had to be carried at all times when at sea. The commander approved the price of 1s 6d and we presented one to him, which soon found its way into the captain's hands, and from then on we were in business and struggling to keep up with the demand. We found that the most difficult part of the job was making the two buttonholes so that they looked neat and did not fray. They proved to be much more convenient than carrying a lifebelt tied to one's money belt when on watch, and we were able to use the caboose in the 6in gun battery above our mess deck, as my two partners acted as 'disc jockeys' for the ship's tannoy system, which was very convenient.

9 January:

Escorted convoy on northeasterly course to rendezvous with *Royal Sovereign* with a convoy from Suez. Our convoy consisted of two sections, one proceeded to Suez and the other to Java, escorted by *Royal Sovereign*. Many of the personnel embarked in the latter section were taken prisoner of war by the Japanese within two months, including personnel of 242 Fighter Squadron RAF, Sir Douglas Bader's squadron during the Battle of Britain, but he had previously left the squadron.

His mechanic at that time, the late Sergeant James Home of Middlesbrough, was still with the squadron and in 1989 published a book *Their Last Tenko*, which describes the horrors endured by the Far East POWs. The CO of the squadron at that time was Wing Commander H Maguire, later Air Marshal Sir Harold Maguire, KCB, DSO, DFC, who wrote the foreword. The book was written in response to a wish expressed by Sir Douglas Bader in 1982 to know more of the fate suffered by members of the squadron after he left them, but tragically he did not live to read the published book.

Another passenger onboard *Empress of Australia* was Victor (Candy) Syrett of Sooke, Vancouver Island, BC, who, like Ken Stofer of Victoria, BC, and many others, paid his own fare to the UK to join the RAF in 1940. 'Candy' died as a POW in Japan in February 1943, a year after arriving in Java, and Ken Stofer decided in 1984 to write a book, *Dear Mum*, based on his letters to his mother. The book was published in 1991, and contains a photograph of *Ramillies*. It is currently on sale in Canada and the USA and is available from a publisher in the UK, part of the proceeds going towards establishing a scholarship in his memory at the Edward Milnc Community School, Sooke, BC.

21 January–21 February: Kilindini, Mombasa

An Eastern Fleet was now being formed under the command of Vice Admiral Sir James Somerville and was based on a battle squadron of *Warspite*, *Revenge*, *Resolution*, *Ramillies* and *Royal Sovereign*, the light aircraft carrier *Hermes* and some County-class cruisers. The fleet did not go to sea for a month and we were not then aware that Vice Admiral Somerville was at loggerheads with Winston Churchill, who was demanding that the fleet carry out sorties (showing the flag) eastwards, in spite of the fact that no proper air cover was available (as had happened with *Repulse* and *Prince of Wales*).

BOAC were still operating a flying-boat service between Cairo and the Cape and it was very interesting to watch them landing almost alongside. One of them, *Canopus*, was a regular visitor.

Fleet proceeded to sea and carried out exercises in the western Indian Ocean.

1 March: Addu Atoll, Maldive Islands

Refuelled from Fleet oiler *Plumleaf*.

Sandy atoll covered in coconut palms. Very clear water showing sea bottom. Mobile Naval Base Defence Organisation manned by Royal Marines.

Crossed Line 2 March.

4–6 March: Colombo

7–22 March: Trincomalee

Ramillies at anchor to act as guardship. Overflown almost daily by squadron of FAA Fulmar fighters, the only air defence in Ceylon at that time. They were shortly afterwards replaced by squadrons of Hurricanes. Small canteen at naval base selling warm beer, but usually a run ashore was a foray into the countryside on hired bicycles.

Crossed Line 24 March.

25–26 March: Addu Atoll
Refuelled from *Plumleaf.*

Joined part of fleet, Force B. Periodic attacks by Japanese carrier-borne bombers.

Crossed Line 29 March.

29 March: Addu Atoll
Crossed Line 4 April.

Force A, which had been joined by aircraft carriers *Indomitable* and *Formidable*, was at sea southwest of Ceylon. During Easter week the sloop HMIS *Indus*, aircraft carrier *Hermes*, destroyer HMAS *Vampire* and corvette HMS *Hollyhock* were sunk east of Ceylon by carrier-borne aircraft. On Easter Sunday, 4 April, cruisers *Cornwall* and *Dorsetshire* were dive-bombed and sunk whilst proceeding south to rendezvous with *Ramillies* and Force B. Force B suffered bombing attacks during search for survivors in flat sea. No survivors sighted by *Ramillies*.

8 April: Addu Atoll
Crossed Line 8 April.
Under air attacks again.

14–16 April: Kilindini
Embarked a number of survivors from *Cornwall*, some of whom were South Africans for passage to Durban

21–28 April: Durban
Berthed alongside 'R' shed with a welcome from 'The Lady in White', international concert soprano Perla Siedle-Gibson, whom I subsequently met several times during the two years I served at NHQ Durban. Durban proved to be the ideal spot to relax with its beautiful seafront, embracing the sunken gardens, amphitheatre, Medwood Gardens, Mitchell Park and Botanic Gardens on the Berea, the Old Fort (GHQ of the MOTHS – Memorable Order of Tin Hats, a South African ex-servicemen's organisation equivalent to Royal British Legion), an Indian market and the esplanade with many high-rise hotels. The municipal orchestra played at a bandstand on the seafront voluntarily on Saturdays and Sundays, when members of the public could request songs and were often able to show off their talent in front of the microphone.

The Playhouse cinema in Smith Street with its starlit moving roof (similar to the one in Cape Town) was a popular venue for an evening out, with a spacious foyer with bar and, on the upper floor, a restaurant and bar. The hospitality was second to none, with invitations to residents' homes, etc, and several canteens managed by voluntary organisations, the outstanding one being the South African Women's Auxiliary Service, which was run broadly on army lines, but members wore khaki uniforms bought by individual members.

A *Book of Thanks to SAWAS* (limited edition), edited by the late Captain E A S Bailley, CBE, DSC (CO of the destroyer *Paladin* in the early '40s), was published in 1980, containing the names of over 6,000 men and women who visited South African ports between 1940 and 1946. It contains a special chapter on Operation Ironclad (Diego Suarez, May 1942) in which *Ramillies* took part as the flagship of SO Force F, Rear Admiral E N Syfret.

Operation Ironclad

As naval bases in India and Ceylon could become untenable due to Japanese air attacks and shortage of defence fighters, it was realised that if the Japanese got a foothold in Madagascar (French), the supply lines to the Middle East could be cut. Operation Ironclad was mounted to forestall this under the overall command of a South African, Rear Admiral E N Syfret, who had relieved Vice Admiral Somerville as SO Force H at Gibraltar. He flew his flag in *Ramillies* with Major General R Sturges, RM, in command of land forces. A slow convoy of Ministry of Transport ships forming the Cape Town section joined up with the Durban section on 25 April and proceeded north escorted by 8in cruiser *Devonshire*, three destroyers, three corvettes and four minesweepers. A fast convoy sailed from Durban on 28 April, escorted by *Ramillies*, *Illustrious*, *Hermione* and six destroyers, to rendezvous late evening on 4 May west of Diego Suarez and now joined by *Indomitable*, the whole becoming Force F.

In foul weather on morning of 5 May, landing craft began to put commandos and other troops ashore, who made steady progress across the island, and the airfield was bombed by carrier aircraft. French S/M *Heros* escaped to sea and was sunk on 6th by aircraft from HMS *Illustrious*. Corvette HMS *Auricula* was damaged by a mine in Courrier Bay on 5th and sank on 6th.

At about 2000 on 6th, fifty Royal Marines from *Ramillies*, commanded by Captain Martin Price, RM, sailed from anchorage in destroyer *Anthony* at high speed and, after running the gauntlet of shore batteries in the dark, landed on the quay at Antsirane. After storming the French army barracks and taking the troops there by surprise, the Marines captured the arsenal and took 500 prisoners. *Anthony* again ran the gauntlet to leave harbour and return to the anchorage. I was on the bridge during the first watch and I remember that as *Anthony* crashed through the boom at the harbour entrance she was picked out by a searchlight at the shore battery, which was extinguished almost immediately by an 8in salvo from *Devonshire*.

The 12in gun batteries in the forts on the Orangia Peninsular did not surrender until the afternoon of 7th, after some gentle persuasion from twenty-four rounds of 15in from *Ramillies*. A few days later some fairly large drawings were displayed on the noticeboard in the port 6in gun battery in *Ramillies* showing a French soldier sitting 'on the throne' with trousers down and with a caption that a 15in shell is an ideal laxative! By that time the army commander and FAA had secured the rest of the area.

8 May–3 June: Diego Suarez
Anchored in harbour.

On going ashore we could see that a sloop *d'Entrecastreaux*, AMC *Bougainville* and S/M *Beveziers* had been sunk in shallow water. The town was typically French colonial with some attractive houses, but also many with corrugated sheet roofs.

Many of our troops were re-embarked and within a few days the majority of the ships forming the convoys and Force F had dispersed after congratulatory signals had been exchanged. There was relatively little activity during the next three weeks as our forces consolidated their positions and took over control of the area. During the evening of 29th a floatplane was briefly observed flying at a high altitude between clouds, but could not be identified and, after a few rounds of HA had been fired, it disappeared. Later information showed it to be from Japanese submarine *I10*.

All three partners in 'the firm' had hardly settled in the tannoy caboose after tea on the following evening, when the peace was shattered by two loud explosions in quick succession, which caused the ship to list to starboard briefly. We rushed out to the nearby mess-deck hatch and shouted to those below to close all hatches and watertight doors and to clear the mess deck. Watertight doors were opened and closed each time anyone passed through and main covers were kept clipped on the hatches, with just the escape hatches (manholes) left open.

As it was a 'jam for tea' day, our messes had been unlucky enough to be issued with marmalade, which was in the original large tin and not very popular. The mess deck shelves containing crockery, etc, were fixed to the bulkhead at the end of the mess tables and the explosions had emptied most of them. The first rating to evacuate the mess deck was an HO telegraphist, not a very happy soul at the best of times, who appeared through the manhole with his head covered in marmalade, due to the tin landing on his head as he was sitting at the mess table writing a letter. He obviously did not share our amusement!

Action stations had been sounded when I made my way up to the flag deck and found that the tanker *British Loyalty*, which was anchored nearby, had been struck and was slowly sinking. The Japanese submarines *I16* and *I20*, part of a flotilla which had been active in the area, each carried a midget submarine, that had managed to get past the corvette on patrol at the harbour entrance to carry out the attack, which did not cause any serious casualties.

Two torpedoes had struck on the port side below 'B' turret and the amount of water shipped was causing the bow to become low in the water. The Union Castle cargo liner *Greystoke Castle* was brought alongside next day and for the following forty-eight hours everything that could be moved, such as cable, ammunition, surplus stores, etc, in the for'ard part of the ship, was transferred.

The findings of the subsequent court of inquiry were reported to have included the statement that 'there was insufficient oxygen in the magazine and handling room to ignite a spark'. After temporary repairs and pumping out, the ship was deemed to be sufficiently seaworthy to attempt the passage to Durban, during which luck was on our side and calm weather prevailed.

The only real problem encountered during this passage was the failure of the evaporators to maintain a sufficient supply of fresh water for cooking and drinking, which resulted in many cases of dysentery. Luckily, the fine, clear weather tempted many men to sleep on the upper deck, which facilitated the regular sprint to the heads!

British Loyalty was later refloated, towed to Addu Atoll and used as an oil hulk. Subsequently sunk by *U183* on 9 April 1944.

9 June–6 August: Durban
Ship secured alongside 'R' shed and was eventually moved to Maydon Dock for more temporary repairs before undertaking passage to Devonport for permanent repairs.

Ramillies down by the bow at Diego Suarez after one torpedo hit on the port side abreast 'B' turret.

12 June

Left *Ramillies* as an Acting Yeoman of Signals to join communications staff at NHQ where the Commodore Durban was based. Commodore B C S Martin was previously CO of *Dorsetshire* when she applied the *coup de grâce* to *Bismarck*. On leaving the ship (with mixed feelings after three and a half years) I was advised by the MO that a good cure for dysentery was brandy and ginger and as three-star brandy was available at five shillings a bottle I tried it during the next few weeks and it worked!

My next contact with *Ramillies* was in December when she called in at Durban. I was able to take my watch of two ratings and a dozen Wrens on a tour of the ship, which they thoroughly enjoyed. They were all issued with a tot and a loaf of white bread, which was not obtainable in South Africa, but I did not enquire if any of them had been shown the 'golden rivet'! A few of the signal staff of 1939 were still onboard. One of them, Leading Signalman Tim Reilly, was, as a signalman, my second hand during that period.

Incidentally, some of the Wrens of my watch, who now live in the UK, Netherlands, Spain and South Africa, are still in touch with me fifty years on.

1944

5 May

I left Durban in May 1944 in the 'floating coffin' HMT *Nevasa* on passage to Colombo via Mombasa, where I again met Acting Yeoman of Signals Tim Reilly at the signal station, who helped me to wangle a new Aldis lamp and battery for *Nevasa*, as the equipment was as dilapidated as the ship.

Crossed Line 22 May.

28 May: Colombo

Left *Nevasa* and, after a week in a transit camp, left Colombo by train on 7 June via Jaffna, Coimbatore, Madras and Poona to Bombay in coaches with wooden seats and with more passengers on the outside than inside the train, which stopped at intervals for passengers to brew up the 'char' beside the rails. I arrived at the RIN Signal School (HMIS *Talwar*) in Woodhouse Road, Bombay on 11 June to take a ten-week course to qualify for Chief Yeoman of Signals.

In the nearby Woodhouse Barracks where I was billeted, the wooden beds (charpoys) had the base of the legs stood in shallow tins filled with paraffin, which the prize bedbugs were unable to cross, but they solved that problem by crawling up the walls and along the ceiling and then dropping onto the beds! I had dropped my watch on *Nevasa*'s deck and took it to Green's department store in Colombo and although the manager informed me that the balance staff was broken and that they were unable to supply a new one, he could tell me of several places in India where I might be lucky. When Bombay was mentioned, he gave me the name of a watchmaker and where to find his stall at the end of Colaba Causeway. I succeeded in finding him and he turned one on a tiny lathe and fitted it while I waited. I wore the watch for many years afterwards.

On 21 August I sailed for UK in SS *Strathaird*, which carried a mixture of personnel, including the singer Anne Shelton. Other ships joined the convoy en route at Aden, Suez and Port Said. On the day after passing through the straits of Gibraltar, I noticed a warship astern, which was slowly closing and I was soon able to recognise the old ship, and during the following afternoon, when she was passing through the convoy and was abeam, I climbed onto a locker on the poop deck and showed the semaphore call sign, which was soon answered by a signal lamp. I asked if any staff from previous commission were still aboard and the reply was, 'Tim Reilly here. Who are you?'

After we had exchanged greetings, a ship's officer asked me to go up to the bridge, where I was given a dressing-down by the captain for not obtaining permission to signal from the ship. I realised I was in the wrong, of course, but he said I could carry on with my little chats whenever conditions were favourable.

Strathaird passed *Ramillies* at Greenock and berthed in Glasgow on 13 September, my last view of the old ship. More than fifty years on, I still feel proud to have served in such a fine ship with a ship's company to match.

The latter part of my war service was in Germany on the staff of the Flag Officer Schleswig-Holstein, Rear Admiral H T Baillie-Grohman, DSO, RN, who spoke to me shortly after my arrival at Plön and said that he had seen my face somewhere. He was very amused when I reminded him of the mannequin episode in Malta in 1939, and he hoped it was a happy coincidence that he was my CO when the war began and again at the end of my war service.

Should auld acquaintance be forgot and never brought to mind?

Our lives are passed away from any land
In waters, in the hollow of Thy hand.
Our ways are found by sun and moon and star,
But ever in Thy hand our fortunes are.
Thy dangers hem us in, of every kind,
The seas that shatter, and the fogs that bind.
The wind that heaps the sea; the rock; the shoal;
Collision and fire, those daunters of the soul.
Save us from these, yet if that may not be,
Grant us the manhood fitting to Thy sea.
Anonymous

Extract from Eric Marks's newsletter, March 1995

A cutting from the *Portsmouth Evening News* for Friday, 29 December 1944:

170,000 Miles in Five Years
In June 1944, commanded by Captain Middleton, CBE, the *Ramillies* was one of the heavy ships engaged in covering the landings in Normandy, firing no fewer than 1,002 rounds from her eight 15in guns. Two months later she was again in action against enemy batteries during the invasion of southern France.

During this present war this battleship has served on the Home, North Atlantic, Mediterranean, East Indies, China, Australian, New Zealand, and American and West Indies stations. At one period she spent 49 days at sea out of 51, and during the first five years of the war steamed 170,143 miles, a striking tribute to the Officers and Men of her engineering department.

The name *Ramillies* has existed in the Royal Navy for 238 years, having first been given to a warship built in 1702 as the *Royal Katherine*, but renamed in 1706 in commemoration of the victory won by John Churchill, first Duke of Marlborough, in that year (Ramillies being a village in Belgium). The present ship was laid down in 1913, launched in 1916, and first commissioned in 1917, and is the sixth holder of that name. She joined the Grand Fleet in Scapa Flow in October 1917 and served in the Atlantic, Mediterranean and Home Fleets during and after the Great War. In November 1939 she was sent east and arrived at Wellington, New Zealand, on the last day of 1939, being the first battleship ever to visit that country. It was during this visit that the Maori Chiefs made the Captain the gift of a grass skirt, which provided it was worn in action was reputed to keep the ship immune from harm.

The third ship of the name (really the second by dates), a 74-gun vessel built in 1763, was in Admiral Keppel's action off Brest in 1778, but came to an untimely end four years later when she foundered during a hurricane in mid-Atlantic. Her successor, the fourth *Ramillies*, another 74-gun ship, was built in 1785. In 1794 she was present at Lord Howe's famous victory of 'The Glorious First of June', and in 1799 served during the blockade of the fleet at Rochefort. The next year she took part in an expedition to Quiberon Bay and in 1801 was Admiral Sir Hyde Parker's flagship during Nelson's victory at Copenhagen. Five years later she assisted HMS *London* to capture the French ship *Marengo*, while in 1813, when lying off New London, the Americans attempted to destroy her with a primitive torpedo; she was scrapped in 1850. The fifth *Ramillies*, a battleship of 14,150 tons, was built in 1892 and sold out of the service in 1913. She spent much time in the Med, and never saw action. The present veteran battleship has probably seen harder and more varied service than any of her predecessors, and it is fitting that she should bear the crest of the Marlborough family with its motto 'Faithful Throughout Adversity'.

The real second ship was built in 1748 and was the flagship of the ill-fated Admiral Byng off Minorca in 1756 and in the following year was Admiral Hawke's flagship during the expedition to Rochefort. Sadly she was wrecked off Bolt Head, South Devon in 1760 with a loss of nearly 700 lives.

This poem was painted in large letters on one of the inside walls of the gymnasium in the Boy's Training Establishment HMS *Ganges*, Shotley, near Ipswich, Suffolk, now a holiday camp. The gymnasium was also used for church services, lectures, cinema shows, etc. After eighteen months' training there (Signal Branch), in my case November 1930–May 1932, before joining our first seagoing ships, parts of it left a lasting impression on many of us!

If

If you can keep your head when all about you
Are losing theirs and blaming it on you,
If you can trust yourself when all men doubt you,
But make allowance for their doubting too;
If you can wait and not be tired by waiting,
Or being lied about, don't deal in lies,
Or being hated, don't give way to hating,
And yet don't look too good, nor talk too wise:

If you can dream – and not make dreams your master;
If you can think – and not make thoughts your aim;
If you can meet with Triumph and Disaster
And treat those two impostors just the same;
If you can bear to hear the truth you've spoken
Twisted by knaves to make a trap for fools,
Or watch the things you gave your life to, broken,
And stoop and build 'em up with worn out tools:

If you can make one heap of all your winnings
And risk it on one turn of pitch-and-toss,
And lose, and start again at your beginnings
And never breathe a word about your loss;
If you can force your heart and nerve and sinew
To serve your turn long after they are gone,
And so hold on when there is nothing in you
Except the Will which says to them: 'Hold on!'

If you can talk with crowds and keep your virtue,
Or walk with Kings – nor lose the common touch,
If neither foes nor loving friends can hurt you,
If all men count with you, but none too much;
If you can fill the unforgiving minute
With sixty seconds' worth of distance run,
Yours is the Earth and everything that's in it,
And – which is more – you'll be a Man, my son!

Rudyard Kipling

Note from Ken Williams' son, Keith Williams

Although my father did keep notes of dates and places visited throughout his service, and copies of some signals, he was relying on memory. In some cases where memory had let him down, other members of the HMS *Ramillies* Association (for whom this document was originally written) supplied him with the correct details, which he incorporated into the text. There is, however, one passage which he was unable to amend before his death. I should like to present the document as he wrote it, but have no wish to mislead researchers, so I have decided to add the relevant part of a letter he received from Ted Greenwood of Manchester. It refers to the sinking of *Cornwall* and *Dorsetshire*, described on page 129.

> I think I mentioned to you that the *Royal Sovereign* was 'repeating ship' and I was the Yeoman on watch, and actually made the signal to the *Cornwall* and *Dorsetshire* – to proceed at 15 knots steering 045° until midnight, then to steer 090° until 0400, then steer 180°. In the meantime the remainder of the fleet were to proceed at 15 knots steering due East 090° (from the time the two cruisers were given their orders) until 0400, then to alter course to steer due North 000°. If this manoeuvre had been successfully accomplished, we had hoped to have the Japanese fleet sandwiched in between us all and the cruisers *Cornwall* and *Dorsetshire*. As events have told this was not to be so, for, that same evening as the sun was setting to westward, the Japanese aircraft appeared out of the sun (and so they were not spotted) and dropped their oil bombs from stern to bow, and set the two cruisers alight from stem to stern. Of course we all know the end result which was a devastating blow to us all.

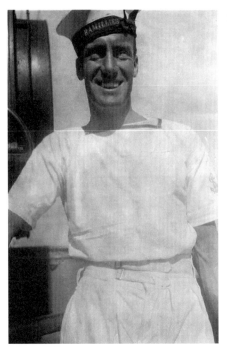

Above left: Ken Williams.

Above right: Ken Williams on the flag deck with unnamed person.

Left: Men of the ship's company on Woolloomooloo Jetty, Sydney, April 1940.

Below left: At Gourdon on the French Riviera in July 1939. Ken Williams is third from the right beside the lady.

The funeral of Boy 1st Class Herbert Iddon, on 21 January 1940 while three hundred miles northwest of Australia.

'Saying goodbye' to HMAS *Canberra* (flagship of Australian Squadron) off Rottnest Island, Western Australia in January 1940.

NAVAL MESSAGE.

Ramillies   FROM: F.O.H.

S. 1320d.
(Established—May, 1930.)
(Revised—January, 1933.)

1, 2, 4 6, 7, 9, 11, 15.

Goodbye and Good Luck. Proud to have had you in the battle with us.
I shall rember your magnificent turn of speed and I still maintain
the Italians made more smoke than you did

1500

REPLY...
Thank you very much. Your signal is much appreciated by all.
We were very glad to give you moral support in your victory

1540
Light   r/L   T.O.R.. 1539   T.O.D...1558   W   7/12/40.

Signals from the Madagascar Operation, May 1942.

NAVAL MESSAGE.

Buboo "F".   S O F.

(A – D.P.O.E.1.2.25.3.34. R S's)

Following messages have been exchanged.

(1) General Sturges   From   S O F.

The capture and occupation of Diego Suarez having been completed
I would like to express on behalf of all in Force "F" our congratulations
to you and the forces under your command for the success achieved and
our admiration at the speed and manner in which it was attained.
The dogged persistance under difficult and trying conditions with which
your Brigades and Number 5 Commando undertook long forced marches and
engaged the enemy in his prepared positions was an inspiration to us.
To all units, and to the 2 9th Brigade in particular whose casualties
have not been light, we offer our sympathy for the loss of messmates.
I would be grateful if you would convey to all concerned my personal
congratulations on a job well done.

0957.

(2) S O F   From   C O C.

All ranks thank you for your kind signal of congratulations. We do not
forget that the R N put us ashore at the right place and at the right
time, then maintained us with re -inforcements and stores in foul
weather. We were subsequently supported to such an extent by sea, air
MXIX and R N landing party that objective was achieved without serious
losses. All ranks are grateful and feel proud to have participated under
you in a successful combined operation.

1200. Ends.

2117/10.

Hand   P/L   T O D... In Transit   AD   10 / 5/42

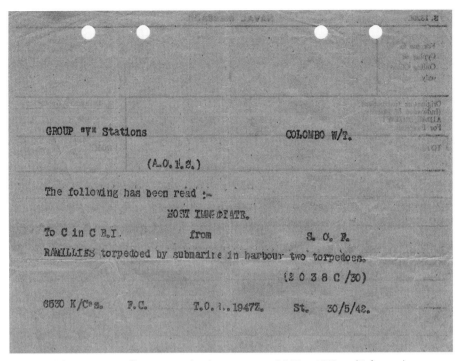

GROUP "V" Stations   COLOMBO W/T.

(A.O.I.S.)

The following has been read :-

MOST IMMEDIATE.

To C in C E.I.   from   S. O. R.

RAMILLIES torpedoed by submarine in harbour two torpedoes.

(2 0 3 8 C /30)

6530 K/Cs.   P.C.   T.O.I..1947Z.   St.   30/5/42.

This signal from Ken D Williams's scrapbook was sent on 30 May 1942 and informs the Commander-in-Chief that *Ramillies* has been torpedoed.

Two photographs from Ken D Williams's scrapbook. He is standing on the right in both photographs.

A naval parade marching through Martin Place, Sydney in April 1940, celebrating the arrival of the cruiser HMAS *Perth* which was joining the Australian Squadron. The marine band from *Ramillies* heads the parade.

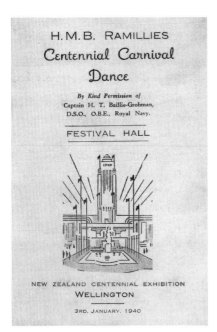

H.M.B. RAMILLIES

Centennial Carnival Dance

By Kind Permission of
Captain H. T. Baillie-Grohman,
D.S.O., O.B.E., Royal Navy.

FESTIVAL HALL

NEW ZEALAND CENTENNIAL EXHIBITION
WELLINGTON

3RD. JANUARY. 1940

Right: On the day prior to the Centennial Carnival Dance held in Wellington for the *Ramillies*, the local paper ran a short story asking local girls to turn out.

Left and below: The programme for the Centennial Carnival Dance held in Wellington in honour of the ship's company.

TURN OUT, GIRLS!

H.M.S. RAMILLIES DANCE

MR. HAINSWORTH'S REQUEST

2 JAN 1940

A memorable function is expected in the Festival Hall of the Exhibition tomorrow night, when the ship's company of H.M.S Ramillies will be at home to the people of Wellington. Making the announcement today, the General Manager of the Exhibition Company, Mr C. P. Hainsworth, said that by the kind permission of the ship's commander, music would be played by the ship's band. There would be dancing from 8.30 p.m. till 1.30 a.m. All members of his Majesty's forces would be welcomed and supper would be provided.

The invitation was directed particularly at the girls of Wellington, who were asked to attend this outstanding naval occasion, said Mr. Hainsworth. Some slight apprehension was felt, lest there should be a shortage of partners for the ship's company, who were anxious to repay the hospitality which had been extended to them since their arrival in Wellington. It was hoped therefore that as many as possible of the local girls would attend the dance.

Arrangements had been made by the Exhibition and Playland authorities, in conjunction with the Government, not only to admit members of the forces in uniform free of cost, but to supply the visitors with some 23,000 tickets for free rides on the main Playland devices. When they had exhausted these tickets, facilities would be provided for them to obtain further tickets at a greatly reduced price.

Tomorrow evening was therefore expected to be a gala one at the Exhibition.

H. M. B. RAMILLIES

- Programme -

(C.P.O., E. A. CHERRY · · · M.C.)

1. Quick Step	12. Rumba
2. Waltz	13. Slow Fox Trot
3. Paul Jones	14. Tango Waltz
4. Slow Fox Trot (Excuse Me)	15. Lambeth Walk
5.	16.
6. Quick Step (Card Dance)	17. Quick Step (Statue)
7. Valeta	18. Waltz
8. Fox Trot	19. Fox Trot
9.	20.
10. Tango	21. Paul Jones
11. Quick Step	22. Tango
	23. Waltz

INTERVAL OF 15 MINUTES.

"God Save The King"

Life in the Navy was not all sea and swabbing decks. A football team in Malta photographed in April 1939 with Williams at the front.

Relaxing at Stanley Bay, Alexandria, in October 1939.

Bernard Mallion, Ordinary Signalman 1943–44[24]

I was an ordinary signalman and my job was to work in communications. I joined the ship in 1943 at Scapa Flow and left her in 1944 after the Mediterranean operations. I then went to the Pacific in a different ship.

Bernard Mallion.

At the end of my Signal School training at HMS *Scotia*, I was drafted to the Portsmouth communications base, HMS *Mercury*, which was located at Leydene House in the countryside, near Petersfield, Hampshire. The base was used as a holding depot for signalmen and telegraphists whilst awaiting allocation to a seagoing ship. I was not at *Mercury* many days before I was called over the tannoy to report to the regulating office, where I received a draft to HMS *Ramillies*, a battleship of the *Revenge* class. The initial procedure for such events was to notify the various departments, eg, catering, stores, sick bay, pay office, etc, which are a part of every barracks, that you were now on draft, and then to be on standby with all kit and hammock to await transport. This tedious procedure was known as the Draft Routine.

Bernard Mallion in his youth.

With the huge expansion in the Royal Navy at this stage of World War II, many naval training establishments had been set up in the Portsmouth area to provide the necessary manpower. On any one day there could be up to several hundred naval ratings en route from barracks to ships located in various parts of the world, a situation that required much organisation. The organisation was centred on the Royal Naval barracks on Queen Street, Portsmouth, and the first stage of my journey to reach *Ramillies* was to be taken by lorry from HMS *Mercury* to RNB in Queen Street. Upon arrival, which was the same as the Draft Routine referred to above, [it was] just as tedious, but necessary, to let the various departments know that I was here. Failure to do so meant that you were not catered for, so no food or place to sling your hammock. Inevitably, it did sometimes mean that you had a medical examination by different doctors on two days' running, likewise for the dentist, and probably tested your gas mask in the gas chamber two days on the trot.

All was OK at RNB Portsmouth, except for some reason that my hammock went missing, so I was issued with a spare one for one night. We were accommodated in what was known as 'P Hut', a rather crummy old wooden building, very overcrowded, but as most of us were only passing through, as it were, nobody was much bothered about it. I was advised during the evening that I would be on my way early in the morning, travelling with about twelve other ratings in the charge of a chief petty officer. I was also reminded not to forget to carry out the Draft Routine before leaving.

The standard kit for a naval rating is quite substantial, and comprised a large kit bag containing uniform clothing suitable for all weathers from winter North Atlantic to the tropics; a heavy canvas hammock containing a palliasse and blankets; also a ditty box or small attaché case for personal items. Small wonder then that handcarts for the transport of the above from A to B were provided in large numbers at most naval barracks. So early in the morning, Draft Routine done yet again, kit loaded on a handcart, I made my way to the lorry park to await transport to Portsmouth Harbour station. There I made the acquaintance of the other ratings with whom I would be travelling, plus the chief petty officer who would be responsible to ensure that we reached our final destinations. I also learned that our destination was likely to be Scapa Flow, a long journey ahead, and that we had to reach Euston Station by 10am. It was a short journey to the harbour station, where, with kit stowed in a luggage van attached to the train, we were soon on our way to Waterloo.

The chief petty officer had a word with us about our conduct when on draft, and that as we had missed breakfast due to early start a sandwich pack would be issued shortly. He also asked if any of us lived in 'The Smoke', as London was generally called in these days. There was one among our number who lived in Lambeth.

Our train arrived at Waterloo about 1910. Throughout World War II, free transport between the principal London termini was provided for all members of the armed forces by army lorries. One of these lorries quickly took us to Euston Station where our train was already at platform 1, and we were urged by the CPO to get our luggage into the luggage van as soon as possible.

Loading completed, he said, 'You have about fifteen minutes to get a cup of tea. Go to the tea stall round the corner, you will get quick service there; I will stand where I can see you and the train. When I beckon you, run to the platform as fast as you can. Our train is the only through-service to Scotland today, so don't miss it.' Off we went as instructed and had nearly finished our mugs of tea when we saw the CPO waving frantically – we ran full pelt for the platform which was only about 30 yards away only to see the tail-end of our train moving off and the barrier gates to platform 1 shut.

I thought our CPO would blow his top, but all he said was that it must have left early, and that he would report to the railway transport officer. He wasn't away long and on his return said, 'Right lads, we are going to have to spend the day in London. You will be accommodated and fed in the Endsleigh Hotel, which is only a short distance away from the station, and I will march you there shortly. You can please yourselves what you do once you are booked in, but keep out of trouble, and make sure you are back at the station by 0930 tomorrow morning.'

We were taken aback somewhat by this news but without further ado, he said, 'Follow me,' and in about ten minutes we arrived at the Endsleigh Hotel.

'Have a nice day', he said. 'See you in the station in the morning and don't be late. I only live half a mile from here so I'm off now to see my wife.' There was a big smile on his face as he left.

I'm sure each of us had the same thought, that he had craftily planned the whole situation, although how he managed to convince the railway transport officer that the train left early I cannot tell. Perhaps a bottle of navy rum changed hands. However, we booked in at the hotel, found out where our room was (it was rather basic, double-tiered bunk beds but clean), paid a visit to the dining room, where we were able to scrounge some scrambled egg on toast, and then pondered on what I was going to do for the rest of the day. I knew very little about London and as my Navy pay at the time was three shillings (15p) per week, paid fortnightly, I was hardly about to paint the town red.

I had chummed up with the chap named Robbie, whose home was in Lambeth, and he said he was going to get a lift in one of the army lorries to Waterloo station which was not very far from his home, and that I was welcome to go with him. It seemed like a good idea to me, so off we went to Euston station and we were soon on a lorry to Waterloo. It was quite a long walk from there to Robbie's flat and on the way he said, 'My Mum will be surprised to see me, and maybe she will lend me a few bob.'[25] Sadly, there was nobody at home. Our thoughts then turned to what to do next.

I said to Robbie, 'I have an uncle who is a baker in a shop somewhere just off Regent Street, near Liberty's. I've never been there, but I would like to see him if possible.'

'We can but try,' he said, 'but we will have to walk back to Waterloo and start lorry-hopping again.' So retracing our steps and with Robbie leading the way, we soon found Regent Street. With incredible luck we spied a bakery in a side street, enquiring within, and in a few moments Uncle Fred appeared, liberally coated with flour. He was most surprised to see me, as we had not met for about two years, and I don't think he was aware that I was in the Navy. I explained about the problem of missing the train, that we had accommodation for the night, and would be on our way in the morning. We chatted for a while, until he had to go back into the bakehouse to attend to his loaves before they got burned. We said good-bye, and as we shook hands he very generously gave me a ten-shilling note.

I hadn't had such a sum for ages, and on the strength of it we had a pint of beer each (sixpence a pint) at the first pub we came to on our way back to the hotel. There they provided us with the necessities for having a wash, following which we had a good meal in the canteen. We had more than our fill of walking during the day so decided to have an early night, having first booked a call for seven o'clock in the morning.

I had not long been to sleep when I was awakened by the wail of air-raid sirens and the sharp crack of nearby anti-aircraft guns. Reluctantly, I followed the tannoy instructions to go down to the basement shelter, where there were only wooden forms to sit on, making it difficult to get any sleep. The bombing continued intermittently for some hours, but eventually the 'all clear' sounded, and everyone made their way back to bed.

If we hadn't booked a call for that morning, I am sure that we would have missed the train again. However, after smartening ourselves up and enjoying a good breakfast we made our way back to Euston. The fire service and civil defence people were busy dealing with the night's damage, but the station was unharmed. This time we all stayed close to the barrier at platform 1, and as soon as the CPO assured us that we were all present, boarded the train. The journey north was long and tedious, the first stop being at Crewe, where we were able to get a quick cup of tea. Sandwich packs, mostly containing corned beef or spam, were issued from time to time but we slept for much of the journey.

The train arrived at Thurso about seven in the morning, and part of the town hall there had been taken over as a canteen, where we had breakfast. Afterwards we were taken by lorry along to the docks, where we boarded a ferry for Scapa Flow, and on arrival transferred to an accommodation ship called *Dunluce Castle*. I made my way to the regulating office on board and was told to go to number 8 store, where I would find my kit, and go to the shelter deck and await a drifter that would take me to *Ramillies*. The ratings in the store were helpful and gave me a hand to get to the upper deck, saying a message would be put over the tannoy when my boat came alongside.

Whilst waiting I gazed around Scapa Flow, looking excitedly at warships that I had previously seen only in pictures: *Nelson*, *Rodney*, *Victorious*, *Ramillies* and many others. Nearby was the upturned hull of a German battlecruiser from World War I that had been scuttled by her crew after the war ended, but had since been salvaged and was awaiting being cut up for scrap.

An hour or so later the awaited call came; I carried my kit down the gangway into the boat, and we were soon on our way to *Ramillies*. The ship looked enormous as we pulled alongside and I was soon on the quarterdeck of my new home, not forgetting, of course, to salute, as is Royal Navy custom. In less than thirty minutes I was allocated a mess, given a mug of tea and a sandwich, and warmly welcomed by a chap named Brian Duly, whom I knew from my sea cadet days in Hastings.

The ship was like heaven: warm, and lit by red lighting. My immediate impression was, 'This is wonderful, she is going to be a great ship,' and within less than five minutes I had been appointed to the mess deck, and within twenty minutes there were two more shipmates who also lived in Hastings where I came from, welcoming me on board. So it really was a good introduction, and it turned out to be a very happy ship.

My duties were in communications. Communications at sea in those days were quite specific as radio was not used very much, because if a ship transmitted a radio signal, enemy search and listening posts would be able to pinpoint where the ship was. So very little was done in the way of actual radio transmissions. The only exception to that would be an enemy sighting report. So all the communication that had to take place between ships was done visually. The majority of it was done by signal lamp using Morse. Basically, they were either 10in or 20in signal lamps, the front of which was covered with shutters. As you pressed a lever to the right-hand side, it opened the shutters. This was done briefly for dots and with a longer interval for dashes. That is the basics for Morse code, and the entire message could be sent quickly and simply by using signal lamps. You called up the pennant number of the ship that you wanted to speak with and they would reply with a simple flash on their signal lamp. Then messages went to and fro quite easily and comfortably.

I would say 90 per cent of communications between ships was with Morse and lamps. However, we also used semaphore and signal flags. There is an alphabetical group of flags, A–Z, and numeral flags. No messages were sent using plain language: every flag had a secondary meaning. For example, a black flag, which if I remember correctly was N in the alphabetical set-up, flown by a ship, meant 'I am investigating a contact.' Flag G flown singularly from the flagship or senior ship meant 'Resume the previous course' or 'Alter course to continue manoeuvre previously ordered.' So each of those single flags could give its own message. But then in combination, two flags would give an even wider range of instructions, and with three or four even more instructions could be given, to the extent that you then needed a code book to interpret what the message was. The ship carried coders and it was their job to do just that.

I was on the flag deck, which was immediately below the operating bridge. If the captain wanted to send a signal to another ship, the senior signals man on the main bridge, the chief yeoman, the captain would tell him to send the message to so and so, and the chief yeoman would shout down the voice pipe to us, 'Make to Scorpion,' with whatever the message was, and, as I said, it could also be done by flags. We had a great reputation from the captain of being top-notch signalmen. What he did not realise was that we had a kind of acoustic hood from down on the flag deck, and if we stuck our head in this acoustic hood we could hear what was going on, on the bridge above, and we could hear the message the captain was giving to the chief yeoman. We knew with most messages exactly what flags would be required, and we would have those all on ready, so when the chief yeoman sent the message down, they went straight up! I don't think the captain ever figured out how we did it, but we took pride in that.

The ship had lots of lookouts dotted all over the place, but we as signalmen vied with them to spot any suspicious ship or object. We were the first to spot it and report it to the bridge, mainly because we used telescopes, whereas the lookouts were using binoculars which were not quite as effective. There were around twenty-five signalmen on mess 39 but then you had continuous watch, even when the ship was in harbour. You had three signalmen on duty and that was 24/7, no knocking off at midnight to get your head down, so you were working four watches throughout the day, and had to have three signalmen for each watch. If we went to action stations, all signalmen were up there until such times as action stations finished: it needed that number to ensure that you had adequate cover. At action stations we had an emergency compass platform aft so that if the bridge was knocked out by enemy fire, you had a working compass platform with all the ship's controls, signalmen and the like, navigators and another sight which was usually just above 'Y' turret.

In the main, I usually say, because she was such a happy ship, there are so many things that are good reflections. For example, I had only been on board a week when my mother received a letter from the padre saying that I was safely on board the ship and would be looked after and that he would look after my spiritual welfare, etc, which I thought was a very caring attitude to take. It was a ship full of fun, full of skylarks. It went on all the time so there is no specific event that stands out from the others – it was very pleasant.

We never had ear protectors or anything like that. We did wear anti-flash gear, which was white asbestos fibre-type hoods with a face piece to go across the nose and mouth. We also had long-sleeved white gloves. We looked quite funny, although it was necessary because the blast and the flame from the 15in guns was quite serious, depending which angle they were firing from. There used to be hoses running on the quarterdeck when they were firing the after guns, because the flash and heat from the guns would dry the deck up and ignite the wooden timbers over a period of time. It was something we got used to. On the other hand, when we were doing a shoot, you would watch the turret rotating, a little bit tense, and wait for the 'ting, ting' of the firing gong that was transmitted throughout the ship, so that everybody knew there was going to be a hefty bang, and that's how it worked. There were one or two funny incidents on the flag deck. We had a young signalman called Passley, and because we were being fired at, he was taking shelter by the navigating officer's door, a heavy wooden door which ran on runners and rollers. In conjunction with that, there was a 'wonder lead light' hanging down from the bulkhead with a single electric light bulb. We fired a salvo and for some reason the door sprung off the rollers and fell on Passley and at the same time this wonder lead light was shaken out from the bulkhead, and fell and broke close to Passley. In the effort of getting up, he cut his hand, only a little, but he got up screaming, 'I've been hit, I've been hit!' – but of course he wasn't. We always pulled his leg about that for a long time afterwards.

I am sad that she has gone and most of the people with her have gone now too. It was an honour to serve on her and a tribute to the people who built her.

CHAPTER 5

The New Zealand Connection

Jim Pollok, Lieutenant

The following interview was conducted for the HMS *Ramillies* Association.

Jim and Fay Pollok.

Jim Pollok was born in Invercargill, New Zealand, in 1918. When the Second World War began, he was studying science at Otago University, before transferring to Lincoln College to begin an agricul- tural science degree. At that stage, he had no idea that the hours he spent in physics lectures would help to equip him for his role in the war. A year later Jim saw an advertisement in The Press *calling for volunteers for the Royal Navy, for a confidential unclear course and arduous conditions. He put his name forward.*

I was completely in the dark. When we were called up, we were called up in civvies and, at the end of 1940, we went to Auckland University in the summer vacation. Something was in the offing and when we got there, lo and behold, if it isn't electronics. All this electricity and magnetism that I'd learned at Otago all of a sudden became very important. But anyway, we had an odd sort of a chap leading us through the elements of electronics, and then just in the last week after the two or three months they spilt the beans – here is a wonderful new electronic device that can see through the dark, through the murk, through the smokescreen, and can give the range and bearing of either ships or aircraft.

Was it called radar at that stage?
No, it was called Radio Direction Finding (RDF). And then they said, well, with all this high-flown stuff, we'd better make you into sailors. And I got a proper, puk- kah naval uniform. I went to Bond Street, Gieves Naval Tailors, you go along there and they measure you up, proper tailors,

Officers of HMS *Ramillies* drawn up by the 15in guns, 'Y' turret, for inspection by the First Lord, A V Alexander, in February 1944. Jim Pollok is the seventh officer from the right.

and they fit you out with a hand-crafted naval uniform. But this little thin stripe doesn't carry much weight, you know. Not in the hierarchy. You're still, as it were, on the bottom rung, but it's a different ladder.

The captain of the Signals School appointed them to different posts. Jim was sent to the battleship HMS Ramillies *as radar officer.*
Just me, Wavy Navy, temporary acting sub lieutenant appointed as radar officer, HMS *Ramillies*, refitting in Devonport. I travelled down there and then reality hits you, clean before the eyes – just before that Plymouth had been bombed, so it was simply a city of rubble, and I can remember picking my way over the great chunks of masonry to get to the dockyard where the ship was. It struck me as for real. The war in Europe was real; the war in England was real. When I say the war, I mean the bombardment.

Had you had a real sense of that before you got to Plymouth?
Oh no, not at all. It was pretty dastardly, pretty dramatic, pretty impressive. I remember somewhere along the line calling in at a NAAFI[26] shelter, which was really just tarpaulins rigged up and very dark and dim inside, and all blacked out outside, for a cup of tea. And there was the old English cup of tea as strong as it comes, and you down that and then you continue on your way. I picked my way down to the dockyard. Nothing had been cleared up. The bombing was recent.

At the time Jim joined the Ramillies *it was undergoing a refit that lasted for three months. As well as older equipment, a new radar set was installed, long-range surface-warning radar that was state of the art.*
It put the Royal Navy streets ahead of its opponents. So here I am, still a rookie, and I have this absolutely top-class surface-warning set. I was very excited about this. In practical terms it meant you had a much less anxious time of it. You could depend on this set. It was on the top of the mainmast – in order to get maximum energy to the aerial they actually built the transmitter on a platform on the mainmast about 100ft up in the air, so I made a point of always climbing up the mainmast to see the chaps operating the set in the middle of the night to make sure that they were happy and the set was going all right. I had a sub lieutenant to help me and there were three petty officer radar mechanics. So we made a team of five that had to keep the sets going. Then we had about fifty operators.

Soon after the ship went to sea, Jim was promoted to lieutenant. He quickly developed positive feelings for the Ramillies.
It was a happy ship. It's indefinable. The people in it make it a happy ship, and a lot depends on everybody. If you come onto the upper deck, from the captain

down, everybody contributes to making it a happy ship, the morale in the ship, the general atmosphere. We had a good long time to shake down because we were at least three months in dock and so you get to know one another. A ship is a marvellous thing. A ship won't work unless you're all working – if you're all contributing, it's absolutely marvellous. The moment you leave port you are on your own, you either sink or swim, I mean the whole show has to work, it's an independent unit that's buzzing with activity. Once you put to sea you're on your mettle, because you are now responsible for staying afloat on the ocean. In actual fact you are a floating magazine. You have all this enormous high-explosive cordite and shells stored in your magazine, and you only have to be hit and the whole thing goes up. But you know you're oblivious, you don't even think about it, you don't think that you can be sunk, it's the last thing you think of.

For several months the Ramillies *was based with the Eastern Fleet at Mombasa on the coast of Kenya. Then, unexpectedly, they were on the move.*

We think we're in the Indian Ocean for the rest of the war. All of a sudden a signal arrives from the Admiralty to say the ship's got to come back to England, and after that it's all a question of what's up? Rumours are rife, especially on the lower deck. We were obviously going back for a purpose – they wouldn't pull us out of the Eastern Fleet – we'd only just arrived four or five months before. And there was all the talk about a second front. The word got around that maybe we were in for something worthwhile. I was made aware then that things were afoot, because as a radar officer I had to know a thing or two, and so I knew that we were heading for Normandy, eventually. You can't disguise the fact. Eventually we're up at Scapa Flow and all of a sudden we find that we're visited by First Lord of the Admiralty and lined up on the quarterdeck to meet him. What's he doing coming out to see us? We'd never seen him before in our lives. And then before we could say Jack Robinson, King George VI arrived, well, you know a King doesn't normally come, so by now you couldn't sort of hide things. And blow me down if we don't get a signal to say that Lord Montgomery will be on board the *Howe* and that he wants to address all those who are free to attend, and I get in a cutter and go across to the *Howe*, which is the number one modern battleship, and there standing on a capstan is Lord Montgomery, and he hops up there and tells us we are in for glorious things and that the German fighters are great fighters, but the British fighters are better ones.

By now we are getting pretty close, but at the same time we're exercising every day, just about. We sail out to sea and we let off these enormous guns, 15in, which we hadn't actually fired before. They're big guns. They let off a big bang. I have a friend who was in landing craft at Normandy and he referred to the fact that he could hear these things going off overhead. We were practising on targets out at sea. And then we went down to the Clyde and we did the same thing. This is going to be a bombardment, and so what you do is you have a fixed target and now you have to locate that target as accurately as possible and fire at it with these enormous guns. On D-Day the *Ramillies*' position in the bombarding force was off Sword Beach, along with another battleship HMS *Warspite*, and HMS *Roberts*. The ships were on the most vulnerable, and therefore the most strongly defended, flank of the force. Their primary task was to knock out enemy coastal defences.

We were all keyed up. We'd been working up for a couple of months at least. Off the Isle of Wight there was a great collecting centre of naval vessels, not just warships – which are there in their hundreds, because you've got battleships, cruisers, destroyers and frigates, all armed to the teeth, but you've also got landing craft full of infantrymen, landing ships which carried landing craft hoisted out, you've got landing craft tanks, carrying tanks, you've got a whole armada of vessels. So we all assembled.

It was in the evening that the captain, Captain Middleton, comes on the blower and tells us that we're heading for Normandy. We now know from the horse's mouth that we really are crossing the Channel and tomorrow morning at dawn we will be opposite the beaches of Normandy. And in the morning we will be at action stations. I had a false sense of security as far as the ship was concerned. It's so big. You just feel so secure in such a large vessel which doesn't feel the motion of the sea very much, so I was in reflective mood.

Ramillies was fitted with jamming equipment to interfere with the enemy's coastal radar, and it was Jim's job to switch this on. By D-Day the crew were ready for action. He recalls the journey across the Channel as uneventful.

Here am I, this little scion from New Zealand, I'm pacing the quarterdeck of a battleship, I've got nothing else to do. The whole blinking show is set up, the whole thing, the targets identified, the guns are ready. The radar sets are ready; the jamming equipment's all ready to be switched on. We're not there yet. It's evening and I'm pacing up and down the quarterdeck and I'm simply reflecting. This jolly battleship is so stable that I hardly feel a thing. I'm not talking about glory or courage at this juncture. I just know that my ship is heading across the Channel, that I'm responsible for the radar gear, everything's in place and it is a big occasion, and it's nice to be part of it. We got into position in the evening.

When Captain Middleton announced that the *Ramillies* was at last heading for Normandy, he added an unusual rider. In 1940 the ship had docked in Wellington harbour before escorting the first echelon of New Zealand troops to World War Two. During the visit, the Ngati'poneke Maori Association entertained the ship's company and presented a *piupiu* made by Pirihia Heketa. At the time of the presentation the *Ramillies* was blessed – as long as the captain wore the *piupiu* whenever the ship was in danger, no harm would come to it or to any member of the crew. When the first detachment of troops pulled away from shore, everyone sang 'Po Atarau'/'Now is the Hour' in Maori and English. This became the ship's song. It's then he used the famous words – 'and I shall be wearing the Maori skirt'. The reason he says is that this is the greatest morale-booster on the ship, this is going to protect the whole ship's company and the ship from any harm, and it's quite remarkable.

Did you know anything about it before he said that?

No, I didn't know a thing about the Maori skirt. I don't know what I thought. I suppose I must have thought it was a bit odd. It meant a whole lot to the crew, primarily in the lower deck. The ship had been to Madagascar before, and there's a story about the Maori skirt and the Madagascar campaign. That was before I joined the ship. The ship actually got torpedoed then and they said that was because the captain wasn't wearing the Maori skirt. But it didn't sink, and that was because the Maori skirt was locked up in his cabin. And each draft of seamen coming on board the ship sooner or later all heard something about the Maori skirt and – 'What on earth is this Maori skirt?' – 'Oh, that's what the skipper wears, and when the skipper wears it, we're all right.' And Captain Middleton was brave enough to wrap it around his loins when he went up to the bridge at action stations on D-Day.

Jim did not see Captain Middleton wear the piupiu, *but a friend who was a Royal Marine bugler on the* Ramillies *has sent him a signed affidavit saying that he saw the captain wearing it on D-Day.*

There's always a Royal Marine bugler on the bridge of a battleship to sound off the various calls which are made from the bridge to the ship's company. It's really a relic of sailing days before you had modern means of communication. So he's up there, and he's there when Captain Middleton comes up on the bridge and he's wearing the Maori skirt, all right. It's quite extraordinary because Captain Middleton was all of six foot tall and he wore a monocle. So he was a sort of archetype, you know, English naval officer and gentleman. He was quite pukkah, he sensed all this stuff about the Maori skirt – and after all, we didn't know what we were in for, really. We knew there was a dangerous coast for sure, and anything could happen to the ship. The batteries could aim at a ship, but also Le Havre was there and all these E-boats and U-boats and submarines and things. I mean it wasn't exactly a pleasant location. The thing is that this ship came through two world wars unscathed. A lucky and a happy ship.

Ramillies *did escape harm on D-Day, unlike a vessel close by. Torpedoes from E-boats hit a nearby Norwegian destroyer, the* Svenner, *which sank with the loss of thirty-four lives.*

There's a sudden commotion and someone pokes his head around the door and says there's a ship sunk, so I go out and then see with my own eyes the

Svenner, broken in two and sinking just a hundred or two hundred yards away from the *Ramillies*. Just sank before your eyes. And that was perhaps the most dramatic D-Day moment for me. It was just part of the drama of the day. There's nothing you can do about it. You say, 'It's copped it.' You know there are men in the water, even if you don't see them.

The day after D-Day *Ramillies* returned to Portsmouth to take on more ammunition, and then sailed back to Normandy. The enemy coastal batteries were not the only targets. The battleship was also instructed to support the attack on the town of Caen, some kilometres inland from Sword Beach. The bombardment of the city and its rail marshalling yards was relentless.

Ramillies became the major bombarding battleship, I'm sorry to say wreaking havoc on the city of Caen, because the Germans were using that as a hinge, a point of resistance for the whole of their campaign. It was obviously within range of the ship. They reckon these 15in missiles weighed close on a ton each, and you're hurling them through the air. The talk on the ship was simply that we were doing our stuff, banging them off, to the extent that after about ten days or so the captain posted a signal which I've always remembered – and the Royal Navy has its own special language which it conjures up particularly when it sends signals, and so this read, and I can see this on the noticeboard, '*Ramillies* to Admiralty. My thousandth round has just rung a merry chime on Caen.' So that's the language used in warfare. And back comes the signal from Admiralty to *Ramillies*, 'Well done, *Ramillies*.'

I've subsequently reflected on what those thousand rounds of 15in high-explosive meant for Caen. It depends how you view it. If you're not particularly warlike, you realise you've wreaked an awful lot of destruction. I don't exactly enjoy the captain's signal. I can understand how it had come to be written. When I see the destruction of warfare I don't enjoy it, and this is just the physical destruction, but along with that goes the human obliteration, there is no other word for it.

Jim Pollok's association with his old ship and its piupiu *did not end with the war. In 1993, at a reunion of the* HMS Ramillies *Association in England, he learnt that the* piupiu *had been lost when the ship was broken up. As the only New Zealander present, he was asked to find a replacement. Back home, he made contact with the Ngati'poneke Maori Association and met Riria Utiku who, with her late husband, Rangi Katakua Utiku, had been in the performing party on the* Ramillies *in Wellington in 1940 when the* piupiu *was presented to the ship. Riria still had the* piupiu *that Rangi had worn on that occasion and generously offered it as a gift to the* Ramillies *Association. Ngati'poneke held a ceremony and church service and the replacement* piupiu *was blessed before Jim took it to England, where it is now on permanent display in the Royal Marines Museum at Southsea.*

From the battle for Normandy, the Ramillies *was sent to the South of France to support a further landing which faced no real opposition. In October 1944, after four years at sea, Jim Pollok was given leave to return to New Zealand. From the day he left the* Ramillies *he missed the ship and his friends among the crew. After a couple of months at home, he joined* HMS Indefatigable *in the Pacific. He was on the ship when it sailed into Tokyo Bay after the Japanese surrender.*

After the war Jim completed his PhD and became a soil scientist at Massey University. In 1975 he married Fay Fairbrother, a schoolteacher. He reflects with satisfaction on the contribution he was able to make on the Ramillies *at the time of the Normandy invasion.*

I've been digging up the records. I found this flimsy, which is a sort of a piece of paper the captain has to write whenever someone leaves the ship.

Dated 1st October 1944:

This is to certify that J A Pollok has served as Lieutenant Special Branch Royal New Zealand Navy Volunteer Reserve under my command from the 23rd day of August 1943 to the 2nd day of September 1944, during which period he has conducted himself with zeal, ability and to my entire satisfaction. By his personal application he has brought the radar equipment to a high pitch of efficiency and operational value. Determined to surmount all difficulties.

Signed G B Middleton, Captain, HMS *Ramillies*.

So I evidently had something to do with bringing the radar equipment to a high pitch of efficiency and operational value. But it was all done by an amateur!

Mick French: The legend of the grass skirt

HMS *Ramillies* went to New Zealand as the senior escort ship to take the first echelon of troops from Wellington to Port Suez in 1940. Having been the first-ever battleship to visit New Zealand, close friendships were formed that last to this day. The Ngati'poneke Maori Club, which started in 1937, was invited to attend various events on the ship and, likewise, the young dancers entertained the officers and men, talking about aspects of their culture.

The committee of the club arranged to present a grass skirt known as the *piupiu*, to the ship. Captain H T Baillie-Grohman and five senior members of the Ngati'poneke Club attended the presentation ceremony. The *piupiu* was a sacred item, having been blessed prior to the presentation. Later, the following verse was coined to accompany the *piupiu*.

> In Wellington this ship is blessed, with full Ma'ori tradition;
> Skirt of grass was given to her, to guard her on her mission.
> In action and in battle sway, this ship will have no hurt,
> Provided that the captain wears this Maori skirt.

When *Ramillies* left Wellington on 6 January 1940, a large crowd had gathered on the wharf together with a military band and the traditional Maori farewell, 'Po Atarau', better known to us as 'Now is the Hour', was sung as the ship edged away from Pipitea wharf. This was a most stirring event and no one on board or ashore will ever forget it. By all accounts, there was hardly a dry eye left among any of those present.

The good-luck charm seems to have worked, as within a few days in a convoy on the Indian Ocean, a soldier fell overboard. Before the 'Man overboard' signal could be hoisted, the troopship *Rangitata*, with a remarkable piece of seamanship, pulled out of line, put her engines full astern, stopped, lowered a lifeboat, and picked up the lucky individual.

There are witnesses to the fact that on D-Day, while bombarding the coast of Normandy, and particularly the enemy gun emplacements at Benerville, Captain Middleton was seen wearing the *piupiu*, and that, indeed, no harm did come to the ship or the men, especially when three torpedoes, mentioned elsewhere, narrowly missed the ship, one passing down the starboard side, and two down the port side. Unfortunately, the Norwegian ship *Svenner*, stationed astern of *Ramillies*, was hit and sunk.

During the Allied landings in southern France, where once more the now battle-worn *Ramillies* played a part, the *piupiu* was reportedly worn by the captain, although there is no clear evidence of this. But again no fatalities were recorded. After the war, the *piupiu* went missing, and no trace of it has since been found.

In 1993, at the third HMS *Ramillies* reunion, it was decided to seek a replacement. Former Lieutenant Jim Pollok, RNZNVR, who was on board *Ramillies* during D-Day, volunteered to seek a replacement. He succeeded in contacting Mrs Vera Morgan, a member of the original club, who contacted further members, one of whom was Mrs Meri Mataira (née Black), who actually wrote down an account of the original presentation, and Mrs Riria Utiku, who, with her late husband Rangi Katakua Utiku, were performers on board the ship in 1940. Mrs Utiku donated her late husband's *piupiu* as a replacement, as she had no son to pass it on to.

This, then, kept a living connection with the original *piupiu*. After a small church service of blessing, at the Ngati'poneke Club, the *piupiu* was handed over to Jim for delivery to the next *Ramillies* reunion in 1994. The replacement *piupiu* is now held in trust by the Royal Marines Museum at Eastney, Portsmouth, and is taken each alternate year, in a smart oak wooden case, to the Portsmouth reunion, where it is revered by all. A legend, or was it good luck? We know what the crew believe!

I am indebted to Jim Pollok and to the late Ken Williams for the information given above.

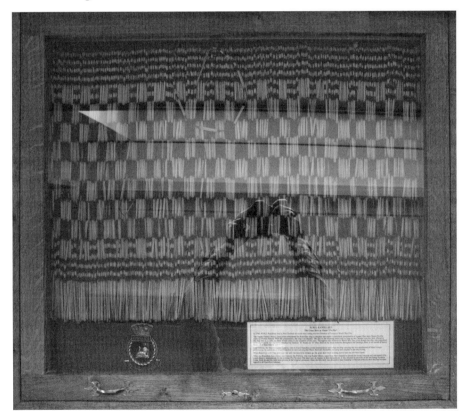

The replacement *piupiu* in its case now held at the Royal Marines Museum in Portsmouth.

J Allan Edwards, Merchant Navy: Timetable of troop convoy US.1 as observed from RMS *Empress of Japan*

Sailed from Esquimalt, British Columbia, on 4 December 1939, on *Empress of Japan* and arrived in Sydney, Australia, on 20 December ready to commence trooping, then proceeded to Melbourne. Sailed on 11 January 1940 with Australian troops to join convoy US.1 from New Zealand.

Ships in convoy: *Orion* (commodore), *Empress of Japan*, *Dunera*, *Sobieski*, *Empress of Canada*, *Orcades*, *Otranto*, *Orford*, *Rangitata*, *Strathaird*, and *Strathnaver*. Our escorts were HMS *Ramillies* and HMAS's *Australia* and *Canberra*.

16 January: Early morning dummy attack by the cruiser escort on the convoy.

18 January: 0500 hours, cruisers made a throw-off shoot on *Ramillies*, convoy formed in line ahead for entry into Fremantle.

20 January: Sailed for Colombo, *Australia* and *Canberra* steam by in farewell. Escorts are HMS *Ramillies*, HMS *Kent* and French cruiser *Suffren*.

21 January: *Orcades* lost a man overboard at noon who was picked up by *Rangitata* in short order. Convoy diverted while a tanker stopped, and was inspected by *Kent*.

A view from the forecastle towards ships of the first convoy to leave New Zealand and Australia for the Middle East.

24 January: *Ramillies* paid a musical visit to convoy today, steaming alongside each ship with her Royal Marine Band playing.

26 January: *Kent* made a dummy attack on convoy. *Ramillies* defended with a heavy smokescreen, and 15in gunfire throw-off shoot at *Kent*. Most impressive!

29 January: *Kent* made a throw-off shoot at *Ramillies*. Convoy reformed for entry into Colombo.

30 January: Arrived at Colombo and moored in harbour to buoys.

1 February: Convoy sailed at noon, being joined by French troopship *Athos* and eleven escorts, among them being *Ramillies*, *Sussex*, the carrier *Eagle* and HMAS *Hobart*.

7 February: Joined by HMS *Westcott*.

8 February: Arrived at Aden and entered harbour.

9 February: *Orion*, *Orcades*, *Empress of Japan* and *Strathnaver* with *Sussex* and *Westcott* proceeded into Red Sea.

12 February: Arrived at Suez.

CHAPTER 6

Operation Ironclad: Madagascar, 1942

Raymond Hedgecock, PK/X110182: The diary of a stoker

An extract from March 1942, Operation Ironclad.

30 March 1942: Fleet Base, Addu Atoll
Expected action with Japanese fleet at pm tomorrow, 31 March 1942. C-in-C
Admiral Sir Percy Somerville on HMS *Warspite*.

Battleships: *Warspite, Revenge, Royal Sovereign, Resolution, Ramillies.*

Aircraft carriers: *Hermes* (later sunk), *Indomitable, Formidable.*

Cruisers (more joining): *Cornwall* (later sunk), *Enterprise, Colombo, Dorsetshire*
(later sunk), *Glasgow, Emerald, Caledon.*

Australian destroyers: *Norman, Nestor* (later sunk), *Vampire* (later sunk).

Also some twenty Royal Navy destroyers including HMS *Anthony*, some
Dutch destroyers and cruisers.

Fleet moves to sea. We proceed to draw out Jap naval forces, to our Main
Fleet awaiting in the Bay of Bengal, but had to retire as there's too many Jap
planes for us. They try to crash onto the decks but all they do is hit the oggin'.

17 days at sea
Ramillies to proceed to sea when fuelled to try and intercept Jap convoy off
Sumatra. Oh for some snow! Action stations 0300 air attack, Jap planes
shadowing us. Continue action stations all day then the fun starts. We are
heading for five aircraft carriers and escorts. Do we nip exit Rammi? Skipper
tells stokers it is up to them to get the ship away from [Japanese]. Arrive in
Addu Atoll, sixteen days at sea. *Ramillies* to do an eighteen-day patrol from
1700 tonight.

Japanese fleet
Three battleships, eight 8in cruisers, six 5.9in cruisers, five aircraft carriers, five
seaplane carriers, twenty-five submarines, fifty-five destroyers.

First submarine attack 1400 hours 30 March 1942. Four submarine
attacks on 1 April.

Attack on Madagascar

HMS *Ramillies*, Straits of Madagascar, 2 May.

Speech by skipper 1115 hours:

'Convoy, which we are escorting, will pick up slow convoy tomorrow, escorted by HMS *Indomitable*. Troops to attempt landing covered by aircraft from aircraft carriers, *Illustrious* and *Indomitable*, cruisers *Devonshire* and *Hermione* (later sunk) and destroyers to go in close. HMS *Ramillies* to lay off and bombard shore batteries, also to protect landing troops from hostile surface craft.'

ZERO HOUR 0430, Tuesday, 5 May

Troops landed successfully, light machine-gun fire. Shore batteries open up on cruiser *Hermione* soon silenced by naval gunfire. Planes from carriers bomb aerodrome successfully. Little resistance has been met yet by our troops. Valentine tanks go into action against machine-gun post, East Lancs regiment meet heavy machine-gun fire on landing on the beach. Major General Sturges lands from HMS *Ramillies* with Royal Marine bodyguard. Commandos meeting little resistance, advancing steadily.

Landing troops include: Royal Marines (Commandos), Royal Scots, Argyle and Sutherland Highlanders, Seaforth Highlanders, East Lancs, South Lancs, Cameronians, 9th Independent Brigade.

Wednesday, 6 May

Patrol kept up and down the coast by *Ramillies*. Major General Sturges, RM, land with Royal Marine bodyguard. Troops still advancing towards centre of the town. 3pm, resistance still very heavy outside city by machine-gun fire, and artillery. HMS *Lightning*, *Laforey*, *Devonshire*, *Hermione*, bombard town from coast, our aircraft bomb at the same time. Our fighters shot down three bombers. Town can be seen burning fiercely.

Royal Marines landing party leaves *Ramillies* on destroyer HMS *Anthony* to try and crash boom and attack from the rear to relieve pressure on commandos who are encircled near the city. We move away and bombard if this movement is unsuccessful.

Thursday, 7 May

HMS *Ramillies*, *Devonshire*, *Hermione*, and destroyer escort steaming up and down coast awaiting word of landing party.

0925 action stations sounds. First salvo of 1000 successful hit by second salvo. We keep bombarding until the French give in. Troops then occupy the town and naval base of Diego Suarez. We await word to proceed into harbour.

1500 hours safe to proceed into harbour. We, *Ramillies*, enter harbour. Wrecks of all we have sunk lies all about us. Seamen rescue a dog chained to a half-submerged sloop, *Admiral Sharney*. The dry dock had been sabotaged and left flooded with a large German supply ship also scuttled in the dock. We make the Germans remove the dynamite and four 250lb bombs which have been placed all over the ship. They don't seem to like it. Nor do we!

Start coal fires to pump out the dock by hydraulic pumps, this goes on till 18 May, then the dock is dry and the German ship remains to be pumped out, with more bombs in her hold. Water stopped them from exploding. Good oh, up to now, but fed up with this place. Mr Churchill sends us personal message and allows us to write home and tell our people about it. Our 15in guns put the finishing touches to the 'Froggie' resistance. They didn't seem to like the ton of muck we slung into their shore batteries. Serves them right by wasting our time fighting, we could have been still enjoying ourselves in Durban!

Saturday, 30 May
HMS *Ramillies* hit by torpedoes fired by unknown submarine. We are sure to go into dry dock now. About time too. Commander says engine room ratings saved the ship. Rip in side of ship 15ft by 25ft, plates ripped right off with force of explosion. Commander tells us that it was a Japanese two-man submarine which hit us, as they shot the two officers ashore at Diego Suarez.

3 June
After much hard work and sleepless nights we are fit for sea. We proceed to Durban having one air attack, two submarine attacks, and a light surface attack, all of which were repulsed by escorting destroyers, HMS *Duncan*, *Decoy* and *Active*. All's well that ends well. Look out, Durban, here we come.

9 June
We arrive in Durban and proceed to make whoopee in a big way. Big fight at dance between us and *Valiant*. I had a big peeker. It was 'good oh!'.

15 June
Proceed to dry dock. What a gash! We had been ripped open from top to bottom, Skipper praises the engine room branch for getting the ship seaworthy, and tells us we have been very lucky as the torpedoes entered our magazine but the inrush of water stopped them from blowing the ship sky-high. The dockyard officials say we are in a worse condition than any of the other ships, which have been hit in Durban, ie, *Valiant* and *Barham*.

17 June
Great news: we are all getting seven days' leave, all expenses paid. The people of Durban are taking us out to the country in pairs at their houses and farms. What a week. Myself and Bill Taylor go to a farm at Glencoe and they could not do enough for us. Bought us trousers, shirts and silk under gear. Took us

out everywhere in their cars and would not let us pay a penny. They were sorry to see us go and have since asked us up again, so I hope some more Jap subs are outside waiting for us. We think we are going to the States on 7 August. I hope so, it will mean another holiday.

Tom Tweedy, Engine Room Artificer: torpedo strike at Madagascar, May 1942

Tom Tweedy.

We led a convoy from England round the Horn to Madagascar. I seem to remember that this was an important mission and that we had an admiral on board. The troops went in early in the morning and the ship opened fire (broadside) on Diego Suarez. I was on watch looking after the ship's generators. When the ship fired she used to roll – it felt like she was going over, but then she righted herself. The noise was almost unbearable.

The captain gave us a running commentary over the ship's PA system: 'We're firing ashore with the army directing fire. We've made a direct hit ... ,' etc. I don't know how long the fighting went on for; it seemed to be several hours. You were frightened, but didn't have time to think about it, you had your duty to attend to. Finally, the captain announced that Diego Suarez had surrendered. He told us that we could 'write home to our families and tell them we have taken Madagascar'. The whole ship's company cheered and I think that we 'spliced the main brace', in other words, we all got a tot of rum.

We had four meals a day and were never hungry, although we had no fresh food after the first week or so at sea. Everything was tinned or rehydrated. There was plenty of tea (no coffee) and the watch-keepers drank a special brew called 'kai' (made from a block of dark chocolate mixed with water and condensed milk). There was plenty of water hanging around the engine room in cloth bags with small spouts to drink from. On Fridays they gave us soup mixed with a laxative which kept the ship moving, so to speak! My mates and I never touched the stuff!

Anyway, on this particular day we were relaxing after supper in the mess. Some men relaxed by walking on deck, some were catching up on their laundry, others listening to the radio. The radio was on most of the time and I seem to remember it was mainly playing Max Miller. I was writing a letter home, and there were probably nine or ten of us in the mess at the time. Suddenly, two very loud bangs shattered our reverie; it was a bit like the ship's guns going off. The whole ship rolled and the lights went out, plunging us into darkness. When watching the films of sea battles, I have always commented that they never managed to reflect the true horror of being hit – the sudden plunge into blackness.

We called to one another to see if we were all all right and then tried to work out how to get out. It was difficult to get your bearings, but then one of my mates called out that he'd found an opening. We all edged towards the sound of his voice and he told us that the doorway had been damaged and that we would have to crawl through a small space. I don't remember any noise or panic, we just took it in turns to squeeze our way through the collapsed doorway by the kitchen until we were all out. We then made our way up the ladders and onto the deck. Here's the funny thing; later, when we were able to go below, we returned to the mess to see what damage had occurred to the doorway. There was a curtain on a pole over the door and this had collapsed at an angle, blocking the door. If only we had had a little light, we could have just lifted the curtain and pole out of the way and exited easily, rather than limbo-ing under the pole! It gave us all a good laugh.

And so we had made our way to our 'action and repair' station on deck, and met up with one of the watchmen who was on duty near to where the torpedoes had struck. He had no recollection of making his way on deck, but he said that he didn't think that his feet had touched the ladders all the way up! A ship nearby had been hit and was sinking. Someone was calling from her, '*Ramillies, Ramillies*, submarine on port side.' It was utter confusion, but nobody panicked. We just waited by our stations until the senior officers arrived to give orders. We were very lucky that day. One of the torpedoes hit the cordite magazine and we should have gone up like the *Hood*. As it was, we beached

Above and right: Tom Tweedy and other crew members relaxing at Mombasa and finding a spot in the sun off the African coast.

Millie and a diver (mechanician) was sent down to assess the damage. There was a massive hole to the port side, which we were able to block with collision mats. Battens were used to shore up the bulkheads to stop them caving in. We then steamed slowly to Durban so that repairs could be undertaken. We lost two or three of the collision mats on the way, but we made it.

On reaching Durban, we hit another problem. The weight of water in the nose was dragging it down to such a degree that we couldn't get the ship over the harbour bar. The captain ordered all hands to the stern in order to lift the *Ramillies'* nose sufficiently to get her over the bar and into the safety of Durban harbour. Once in dock, I went to have a look at the damage. It was amazing; you could have driven a double-decker through the hole in the side! Inside, some of the 15in cordite bags were punctured and there was shrapnel damage, but none had exploded. I also recall a small bump in the deck. We had been very lucky; I think that our captain must have been wearing the grass skirt that day!

I remember two leaves whilst the ship was in Durban (two weeks apiece). I also remember that the Women's Voluntary Service really looked after us, taking us out to dinner and so on. So we enjoyed a pleasant stay in Durban before sailing home to Liverpool.

Ron Lamming: serving on *Ramillies* in 1942

My name is Ronald George Lamming. I was in the Royal Navy during the war and served on many ships. I was in the Navy barracks on 10 June 1940 when I was drafted to *Ramillies*. She was in the Med at the time and as no ships were going past Gibraltar, we had to go the long way round the tip of Africa. So we sailed in the liner *Stirling Castle* going first to Durban, South Africa. When we got there, there was no accommodation and luckily the CPO who was in charge of the draft and looked after us during the voyage arranged to have me and Gerald Alcock accommodated in the police station. We slept in a cell where they made us as comfortable as possible and gave us a hearty breakfast. In the morning we waited for the CPO to arrive with a car. He told us to jump in and there was Mrs Howse, whose husband was the chief adviser to the town council in Durban. We stayed with them for the duration of our stay in Durban.

As the *Stirling Castle* was not going any further, we joined the *Ishmael*, which was a merchant ship being used as a troopship, and sailed firstly to Mombasa in the Indian Ocean, finishing up at Bombay. Again, there was no accommodation, so we slept in the cricket-ground pavilion. We stayed there while anti-mine gear was fitted round the ship's hull. From there we went to the Suez Canal, where we at last joined the *Ramillies*.

On *Ramillies* I was made a member of the 4in gun crew as a loader. During our trips through the Med, we were attacked quite a few times by Italian planes. We fired at them, but they would never come very close – they were not like the Germans. Then we got called back to the UK for a bit of a refit and then we were off to South Africa. We went up to Mombasa and joined with another ship doing patrols, trying to find the Japanese, whose fleet we thought was out there. Luckily we never found them, which is a good job, as I would not be here today if we had, because *Ramillies* was such an old thing. It had big guns and everything, but it was so old and so slow I'm afraid we would have been in for it.

After that we sailed down to Durban, and set off for Diego Suarez to stop the Germans taking over Madagascar. The Vichy French were already there and we were worried they would go over to the Germans, so we went into Diego Suarez and landed a troop of our Royal Marines who took the port over. The army had already secured a lot of the island, but we took Diego Suarez over.

After a week, a plane flew over, but no one could identify whose plane it was, so the captain pulled up anchor and we sailed a little outside the bay, and then came back in again and dropped anchor. I have always said that we should have stopped out if the captain was not sure if it was a Japanese plane or not. As things turned out, at 8 o'clock that night, there was a terrific bang whilst I was having supper. Luckily, the torpedo was right forward on the bows and we all rushed up on the upper deck and went to action stations. I was at my 4in gun station, but it wasn't any good, because we had no idea where the submarine was, and it was pitch black, but we did not want any lights because that would have given our position away, so we were stuck there and could do nothing.

The two corvettes in the harbour were having their boilers cleaned, so they had no power and couldn't do anything, I don't think they could have done anything anyway, so we were stuck there knowing that there was a sub in the harbour. After half an hour, maybe longer, another torpedo was fired. Luckily for us, it hit an oil tanker that was with us, which was unlucky for them as the torpedo was meant for us. We later found out it was a Japanese miniature two-man submarine.

Next day they set about emptying the ship, taking all the 15in shells off, as they weighed nearly a ton each, and because of where the ship was anchored, there was not a lot of water underneath. The crew got the ship afloat again, so it could be repaired temporarily, and we could return to Durban. Again we returned to Durban, and once more we saw our friends that we loved, and after a fortnight or so we sailed again.

Everyone was hoping we were going to America although we lived in UK. But we were off to Liverpool, England. When we got to UK we docked and went in and were paid off and went down to Royal Naval barracks again. I have been in quite a lot of ships after that as I did seventeen years altogether, in the Navy. *Ramillies* was not a bad ship, but it was so old there were times when there was no fresh water to get washed in and things like that. You had one bucket of water a day to get washed in, shaved and everything, including washing clothes, as you had to do your own. If you wanted a shower you went down, but that was with saltwater. The shower got rid of the dirt, but left you covered in salt.

Anyway, that is all I can tell you about *Ramillies*. Towards the end of the war I finished up minesweeping. I went over with the D-day lot as part of the 2nd Flotilla to lead all the others in and luckily we got away with it. I swept twelve mines in our flotilla, and happily I am still here to tell the story.

Ramillies with *Resolution*, *Royal Sovereign* and *Revenge* in the Indian Ocean, March 1942.

CHAPTER 7

Operation Neptune: D-Day, June 1944

Joan Mallion, wife of Bernard Mallion[27]

It was 6 June 1944 and I left home quite early as usual, so I didn't hear the radio news that morning. I worked at a dental surgery on Hastings seafront. My first job on arrival was to go to the second floor and prepare the surgery for the arrival of the dentist and his first patient. On opening the curtains I looked out to sea and what a sight met my eyes. The sea, normally devoid of ships, was a mass of vessels of all shapes and sizes, as far as the eye could see. It is something that I will never forget. A friend called in a little while later and told me that the Allied forces had landed in Normandy – it was a day we had all been waiting for. The ships I could see must have been heading for Normandy as a back-up for all the forces already there.

A few days later I read a communiqué in the national newspaper and I quote, 'HMS *Ramillies* lost her temper and opened up with all her heavy guns and fired for fifty minutes.'

I now know that Bernard was in the thick of it, and I prayed for him. Of course, we were not married then, just going steady, as they say.

Ben Platt's diary: June to September 1944

Saturday, 3 June 1944: Greenock
We were told, 'This is it', and afterwards in the mess the lads studied and pondered how and where we were going to invade, as though we were all admiral ... very amusing. No one seems to be very worried, but they think we have a lot to do. And so do I! The majority of them prefer being on the ship, instead of in the army.

We met thirty-six merchant ships and sailed with them for over eight hours. That made our force three battleships, nine cruisers, and twenty-six destroyers. Total seventy-four ships. We left them seven o'clock, time now eight o'clock.

The BUZZ says ZERO HOUR four, Monday morning 5 June. Some say at exactly four years ago we left DUNKIRK.

Got action rations today, consisting of four barley sweets, six Horlicks tablets, one packet chewing gum. I also bought eight bars chocolate and eight packets gum at canteen. We also got lifebelt light, just in case.

Sunday, 4 June

Got up at 3, visibility very poor. Passed convoy of forty-two merchant ships, at 10 o'clock. Told an hour before, that the weather had cancelled the invasion for twenty-four hours. The only grumble the lads have, is that it means one day longer to leave. Two o'clock passed, thirty-four more ships, weather very poor, and raining. Dawn, action stations at five in the morning. Time now 9.30. Direction we are going in is due south. The sun is shining now, but there is plenty of ground swell. I expect there are hundreds of ships turning round, all feeling as we do. At one time today, one could count sixty-four ships alone.

Ships today:	
Battleships	2
Cruisers	7
Destroyers	20
Merchant	76
Total	105

Monday, 5 June

Dawn action stations at five. Secured at six. The captain said that the action was to be carried out and that he would wear the Maori skirt, and for us to do our best. Met three Yank battleships and two French cruisers at 12 noon. Passed forty landing craft at 12.30 and twenty merchant ships, two tugs and eight destroyers at 5 o'clock. Real action stations tonight, till I don't know when.

About 7.30 tonight, we all meet just off the Isle of Wight and as we are faster, we just stooge around, and then head straight south, together with the 15th and 40th Minesweeping Flotilla, who will sweep a path for us. We lay off the coast till it is light enough for aircraft to spot for us, and then slowly and accurately bombard the batteries, and if the 16in battery starts firing, the *Warspite* has to attend to her. We stay until our ammo is done, go to Pompey for more, and return.

Every night, we anchor off shore with hands fell in, as for entering harbour, and the band playing to boost up the soldiers. We also get a personal message from Eisenhower.

Gliders, and planes carrying paratroops, will be coming over all night, and we have not to fire at anything, unless it attacks us. Closed up at action stations at 9.30.

Tuesday, 6 June

Spent last night in second degree of readiness till 5.00 – the ACTION. The cruisers opened up first, as it was not light enough for a plane to spot for us. At 5.45, three torpedoes were fired at us, and all missed, but one hit a Norwegian destroyer amidships, breaking her back. She went down in three minutes, showing her stern and bows above water. Two German destroyers attacked us, and we got vengeance by blasting her with our 15in guns, and she sank. E-boats were reported, and one sub, no planes. We engaged our battery target, and completely silenced it.

Troops went in at 7.30, thousands of them. The paratroops landed during the night and attained their allotted objective.

We have been bombarded all morning, I was nipping around with 6in shells, at 5.30, and cordite at 6. Went into galley at 8, just after fifty Bostons ha[d] passed over, plenty of air cover.

I have just come down from the upper deck, after seeing a plane come down in flames, time 2 o'clock, lovely and warm just lying off the coast about 3 miles.

Came down to the mess for a wash, at 4. The first for twenty-four hours, and found one of the ship's cats, fast asleep!

Heard the news, and saw about two hundred gliders going in to attack, a most impressive sight.

Told to work the middle watch, and finish till Thursday, not very lucky, am I ?

Returning to Pompey for ammo, and fuel. We have fired 225 15in shells today. We are going with the monitor *Lord Roberts*, to Pompey, arrive noon tomorrow. Hope to have a run ashore, and get some mail.

Wednesday, 7 June

Reached Pompey at 8 in the morning, but I was fast asleep. I woke at 1, had dinner, and slept again from 2 till 6.30, time now 7. Last night passed very quiet, it was very hot in the galley.

Started ammo'ing at 8, just finished. The blast from the guns has smashed our boats. A PO, who went ashore, brought a paper that said the ship had fired the first shot.

Going out again in a half hour's time. No shore leave.

Thursday, 8 June

A ship blew up against us at 1 o'clock, we were told it was loaded with ammo. Action stations sounded, suspected E-boats, and destroyers. Being on the first watch. Our coastal forces engaged the destroyer, and sank one. I saw a body float past, late last night, it was pretty gruesome. About 5.30, we opened fire at something. Hands went to breakfast at 6, and we dropped anchor at 6.30, and we start bombarding at 7.30. Did our 'shoot' quite well, and went on the upper, and saw dogfight. The Jerry was shot down. One came down and machine gunned us. Saw a wonderful sight of ammo going up. This was at 2, and smoke still rising from it now, time is 6.30.

The ship was mentioned on the 1 o'clock news. We have been shooting all afternoon very steady. I turn to in the galley at 8. At 8.30 two FW190s dived and bombed the beach, and every ship opened up at them. They soon beat it.

Alarm, 'To arms, to arms', went twice during the night, so I slept near my action station, on the torpedo mess deck.

Friday, 9 June
Three air raids, up till now, 10 o'clock. Eight bombs dropped close at 5, but I slept on. We have been bombarding all day. We had several air raids, and I expect one of our pilots got a shock. He came over, and didn't give his recognition signal, so everyone of our guns opened up at him. Luckily we missed! The last raid lasted three hours.

Saturday, 10 June
We have been bombarding rail installations all the day, and have put in some very good shooting.

Sunday, 11 June
We have only had one raid up to now, 1 o'clock, and have done no shooting. We are going to bombard a bridge and rail installation, 11 miles away. We hope to fire 450, 15in shells between 10 tonight and 6 in the morning.

Monday, 12 June
Had just one raid today, and it is getting rather monotonous. We had an E-boat alarm last night, it lasted an hour.

Tuesday, 13 June
Fired 250 shells last night at Caen and another sixty this afternoon. We had several near-misses with bombs last night, and have had two raids today. Fired another twenty 15-inchers before 12 midnight.

Wednesday, 14 June
Everyone is getting choked. It is the same every day. Air raids, bombardments, and E-boat attacks, and no sleep till 5 in the morning. Jerry is a good bloke when it gets dark, but when it's light, you don't see much of him.

We have just fired twenty-five 15in projies, at some German camp. Saw a blazing ammo ship last night, and did it go off with a bang.

Thursday, 15 June

Nothing happened this afternoon till we started shooting at a 6in battery. We silenced it, and be damned if another battery didn't fire at us! They got too close, so we went into action, going astern. We quietened them.

Friday, 16 June

Nothing happened, only three raids, and a few mines dropped.

Saturday, 17 June

Got first mail for a fortnight, and in the afternoon fired thirty-eight shells. One was our thousandth round, and it got a direct hit. Mentioned five times on radio today.

Sunday, 18 June

Set sail for Pompey. Arrived 2.30.

Monday, 19 June

Tied up alongside and I went ashore and got canned.

Tuesday, 20 June

Went ashore, and met Derby's sister Lynn, and had a very good time.

Wednesday, 21 June

On duty.

Thursday, 22 June

Went swimming at Gosport. At night, went to Dorking, and got drunk.

Friday, 23 June

Went to Derby's again, and got happy again.

Saturday, 24 June

Duty. Left jetty, and have no leave, we are at a minute's notice.

Sunday, 25 June

Nothing happened. I saw two doodlebugs.

Monday, 26 June

Done nowt but rain.

Tuesday, 27 June

Duty. No leave.

Wednesday, 28 June
Duty. No leave.

Thursday, 29 June
No mail.

Friday, 30 June
Duty. Pay day.

Monday, 3 August
Sail to Gibraltar, arrive 10 August.

10 August
Sailed from Gibraltar to Algiers, arrive 11th.

11 August
Sailed from Algiers to Toulon. Told that 'This is it again.'

13 August
Our force is one battleship (US), six cruisers, nine aircraft carriers.

DAWN, action stations at 4. Bombarding at 6. Everyone thought that this would be worse than Normandy, but is OK up to now. We have only fired twenty shells, it's now 1pm, and it has just come over the wireless, that there has been another landing. Captain told us that on our Sector RED, the troops have gone a mile inland.

Churchill came past the ship. A Jerry plane had been over five minutes before.

Wednesday, 16 August
Fired twelve rounds at a fort, and an unusual thing happened. They waved a white flag, and came out and gave themselves up to the ARMY. Our shells, at a range of 6 miles, were within 50 yards. They blew in the fort walls, and blew out two guns. The admiral signalled us, 'Never has so much been achieved by so few in so short a time.' Set sail for Corsica at 7.

Monday, 21 August
Still at Corsica.

Wednesday, 23 August
Left at 9.30 at night to go to Algiers.

Thursday, 24 August
Received an order to go back to the OP area. Everyone chocka.

Friday, 25 August
Arrived OP area in the afternoon. Bombarded straight away. Fired thirty-eight, target destroyed.

Saturday, 26 August
Bombarded again. Forty-eight shells.

Sunday, 27 August
Got a surprise. A Yank destroyer sighted a boat, and it contained thirteen Jerry with a white flag. The destroyer picked them up and brought them aboard. Me, I saw them quite plain. There was more lads on the upper deck than there was when the King passed us at Scapa.

The Jerries have a mess on their own, and have a sailor messman. Just after they came aboard, we had a shoot – forty-nine shells. The spotter plane went down to look at the target, and some men in a slit trench fired rifles at him. Now, after destroying a lighthouse fort, and a battery, the men in the trench have lost all interest in the war.

Tuesday, 29 August
Left Corsica 29 August, arrived Algiers 31 August.

Thursday, 7 September
Left Algiers for Gibraltar.

Friday, 8 September
Arrived Gibraltar.

Monday, 11 September
Left Gibraltar for Greenock

Sunday, 17 September
Arrived Greenock, 17 September. At Greenock till 19 December.

To Pompey, 21 December.

I left *Ramillies* on 12 October 1945.

Squadron Leader George 'Jock' Louden: D-Day, 6 June 1944

An account by Squadron Leader George 'Jock' Louden, MBE, Mentioned in Despatches, navigator on Douglas Boston 111A aircraft 'L' of No. 88 Squadron, flying from RAF Hartford Bridge, Hampshire, in the No. 2 aircraft to the leader, Wing Commander Paddy Maher, DFC, our Squadron Commander, and supported by No. 342 French Lorraine Squadron to lay a covering smokescreen down at sea level for the Royal Navy bombarding battleships and also for the troops landing on the beaches at first light.[28]

On the evening of 5 June 1944 the bar was closed in all the messes at 1800 hours and we were all ordered to have an early night. The battle order was pinned on the noticeboard, which indicated that our crew were flying No. 2 to the leader, who was our Squadron Commander Wing Commander Paddy Maher, DFC. There were twelve aircraft listed for 88 Squadron and also twelve aircraft for 342 Squadron.

For some reason I found myself alone in the officers' mess so I went to find the other boys at the tented site we occupied. When I arrived there was a strange silence over the area and I thought I was missing something. I then went to the field latrines at the rear of the site and found almost everyone there discussing the situation, those not 'sitting' were standing in front of those who were 'sitting'; eventually we got to bed for a while, but no sleep.

At 0100 hours on 6 June we had the usual big 'fry-up' early breakfast in the mess, then to the briefing, and out to our aircraft – 'L' for Louden!!! At 0436 hours we were airborne and heading for the 'big one'. Our task was to lay smoke at sea level (for which our craft had been specially adapted with canisters in the bomb bays and funnels projecting out through holes in the bomb doors), to protect the Royal Navy ships and also the invasion troops as they forged ashore.

The code names of the beaches were 'Gold', 'Juno' and 'Sword'; No. 342 Squadron were to cover the Yank invasion at the far end of the beachhead landing area.

We flew from Hartford Bridge to Selsey Bill at about 500ft and descended to wave-top height as soon as we reached the Bill, then on course for the beachhead. I was to call up the battleship *Ramillies* on the radio transmitter whilst en route and inform them that we were ready and about to lay smoke. I am still awaiting their reply! However, as we flew below her decks at sea level, the *Ramillies* acknowledgement was to give us everything she'd got by way of tracer gunfire, what-have-you, this despite the fact we were painted like a humbug (this being the black and white stripes, painted overnight, under the wings and fusillade of the aircraft, the markings of the 2nd Tactical Airforce).

Our next pin-point on the lead into the beach area were the battleships *Warspite*, *Rodney*, and *Renown*; they handled us more gently. However, one cannot blame those itchy trigger-fingers on the *Ramillies* when one considers the sea-to-shore battle going on. We were in the middle of it and catching it from both Jerry and our own forces. We found out afterwards that commanders were anticipating 75 per cent losses from this smoke-laying operation.

Our final pin-point before hitting the beaches was a naval monitor, this was merely a barge with one bl**** great gun. My memory at this time, just for a laugh, is that as we flew below the deck height of the battleships I could hear their big guns going 'wuff, wuff, wuff' at the enemy, whilst the naval monitor was covered in black smoke and it was delivering a massive 'crump, crump, crump' on some Jerries.

We were going in to the beachhead at intervals to lay smoke, and approaching the naval monitor I could see the smokescreen laid by our leading aircraft Wing Commander Paddy Maher. We hit the beach slightly to the northwest of Bayeux, turned to port and laid our smoke inshore slightly to that laid by Paddy. I'm glad we were on the deck, although I suppose it didn't make much difference, as we were getting attention from our own and the German forces. Having pressed the tit and laid the smoke, we turned to port coming home, and immediately were over the port entrance of Le Havre and we got a rough reception from German E-boats and their defence forces. Then we were home, a fag, a pint and another good meal. A wonderful hairy, scary and sad day. Eh!!!

I shall never forget the sight of the English Channel that day, nor of those mates that 'bought it', what was a proud success.

CHAPTER 8

Boys at Sea

Norman Burns, Boy Seaman[29]

On joining the *Ramillies* I was a boy seaman, Pompey division, No. PJX631345 HO (hostilities only). Not servicing boy seaman, full-time. That's what I was when I joined the *Ramillies*. I joined February 1944. I did training at HMS *Collingwood*, Fareham, that was for ten weeks, November to February.

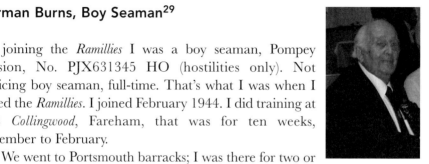

Norman Burns.

We went to Portsmouth barracks; I was there for two or three days on a draft. From there we got the train from Portsmouth Harbour – we were not told where we were going, but ended up at Thurso late at night, where we caught a lighter which took us to Scapa Flow where we joined *Ramillies*. I had a kit bag and my hammock and we had to wait the right opportunity to get aboard, as the lighter was right by the gangway. I was amazed at what I saw. I had never been near a ship, let alone on a ship, and a battleship, I was amazed, I really was. I was in awe of the surroundings. From that, I got used to it in the end.

I did enjoy my time with the fellow mates who joined with me, especially my great friend, Alfred Booker. We were both seventeen-year-olds when we met and gelled together, and ever since then to the present day we have been great pals. We left the Navy and went our different ways, he brought up a family. I was a Bournemouth lad, and returned there, and brought up a family, but we kept in touch. I saw the advert for *Ramillies* reunion in the *Navy News* and joined.

On board *Ramillies* it was a working partnership and I was on top side, looking after and renewing Carley floats, the davits, and the lifeboats, cleaning them and painting. One of our first jobs, I always remember, was to chip off paint from the ship's side, working off staging. There were two boys on each stage, lashed together because the bow of the ship goes in, and we were chipping, no spectacles, no earplugs. We finished that after two or three days, then we red-oxided it from the same stage.

We had never fired a broadside, we had gunnery practice with the main armaments, but this particular time I was near a TS station amidships where the pom-pom was. We had spotter planes that used to tell different ships where the enemy was. I remember this one telling us there was a Panzer division in the woods. The main armament were brought to bear broadside, and the skipper came on the loudspeaker, and said he would fire the first salvo from the bridge (which he did). As he fired, the ship lifted up out of the water and down again. We continued firing for quite some time.

I can only say one thing really, I would not have missed it for the world. As I contemplate now that I have retired, I can say it changed my outlook on life. Many people that have not been in the Forces don't realise the comradeship you have for one another, especially in wartime, even people you hate, as you can't like everyone on board; there were people you disliked, but even they rallied around and helped you, and I would not have missed it for the world. Although it was wartime, it was wonderful, that's all I can say, wonderful. My wife now often says, 'How can you remember all these times in the Navy, some sixty years ago, yet you can't remember what you had for dinner yesterday?'

I say, 'I don't know.' When Alf and I get together, it annoys her, as we go on talking about things that happened sixty or seventy years ago when we were seventeen.

The *Ramillies* shipmates and firm friends, Norman Burns and Alf Booker, by the twin 15in guns that stand in front of the Imperial War Museum in Lambeth, London. The gun at right was from *Ramillies*.

Harold Ball: one of the last giants

Harold Ball.

It was with anticipation and excitement, suitcase in hand, that I made my way to London Road railway station, Leicester, to board the train to Portsmouth. I was bound for the RNBI, after which I would join HMS *Collingwood*, for some ten weeks' training. It was by far not all 'beer and skittles' either at RNBI or at *Collingwood*, but we weathered the storm, and finished training to join the ship in May of 1943. It was not a totally new experience to me to board one of these ships, as my father, being a petty officer in the Royal Navy, whose last ship was *Newcastle*, had given me plenty of opportunity on Navy Days to go aboard such ships, one of which I remember was the ill-fated *Hood*.

But to actually serve on one is a totally different ball game – but I loved it. I had tried to get into the Navy at sixteen but my old Dad would not hear of it, so I volunteered at age seventeen and a half, and loved practically every minute of it, even though there was a war on. I can always remember Leading Seaman Priest, seeing myself and others up the gangway on to the quarterdeck, on that special day in Portsmouth. Most of the chaps I was with were astounded, and wondered what they had let themselves in for.

We finally set sail in May 1943, saying goodbye to Blighty; we didn't know how long we would be away, but it didn't matter. Our first deployment was in the Atlantic and our first port of call was to be Casablanca. Then, on down to Walvis Bay[30] for refuelling from a supply ship, and henceforth making our way down the west coast of Africa with a couple of U-boat scares along the way. At that time, myself and about fifty or sixty others were attached to damage control, which was a very important job, especially if you happened to 'catch a packet'.[31] We had all done training in Scotland for fire fighting, etc – no health and safety in those days! And it was no picnic dealing with mock-up oil fires in constructed wooden ships.

We finally reached Cape Town, and Durban where we got a spot of long awaited leave. After this we made our way up the east coast of Africa into the Indian Ocean arriving at Mombasa and then on through the Suez Canal, to Algiers, and finally home!

Our next deployment was to be D-Day, 6 June 1944, and then a little later to the South of France, knocking out German gun batteries on the way. After that, my next deployment was to be India and Ceylon in 1945, having by then left *Ramillies* and being shore-based for fifteen months at HMS *Braganza*, during the Indian riots. The troopship we went out there on was the *Stratheden*, a story of which has been told many times.

Another vivid memory is when we were at Walvis Bay, looking over the side and seeing thousands upon thousands of gigantic jellyfish! Another thing

I remember was the German prisoners we took on board while we were involved with the invasion there. I believe they were brought aboard by the Americans for interrogation and soon taken away by them again.

I will always remember the *Rammy* as being a good ship and a happy ship and have been proud, always, to have served in her.

Alf Booker, Able Seaman 1943–45[32]

I joined *Ramillies* in 1943 and left it in the beginning of 1945. As we had just come back from the Med, and they weren't going to be using the ship anymore, they had someone come on board to have a look at it, because we were going to go to the Pacific, but it was unfit, and it would take too long to get it into condition to go out there, so they paid us all off. Not sure if it was just before Christmas or just after, so I will say it was January 1945.

Alf Booker.

It was funny, we pulled up alongside in a little boat, it was getting dark, and out of the gloom we could see this huge ship with massive great guns: 'course we had never seen anything like that before in our lives. 'Oh God!' I said, 'Look at that,' and when we got up on board it was marvellous really, it was like a fairy story seeing this huge ship with great guns and everything; it was incredible really. That was in Scapa Flow. We travelled up to Thurso, that's about as far as you can go without getting your hat wet, and then a little drifter came along and picked us all up and takes you to the ships out there.

Alf Booker as a young seaman.

One of the other things that happened was that the King came up there and came on board the ship, and that was at Scapa Flow. We had to line up in front of this whaler boat, we had to paint the side where he would be looking, the back side we never had time to paint, and the chief said, 'Now then if the King talks to you, you call him Sir, you don't call him chief, cock or anything like that, you call him Sir.' Another person who visited the ships just before Normandy was Monty; he went on the *Nelson*. They put a notice on the noticeboard saying anybody who wants to go and see Monty put your name here and go over there. They only got one name, so we all had to go, and Monty came out and stood on top on [one] of the turrets yapping away, and we were all surprised how small he was, and he looked like he had been all coloured up. The boys used to do all these things, the boys' division will go over and see Monty on the *Nelson*, so that's why we went.

On board the *Ramillies* I had general duties; one thing I had to do, being boy seaman you had to look after one of the midshipmen, and we had quite a few midshipmen on board, the officers used to call them 'Snotties', and I used to look after one, his name was Midshipman Locke, big tall fellow. I used to go and put his hammock up of a night, that's if I had time. If I was on watch I was not allowed to go. In the mornings I used to lash it all up and stow it away for him. Two years later I'm on another ship, quartermaster, and we had a new navigation officer coming on board, and who should it be, it was Lieutenant Locke. By now he was all right, he said to me, 'Old ships, aren't we? Old ships.' It was good.

You were learning all the time. You had to do your watch-keeping same as anyone else, but when you had any time off you were doing knots and splices, all the electrical work, they were called torpedomen in those days, we had to learn all that, gunnery too. You never had any time off and they were very strict with us, the least little thing and you were in the muck. We used to get slack hammock drill, you used to get to the quarterdeck with your hammock across your back and run around the quarterdeck – crazy really, but it didn't do us any harm.

I was on a four-barrel pom-pom; that's how I became an AA gunner. The old chief on board in charge of it, he was a character: he said, 'Have you seen one of these before?' and I said, 'No, only on the news, firing on the news,' and he said, 'This is much better than the bl**** news – you are going to enjoy this.' He said, 'The best thing to do is we will train you to be an AA gunner. AA3 it starts and then 2 and then 1.' He said, 'While you are here you may as well learn the job properly,' and that's what I did, became AA3 and got an extra threepence a day, so I was pretty well off in those days. That's how it started, and it was good.

Oh my God, the noise and the smoke! That's what I never thought of: after you have been firing for a few seconds, I mean there were four firing, and these bl**** canisters coming out, empty cylinders and the smoke going up, it was awe-inspiring, it was. I don't think we shot anything down: we came a bit close, but it was a close-range weapon. There was no point in firing up in the sky, but if they came very low, then everybody used to open up at them.

In those days the Bofor was beginning to take over; we didn't get one on the *Ramillies* but they were taking over, so we had to learn about the Bofors then. Firing one of those really was awesome: again, all the smoke and empty cylinders rolling about the place, and they are red-hot – you couldn't touch them, so you had to kick them out of the way. We used to wear rubber pumps and Norman's shoes caught alight; he was kicking them about and his shoes were smouldering.

I was asked to become a recorder; there are two or three recorders. The orders came down from the firing place, the gunners wait, and he gives an order, somebody else gives an order; all I had to do was write down all the orders the gunner's mate said. 'Course we had a little bit of confusion: there they were swearing and cussing, as you do, and I asked him how to spell a certain word, and he said, 'Don't you start, I got a turret full of comedians now.'

But that was an education there, to see the guns actually working. A huge great breech comes out, right round, and this tray comes up, and there's a shell on the top shelf and a rammer comes out like a great big bicycle chain, pushes the shell into the gun and goes back down, and then up comes the cordite. They measured the cordite out: they are in linen bags and they cut it up; they had to use phosphorus bronze knives down in the magazine as you mustn't make a spark. Anyway that comes up and that is rammed in, out it goes, down it goes, around comes the breech, goes in twists and locks, and there is a chap with a belt with cartridges all round, he pulls one out, and puts it in another part and shuts it up and gets out of the bl**** way. Someone shouts, 'Close the interceptors,' then the circuit is made and then ready to fire, and just before firing they ring a bell. So you had ding, ding, BANG! When you first hear [the noise] it frightens the life out of you, the concussion hits you, bl**** great guns recoil back and then in again. Some of those gunners did get in a state: bleeding ears, noses bleeding.

One of our chaps if he was still here could have told you: he was an electrician; you had an electrician in each turret, because with the blast little things come off or get broken, and he had to be there to repair them, and he used to go round with rag wiping the blood off me – could not have done them any good, they never wore any ear protectors; anti-flash gear, yes, but nothing to protect their ears. Now when they fire a rifle they wear great pads over their ears. With the anti-flash gear, it would get dirty and they had to go and wash it; they had a special stuff to dip it in and hang it up to dry, and that was supposed to keep the flash off your face – whether it did or not I don't know, probably a load of rubbish. We looked a right lot walking round with the anti-flash gear on. When we were on the four-barrel pom-pom we had to wear tin hats too, what a carry on.

Rose Cottage comes about because the jolly Jack goes ashore and meets up with some of the inappropriate women, and he gives them one, and then ends up with a nasty rash on his penis and goes to the doc in sick bay and says, 'Look at this, get 'em out.' I think they used to cure them in about two or three days with penicillin; they used to give them two or three shots, and they were not allowed on the mess deck until they were clear. When they used to come back on the mess deck, people used to walk in front of them ringing an imaginary bell shouting, 'Unclean, unclean.' A jolly Jack knows how to make life interesting, doesn't he? There was a notice saying 'Rose Cottage'; it was up there where we used to sleep. We used to sleep in this 6in gun casement. There was always half a dozen blokes in the cottage, always.

One thing I often think about was just after we joined *Ramillies* as boys, we had our own mess deck: no one else was allowed on there, and we used to go and get food out of the galley. For breakfast this particular morning we had a potful of porridge (the pots were called fannies, I will leave you to imagine why), we ate all the porridge – beautiful. It was really good food on the *Ramillies*. Anyway, we were sitting there and someone said, 'I could eat some more of that,' so we thought who would go up the galley to see if we could get some more porridge, so muggins gets the pot and up I go.

I walk into the galley and the old chief was there writing, stood writing, he looks up, sees me; he says, 'What do you want?'

'Oh chief,' I said, 'I just popped up to see if there was any more porridge going.' He looked up at me and he called over the other three or four young fellows who were doing the cooking and told me to repeat to them what I had just said to him. So I asked again if there was any more porridge. He said, 'I thought I heard that. I have been in the Navy for twenty-three years and no one has asked me for more porridge before.'

I said, 'There is always a first time.' I was trembling.

'Go and give the boy some more porridge,' and then he said to me, 'Any time you want anything more, if we have got it, you will have it.' They used to make a lovely duff, in a deep tray, used to mix it with currants and sultanas, and they used to make it in the steam oven, and it used to be a great slab of this. We used to have a wedge of this and then go to the galley, and he would say, 'I know you want some more.'

'Yes, please,' and we would get more … We used to eat like fighting cocks. The food on there was excellent, every meal was good. But we did all right with the porridge.

As we saw on the plaque it was a happy ship and it really was, and there were some characters on there. They had a weight-lifting class up on the gun deck. One of the chaps on the gun I was on was a massive fellow, well-educated, been to university and all that. One day he said to me, 'Young Alf, why don't you come up on the gun deck when you are off, and we will get you doing a bit of weight-lifting.'

We had this little Welsh fellow, and he said, 'Leave that boy alone, he don't want to grow up to be a muscle-head like you.'

That's the sort of people they were, marvellous. When we were painting ship up on the mainmast, the ship was rolling all over the place, and we boys were up there painting, and two midshipmen down below with binoculars shouting, 'You missed a bit.' They called it holiday, so, 'You have a holiday ahead of you there, so you get your brush and paint the bit missed.' And he would get covered in paint and we would say, 'Serves you right, you sod.' It was all a good laugh.

We went to Algiers. 'Course, it's all Arabs there and the French were in charge of them. They carry these long sticks. And the Arabs used to lift their skirts up and go to the toilet over the end of the dock and that's it. As soon as the hooter went they had half-hour breaks; they'd all be down, plop, then the hooter went for them to go back to work, and the French would come down whack with their big sticks to get them going again. 'Course we would all stand along the ship's side, cheering and shouting. Another thing we did there, they asked if anyone wanted to go to the wild part of the place: we had some French Foreign Legion men to show us round, well-armed they were, and said, 'Don't wander off into any of the alleys because we will never find you again.' So we had a look round there: you'd never seen anything like it in your life; human beings, they were worse than any animal, far worse.

Alec Wickens[33]

When I first saw the ship I thought 'How awesome!' due to the size of it, although I had spent days at sea on other ships as well, the *Clare*, of course; this was the first time you were going to spend a full week on board. I didn't have a problem once I got on board, and any fear was completely lost after speaking to people who had been on board, who all said what a happy ship it was. That was coming through the feelings I had at the time.

Alec Wickens.

She was still called the *Ramillies*, but she was part of HMS *Vernon* which was the training establishment of the Navy at that time … There was still the WT wireless training room, so we were taught Morse code, how to send and receive messages and, of course, semaphore was still being used then.

Although we had been trained in semaphore in previous courses, this was the final course and we would be tested on it. So we were tested on both. General seamanship: when we first arrived we were shown how to sling our hammocks, and trying to get into the hammocks was hilarious, because we were climbing in one side and falling out the other side. So the first two things [we] were shown was slinging and stowing hammocks.

When we first arrived on board ship, we had to give our details to the duty officer, then we were issued with station cards, then hammock-slinging, then we were given our orders for the week, introduced to our instructors. Besides general seamanship, which the training was on board the

Alec Wickens as a boy.

Ramillies, such things as slinging the lead, and reading the lead readings, which is checking the depths of the ship. Then we were tested for swimming. For that we were taken from the *Ramillies* to HMS *Dolphin*. We were introduced to part training in the Davis escape apparatus. We went into the apparatus, but never did the full training; it was just to give us an idea how it felt, and how we reacted to it. Next day we were transported to do squad drill.

Alec Wickens' certificate of proficiency from his time on HMS *Ramillies*.

Freddie Smith, Signalman

The draft, of course, was to the battleship HMS *Ramillies*. Next day I left *Mercury*, located at Petersfield, just outside Pompey, and caught the train for the trip to Greenock, yes, back to Scotland. It was a long journey, but I finally arrived. We made our way (I was not the only one) down to the docks where we were shepherded onto a drifter to make our way out to a massive ship (to us anyway), that was named *Ramillies*. That was the start of the dream that I had envisaged when I left home only six months earlier.

Freddie Smith.

Shortly after our arrival (next day or so) we left Greenock and sailed to Scapa Flow, ahh, what a place ... Hmmm.

By this time I was just seventeen and a half, not knowing what I had gotten myself into, but I survived my first voyage with no ill effects from seasickness, etc, so was quite pleased with myself.

The next time that we left Greenock was to go to the Normandy invasion in June '44. We all know what happened there. In due course, we left the D-Day venue, returned to Portsmouth, had our gun barrels changed, and then headed out for the South of France (Dragoon) invasion slated for 15 August '44. Yes, we did ourselves well there too, and came away unscathed. The Maori skirt that was worn by our captain did get much praise for keeping us all safe.

After our action there, I was still only seventeen years old, still a boy according to naval standards. I had survived two massive naval operations before I was eighteen, then to become known as Ord Sig F A Smith.

The eleven-piece Jazz Bandits ready to burst into action on the quarterdeck.

CHAPTER 9

Life Onboard Ship

Robert Bennett, Stoker, First-Class[34]

Robert Bennett, stoker first-class, no. PKX 665298, P meaning Portsmouth. I joined Ramillies in 1943 and left her just after the South of France landings, where we bombarded Marseilles and Toulon, which was the last action by any British battleship in the last war.

Bob Bennett.

My very first impressions when I saw her in the Gareloch was, 'Oh God, no.' I had completed my engineering training as they called it, with mechanical and engineering courses, earlier on the old battleships *Revenge* and *Resolution* at Southampton, and they were mucky, dirty ships. After the completion of training on these ships, I was drafted to the RN Barracks at Portsmouth to await my posting, which I received soon afterwards. It was awful being in barracks, with a lot of thieving going on. You had to sleep with your boots tied around your neck, otherwise someone would steal them. So when I saw the *Ramillies* out there in the Gareloch, off the Clyde, my heart sank, as she was the same class of battleship as *Revenge* and *Resolution*. I thought no, but she turned out to be a very clean ship, and I was always proud to be a member of the 1,500 or so crew that made up the complement of the ship.

Bob Bennett, a new recruit at eighteen years of age in 1940.

When I first went on board *Ramillies* I went down below to the stokers' mess deck and looked at the chief stoker's noticeboard, which asked for anyone with bricklaying experience to report to the chief stoker. They say never volunteer for anything, but I was so intrigued, I thought, 'Bricklayer, what the hell does a bricklayer do on a battleship?'

I went to see the chief stoker and he said, 'Go and see Taff Ward and Ginger Bates,' two bricklayers who would show me the ropes. These two men, probably ten years older than me, became the two best friends one could wish for. Taffy, in civvy street, had been manager of the Co-op store in Cowbridge near Cardiff, and Ginger had been an electrician down a coal mine near Nuneaton, Leicestershire. He won a BEM for bravery in a pit accident. Unfortunately, Taff Ward died not long after the war of a heart attack, and Ginger died of leukaemia, leaving a wife and children at only about fifty years of age. There is hardly a day goes by when I don't think about these two lovely blokes who helped shape my life.

When the ship went to battle stations, the shout 'All hands to battle stations' would come over the tannoy. My normal duties were down in the boiler rooms as a bricklayer, repairing the brickwork inside the furnaces where fuel oil was sprayed, but my battle station was on a 4in gun, one of several. I passed the shells, which came up from below, by hand to the gun loader, who took it from me and shoved it in the breech and away it went, very, very noisy. In fact the noise was far worse than the 15in guns, it really was ear-splitting; the *Ramillies* made a lot of noise but it did not affect me as much as being next to a 4in gun. I never had any flash gear or ear muffs, although I think the gun layers may have had them, and I think they had it in the 15in gun turrets. Normally, if we were not at action stations, we did almost a nine-to-five job of repairing the boilers. That was the three of us. It was work that I thoroughly enjoyed, hard work, but we were very good friends, and loved every minute of it. The fire clay came in 2cwt[35] sacks and I only weighed about 9 stone 6lbs[36] then, but you just shoved them on your shoulder and went to the boiler rooms, which were below the stokers' mess deck.

There were eighteen boilers altogether in three boiler rooms, A, B and C, with six boilers in each and when we were at sea, fifteen would be lit, or flashed up as we called it and three would be out of commission, and we would work on those three. Each boiler had six oil sprayers which sprayed fuel oil into the furnaces, and the stoker's job, one of many, was to knock carbon off a brick-lined ring, about 2ft in diameter, which had an oil sprayer and steel plate in the middle. This got damaged by the extreme heat from the oil sprayer, and also from damage caused by stokers hitting the bricks with a steel poker, trying to knock off the carbon. We could access the furnace by removing the oil sprayer and steel plate, and crawl on hands and knees through the boiler room into the furnace, which was a space about 10ft long, 6ft wide and about 4ft high, to repair the brickwork. Inside the furnace, when it was shut down and was cool, the oil vitrified and was as sharp as glass when broken, so we had to watch we didn't cut ourselves.

The boiler room itself was airlocked and could only be entered by going into a small compartment the size of a telephone box. This was entered by lifting a heavy steel hatch at the top. To get to this airlock from the stokers' mess deck, you went down a ladder to a hatch on the deck below. You climbed into the airlock and down a vertical ladder, closing the hatch behind you, and then opened a door at the bottom going onto a platform, and then down more ladders to reach the boiler-room deck. The boiler room was pressurised by having huge 8ft-diameter fans situated on both sides, forcing air into the room. The pressurised air vaporised the oil as it was sprayed into the furnaces to create maximum heat.

Going into the airlock, it was very important to open the hatch, go into the airlock and close the hatch behind you, before opening the door, otherwise the pressurised air would rush out, bring flames and intense heat out of the boilers, which would be fatal to anyone in the boiler room. Fortunately, we never had anyone do that, but that's what would happen. There was another entrance to the boiler and engine room which was the officers' lift, and for their use only. If we could get away with it, we used them to bring our materials down when no one was about.

I never did work in the engine rooms, although I did go down into one of them and it was enormous – I think it was the port engine room, which drove two of the propellers out of the four, with the starboard engine room driving the other two. The propellers went through a shaft, like a tunnel, which had to be oiled. There were gauges there to say what the pressure was and all the rest of it. Massive, everything about a battleship is massive.

The hardest part of the job was disposing of the brick rubble from the boilers. This had to be carried up umpteen ladders to the upper deck, and into the gash chute on the side of the ship when at sea, or rubbish bins ashore. All the cement and fireclay came in 2cwt sacks and had to be taken on our backs to our stores in each boiler room – very hard work; also the firebricks. Anyway, doing this work meant we didn't have to clean out the bilges underneath the boiler-room deck plates. We had a den halfway up the boiler room where we would have a cup of tea, sit and have a natter, and do our dobeying. We also had a special place where we could hang our washing, and it was always the envy of other people because our clothes always looked so white, because we used steam to clean them, as well as make tea.

That mainly was a stoker's job, besides looking after the pumps. It was a doddle really, it was hot work, but not really hard work overall. 'B'

Bob Bennett, a little bit wiser in 1943.

boiler room was the hottest with temperature getting up to 130 degrees,[37] quite hot. There was a ventilation system of sorts of course, and you had these huge fans.

As I said earlier, my fondest recollection was meeting the other two bricklayers, Taffy and Ginger. They were older than me, but they taught me the error of my ways, as I was a bit cheeky when I first went in. The three of us used to go out, say in Portsmouth, to the Black Prince, which is still there down a side street, and have a drink. We always went out together even though they were ten years older than me. We served the same mess deck and they were real friends.

Once when we went into action, we had a stoker going berserk in the boiler room and he had to be taken out and put in jankers.[38] I don't know whether it was apprehension when we were in action, but you just accepted it, although some people did not like being down below when we were in action. I don't think I was particularly bothered. I'm not a brave person but I just liked being on the ship.

When the main armament was about to be fired, a loudspeaker system was used over the ship and a bell was rung, but down in the boiler room all you heard was just a thud. That's why to me the 4in guns were a much sharper noise. I don't know what it was like in the turret. The shells were right down below and hoisted up by hydraulics. It must have been horrible down in the room where they stored the shells, one hit and they would have gone up. Of the 6in guns, there were five guns on each side of the ship; half were manned by Marines and half were manned by seamen. The Marines were smart. We got away with going up on deck in boiler suits, but the Marines were drilled and always looked absolutely immaculate in their uniforms. There was no getting away with discipline with Marines on board the battleship.

You had what was called a mess deck, which was a table of very thick timber which could have been teak, about 20ft long. The end would go to the bulkhead where there was a round light to give some lighting. There was a wooden bench on either side. My particular mess was 49, and to my left was 48, and on my right-hand side was 51. There was only about 3ft between each mess deck, and there was I think about six messes in all, split up into compartments. You never had too big a compartment, in case of damage to the ship and flooding and so on. To get out of our mess we had to undo a hatch, go up a ladder, then bring the hatch down, the idea being if the ship was flooding, it would be a watertight compartment. You would go through one compartment to another via a bulkhead door, one on each side.

We had a tailor's shop on board, and as soon as you joined ship you wanted to get away from the horrible uniforms that were issued, and get tidy and see the girls. Making up a uniform cost you about five bob in those days with seven creases down your trousers, something to do with Nelson, I can't remember the details now, or what they were for. A tot of rum was given out each day, which we liked, and which you did not get until you were twenty years old. If you abstained you got sixpence a day extra. My pay when I joined the Navy in 1943 was thirty shillings a fortnight and of that I allotted my mother fifteen shillings, with seven shillings and sixpence to spend per week. If anything happened to me, my mother would get a pension of about fifteen bob a week. I am still here, but we managed. We could go and enjoy a pint or two and things on board were very cheap, cigarettes fourpence for twenty. You could buy all sorts of things like fountain pens, this, that and the other, nick-nacks, all duty-free, of course.

I was down on watch on D-day and the captain had said that food would be in short supply. You could get hold of soup and bread, but meals were not being cooked in the galley, so everyone rushed round to our little NAAFI and bought up all the chocolate, which was in boxes of forty. By the time I came off watch there was only Fry's plain chocolate left, and after five bars I felt like I never wanted to eat another bar of plain chocolate in my life. Probably only about three shillings for the box, the bars were far bigger than they are today. We also had a place called a 'Guffer' bar where you could get soft drinks. You could not take any alcohol on board, apart from the tot that was issued, so we had this Guffer bar which served fruit juice stuff. But something different and just in front of the bar was a cinema screen about 6ft square, with maybe about hundred people on either side watching this cinema show, probably some cowboy film. That was our entertainment although we played crib in the mess deck. Cards and gambling was frowned upon but that's where I learned to play crib – on the ship. But mostly we made our own entertainment, including writing letters home.

I was in the boiler rooms on the morning of D-day, my watch was midnight to four o'clock in the morning, and I came up on deck about 4.15 to 4.20 for a breath of fresh air and the sight I saw was amazing and never to be seen again. Thousands of ships, with the *Ramillies* banging away with her guns. The *Warspite* got all the glory because the name *Warspite* was more famous than *Ramillies*, but we fired over a thousand one-ton shells in the action spread over ten days, and I understand that this was the most number of shells ever fired by a battleship. My memories are of a happy ship and good mates. I could not have asked for better and I was sad when I left her, very sad indeed when I left that ship.

From *Ramillies* I was sent up to Liverpool and boarded a new liner, the *Stratheden*, where I shipped out to Australia. After about a month in Sydney I got a berth on HMS *Reaper*, which was an escort carrier which the Americans churned out like sausages. She was not a fleet carrier like the *Ark Royal*, but a cargo vessel they took the top off and put the flight deck on. Then I picked up a new ship, the frigate *Widemouth Bay*. Our duties in Hong Kong were mainly concerned with minesweeping. They used to call us the 'Blood Boat' because we went into the minefields to mark the lanes out for the minesweepers, and then when they raised the mines to the top, everybody on board the frigate would have a blast at it with whatever was to hand, the 4in gun, a rifle or whatever, and nine times out of ten if you blasted a hole in it the mine sank. Very rarely did you hit the button, but one day they did and, unfortunately, it was only a couple of hundred yards away from the aft end of our ship where we were all sitting having our dinner and whoops! Everything on the table went up in the air.

The other duty on the frigate was escorting merchant ships to China because of attacks by pirates. I ended the war in the Far East, received my demob notice in Hong Kong and was flown home, taking ten days to do so.

King George VI inspecting the engineering department on HMS *Ramillies* at Scapa Flow in May 1944. Bob Bennett is fourth from the left on the front row.

Victor Stamp, Leading Cook[39]

A week before war was declared I was on the cruiser *Frobisher*, and as I got to the ship at the jetty the master-at-arms was there, along with the rest of the crew, and he said, 'Get your bags packed, everybody on this ship is on draft.' We didn't know where we were going.

Victor Stamp.

I said, 'Half my kit is at home, master,' and he said that it would catch up with me some time. The whole of the ship's company was drafted to three different ships *Ramillies*, *Hood* and *Royal Oak*. I was drafted to *Ramillies*. We all know what happened to the *Royal Oak* and *Hood*, so we were the lucky team and I was a lucky, lucky man.

Anyway, we went to the naval barracks, and caught a train at 11pm which took nearly two days to get to Scapa Flow where *Ramillies* was lying. We could not get aboard her that night so we all slept on the jetty until the launches came in next morning and took us to the ship.

Victor Stamp in his naval days.

One week later we set sail, with no idea where we were going and ended up at Halifax, Nova Scotia, to bring a convoy back to Liverpool. We never went into port at Liverpool, but were sent quickly back again to Nova Scotia for another convoy, and back again to Liverpool, and so on. On the third trip, we didn't return to Halifax, but instead went to Iceland and a place called Belfjord, where there was a small army camp. Well, these army chaps were alone, a hundred or so of them, so we went ashore with bottles of rum – tots that had been saved up, and gave them to the soldiers. We made good pals of them.

It turned out we were after the *Graf Spee*, apparently, but we did not encounter any ships whatsoever. We then made our way back to Halifax, and another trip, as we thought, back to Liverpool, but no, this time we ended up in the Middle East at the Suez Canal going east, and it was frightening: soldiers on either side shouting out 'The war is that way,' because Japan was not in the war then. They kept shouting, 'The war is that way,' but we shouted back, 'Yes we know, but we are going this way.' Then it was, 'Have you got any spuds, Jack, we have not seen spuds for months,' so we started throwing potatoes over to them. It was an easy distance as we were virtually in the centre of the canal and we could easily toss potatoes to them.

We ended up at Colombo and who did we bring on board *Ramillies* but Prince Philip as a young midshipman. We then set sail for Australia and New Zealand for convoy duties, bringing troops to the Middle East. We did this until June 1940, ending up at Wellington in New Zealand. We went into the harbour there with a banner the whole length of the battleship saying, 'Well done, *Achilles*,' after the cruiser's part in the sinking of the *Graf Spee*.

At that time our wages were 10p a day, but as chefs and stokers we got double pay, commonly known as sweat money, two bob a day, and I can still see those £5 notes. We went ashore and for every English pound we had twenty-five shillings in New Zealand money. We ended up Sunday night, New Year's Eve, in a dance hall with some girls. At one minute past midnight the girls turned round to us and said, 'Do you want to stay here, Jack, all the pubs and clubs are open at a minute past midnight?' The place was evacuated and we all ended up in the pub.

Fortunately, when we were travelling from Halifax, to Liverpool, I was coming up to twenty years of age and had been in the Navy exactly one year. On the way back to Halifax, the chief cook, George Harding, told me to get out of my whites and into my number 8's, 'You're going aboard HMS *Forth*.'

'Am I drafted, chief?' I said.

'No,' he replied, 'I want you to pass exams for leading cook.'

I said, 'I only got twelve months in the Navy, there are guys with twelve years in and others with fifteen years in!'

'Get aboard the *Forth*,' he says, 'and pass for leading cook.' And I did pass. They sent the signal back to England from Halifax, and they sent a signal back saying, 'Make him up to leading cook,' which was unheard of – a no-badge leading cook with just twelve months' service. I thought I would be drafted off the ship, but no.

I said, 'Look, chief, this is not going to work,' I said, 'Me with just twelve months in, telling others with more years in what to do.' I said, 'I will work in the bakery,' and don't forget in those days the galley was coal-fired, and the bakery was coke, and the coke had to be broken down to the size of a walnut; I can still see that. Every loaf of bread was mixed by machine but moulded by hand for a thousand men. I used to make hundreds and hundreds of loaves and every one was hand-moulded. You had about 200lbs[40] of bread going into the ovens every time, and I used to do this four times every day. On Friday it was Madeira cake day – we used to make 10lb cake slabs for Sunday's tea. That was a speciality and was made by the chief baker, later Lieutenant Commander Boss. Any sticky jobs he'd say, 'There's one man to do that and if he can't do that nobody can,' and that was me. I used to work all night, start at 8pm and work through to 6am as the others came on, and I went off sleeping during the day. If action stations were sounded, you were obviously up on your action stations, which in those days for me was on the 6in guns, carrying shells which weighted 100lbs each. In harbour my station was on an ack-ack gun.

When we returned to the Middle East we came to Alexandria one time, just after the French gave in, and there was a French battleship there called the *Lorraine*, and we did not know what was going to happen. She turned her guns onto us and we turned our guns on to her; we were only a few hundred yards apart – it was frightening. There was no leave, but fortunately some French officers came aboard *Ramillies*, and we thought something was going on and, happily, peace was signed between the two ships.

Then we were allowed to go ashore and my brother-in-law was on board the *Malaya*, which was in our squadron, so we used to meet up in the fleet club in Alexandria to knock back bottles of beer. One time in Alexandria harbour they pointed the 6in guns skyward as far as they could go and they fired, but then we were told to pack up firing the 6in guns as we were firing the side of the ship out.

The memory that stands out most to me in New Zealand was when we went to the Maori village called Otaki. I was one of the fortunate few who actually went to the village. The chief came aboard the ship and presented Captain Baillie-Grohman with a grass skirt, and said that every time the captain goes into action he must wear this grass skirt, and no harm will come to any member of the ship, and how right that man was, because with six years of war, we never lost one man.

One particular time when we came back to the Mediterranean we were sent to Matapan to bombard the coastal area. There was a big fort there, right on the seafront, and by the time we and the *Malaya* left there was not one brick upon another brick, and we never lost one man despite being shot at and torpedoed at by Italian planes.

Coming back to before I joined the Navy, I was a milkman getting up at 4am every morning. The milk came from Corfe Castle and I was always the first one round there when the seventeen-gallon[41] urns were wheeled in, and the milk put into a fifty-gallon trough. The boss man used to dip his measure in it then take it up to his office and test it. He would come back down and say, 'Put five gallons of water in it.' Then we were allowed to ladle the milk into our pint or half-pint bottles. So we had a seventeen-gallon urn, two-gallon buckets of milk, pint and half-pint bottles in a three-wheeled truck, which we had to push around the streets of Portsmouth twice a day, starting at about five in the morning. We used to knock on so many doors of dockyard 'mateys' shouting, 'Time to get up, time to get up.' Christmas time they used to really look after you.

In 1938 when I joined the Navy I said, 'Sorry Bob, I'm leaving.'

'Where you going, Vic?'

I said, 'I'm joining the Navy – we will all be in it shortly'. I said to my mother, 'I am joining the Navy,' and she said, 'What! There are no back doors on ships, you know.'

I said, 'No, but you can jump over the side, Mum.' My father was a regimental sergeant-major and two of my brothers were army – one was unfortunately captured in Crete and a POW for nearly four years, but I brought him home from Gibraltar.

The *Ramillies* was a fine ship, lovely ship, clean, and I had no worries at all and a good ship's company.

Prince Philip, he was only eighteen years old. He had a fairly easy time, but he could not get on with Commander Larkin.

I came home in 1941. Beer was one shilling a pint. I walked into the pub and said, 'All the drinks are on me,' and this girl was sitting there with her mother, and the mother said, 'There is your future husband.'

She said, 'That big-head, he's been away for over two years,' but I bought the mother a whisky, and the girl a lemonade. Anyway, she was courting an airman and, unfortunately, I had only three weeks' leave and had to go back to *Ramillies*. I had been promoted, as I said, so got drafted off the ship to the naval barracks. I started going out with another girl then, but the other girl had dropped her airman by now, and I dated her. Came home on the Tuesday, married her on Thursday, went away on Saturday for twenty months operating from Gibraltar down to West Africa, Freetown.

Vic Stamp presiding over the stirring of the Christmas pudding later in his career in the Royal Navy.

Sid Slatter: AB S R E Slatter, RC2, PJX393413, AC2 Gunnery Control

Sid Slatter.

A recollection from 1943

I left Royal Naval Barracks Portsmouth on 11 May 1943, to join HMS *Ramillies* at Devonport on the following day. Upon joining, we left Devonport for Greenock, then to Scapa Flow. Here we were visited and inspected by our King. Then we left Scapa to go down to Rosyth, and then sail back to Greenock on 3 August 1943. We finally left Greenock, arriving at Casablanca on 9 August 1943 after an awful trip across the Bay of Biscay with HUGE waves coming straight over the fo'c'sle!

We journeyed all the way down the east coast of Africa, making many calls en route. We had our Crossing the Line ceremony on 29 August 1943, finally arriving at Cape Town on 6 September. The next day we again left Cape Town, arriving at Durban on 10 September. We left Durban after a few days, to enter the Indian Ocean, where we completed many, many patrols, and exercises and the like. I have so many memories of the ins and outs of the places we went to.

My action station was the AB unit (the auto barrage unit), which was situated in the 15in target spotter, just one deck above the 15in magazine! One laughable story I have is this ... we were anchored off Kilindini (Mombasa) and we had a 'Hands to bathe' order. Booms were rigged up for water polo games, etc, and scrambling nets were rigged over the side of the ship, to allow the ratings to climb up or down, if they didn't like the idea of diving in, or jumping in, from the deck level, which was quite high. We were at Kilindini at various times up until 16 December 1943, anyway, I think it was around 10 December, but the date is really not so important. I was detailed on shark lookout watch. I was issued with an Enfield .303 rifle with five rounds of ammunition. That was OK as I had spent two years in the Home Guard before joining the Royal Navy. I was watching the swimmers, and also the players in a water polo match that was going on, so it was difficult to concentrate. All of a sudden I saw something in the water! 'SHARK, SHARK!' I shouted, and then the pandemonium set in. The chaps were all clambering on the netting, pushing each other back into the water and climbing over each other in panic. I just could not load the rifle through laughing so much!! The officer of the day then asked me where the shark was. I pointed to the object, and he looked at it through his binoculars and announced, 'It is a BOTTLE!!' He recommended me for being so observant!

When the crew found out it was only a bottle, I was chased round the ship for a bit, and also threatened to be thrown overboard! We left Kilindini on 27

December 1943 to return to the UK. Of course we did not know why, but it was in preparation of the coming D-Day.

Postcript

The first day we were welcomed aboard *Ramillies*, the chief reg petty officer, informed us to 'go ashore and buy a bucket, to survive on board.' This we did. Our section of two hundred ratings had to share just five washbasins and one shower between us! We shaved in them, bathed in them, did our washing in them, so we soon put our buckets to good use! There were thirty chaps in our mess, fifteen to each side of the mess table. There was no room to swing a cat, never mind room to sling our hammocks.

Bill McConnell: memories of his time on the *Ramillies* – Scapa Flow, May 1944

Bill was twenty-one, in charge of the gunnery control systems on the ship, and by this time had nine years of training, having gone to the Royal Hospital School in Greenwich as a boarder at the age of eleven years. He had been on Ramillies for a year and was returning from the Indian Ocean trip where they had been escorting convoys to India. He had his twenty-first birthday in Greenock in January 1944 but was too busy to go ashore. The ship then sailed to Scapa Flow.

Bill McConnell.

I was having breakfast in the electrical artificers' mess when there was a rap on the door and a young sailor who was in charge of the general equipment under the low power room told me that the glass fuses on the large distribution panel were nearly all blown. I knew that these were responsible for supplying the control systems for the 6in and 15in guns.

I left my breakfast and went down to the low-power room and to my horror saw that all the supply fuses were blown. I was standing there thinking, 'What the hell has gone on?' I searched and followed the cables from the supply panel through bulkheads and compartments and to where the tripod mast came through the ship to the lower deck. Here, the cables turned to go round the side of the tripod leg. This meant that the 12-volt and 24-volt supply for the radar, the gunnery system, the control room were going to be affected.

I also saw, wedged into the lead case cables, a metal spike and, surrounding it, hundreds of holes in the cable. Some idiot had brought a dartboard on board and they had played a dart tournament using the cables as a back drop for the dartboard, including the metal spike, which I guessed had held the board in place. I reported to the gunnery and electrical officers that the whole ship's electrical system was dead and they were horrified. I had to report that all of the low-power fuses were blown – the only good news was the compass electrical supply was not affected. We had to run temporary cables to get the power supply up.

Eventually, the decision was made to phone the local base staff in Scapa Flow and get the head of the electrical department to come aboard, who made the decision that the ship should make a high-speed return to Rosyth for repairs. We immediately got a full head of steam and sailed to Rosyth, and anchored just beyond the bridge, and there a team of electricians met us. They came out in a small boat, with cabling and junction boxes, and went straight to the job. The cables that were painted and stuck to the bulkhead had to be pried forward, and the damaged piece of each one had to be cut out. They put in junction boxes, and cut and joined up the cables. As always, the crew from the dockyard were marvellous and completed the job in thirty-six hours. We still had steam up and returned to Scapa Flow, because we knew the King was coming to inspect the ship. We tested the cables on the way back up to Scapa and all were in working order.

The official report said that the ship had to return to port for temporary repairs, and no mention was made of the dartboard incident.

This was just before we started practice runs to Ailsa Craig. Each Friday, for four weeks, we set off for Ailsa Craig to practise our gunnery, returning to port on Monday to take on more ammunition. The people from the Clyde came out waving and shouting to cheer us on, thinking we were on our way to the front. By the time we actually left for France, they had stopped taking notice, and we all thought we were just out on another gunnery practice run. However, on that last day we turned south, and the captain let us know that it was the real thing.

Problems with the 6in shell hoist

On return from Indian Ocean, and while moored in Greenock, we were doing some gunnery tests to ensure that all systems were working. I got a call saying there was a problem with a 6in shell hoist. A man had put his head into the shaft and had been crushed. The poor man's head and body were in the shaft, with just his legs hanging out. By his side there was a telephone used for communicating with the control room. Apparently, he had called down to get the hoist started, but had not got a reply and so had put his head in to shout down to them. The hoist came up and broke his neck and cut his throat. I had to remove a plate to allow the team to get access to the body – it was my bad luck it was an electrical panel, and so the job fell to me. The sailor's kit was auctioned off to provide for his widow. The sailors re-auctioned the kit again, so that the widow could get as much as possible. Since this happened while in dock, he was buried ashore. He was a leading seaman, aged twenty-one years.

After the D-Day invasion, the rifling on the guns had to be changed in all of the big guns, so she went into dock at Portsmouth. The dockyard bosses with bowler hats came on board with the ship's drawings. They met on the quarterdeck with the gunnery officers, and they said they would change all of the guns. A crew was sent on board to remove the plates on top of the turrets, and they were all off by the next morning. A train pulled up alongside the ship with the new 15in guns ready to be installed. They changed the guns, and the ship was ready to go in less than a week. The ship then sailed for Algiers. My next posting was with the cruiser HMS *Gambia*.

Sylvia Turner, wife of Bob Turner[42]

I met my dear husband Bob (Topsy, of course, as he was a Turner) at a St Valentine's dance at a hotel in Windsor, my home town, in February 1943. Bob lived not too far away, and was on a forty-eight-hour leave, as he was to travel to Scotland to begin an Asdic course at Dunoon. He had been in the Navy since August 1941, having decided this is what he wanted to do at an early age, and went along to the recruiting office at Reading. The recruiting officer was a Royal Marine colour sergeant who asked what he wanted to do, and Bob said, 'Join the Royal Navy, please, sir.' The sergeant replied, 'Don't Sir me, I am a colour sergeant; go to the pub down the road, have a pie and a pint, and when you come back to me you will be old enough.' Bob was sixteen years and eleven months old, and one month later his papers arrived, and off he went to Portsmouth, which was to be his home base.

Bob Turner at the start of his career in the Navy.

It was a six-week course in Dunoon, then another two weeks of leave, then off again to Scotland to pick up *Ramillies*. He always seemed to have to journey to Scotland, and although he was issued with a travel warrant, with train times, etc, in wartime, half the trains did not run, and I know that once, when he and some other chaps had to catch a train at King's Cross, there was no train, and they had to obtain a note to that effect and travel across to Euston and pick up a train there, as they were obviously going to be late back from leave.

Looking at some of the records that Bob kept, it appears that *Ramillies* set sail from Greenock on 3 August 1943, and arrived in Casablanca on 9 August, 1,936 miles. It was rough weather, and they were hove to. I seem to remember that because of this storm in the Med, when the ship was in harbour, some of the mooring ropes were snapping. Just before Bob had left, we had been to see that really good film *Casablanca*, and he worded his letter in a way that I knew where they were. Of course, the letters took weeks to arrive, so it would not have mattered had he mentioned Casablanca, but the letters were censored and he used to give his to the padre on board. Bob said that when he wanted a quiet moment, he would sit in the space set aside as the chapel, and in fact when the ship paid off, the padre, Mr Powell gave him a Bible, with a dedication, which we still have.

These following notes, I have recorded the whole journey to Freetown, Walvis Bay, Cape Town, Durban, Kilindini, Manza Bay, Aden, Suez, Port Said, Algiers, Gibraltar, Greenock, on 27 January 1944, a total of 2,213 miles … weather in Greenock, cold; sea, rough; a real contrast to those hot sunny days in the Indian ocean.

Bob said it was too hot to sleep below at night, so he used to get his head down on the cool deck, and look at the sky with its myriad of stars, which must have been wonderful, and a whole world away from what was going on elsewhere.

I believe *Ramillies* cut short her visit to Africa, to return for the South of France invasion to support the American landings and, of course, D-Day. When the ship came back to Portsmouth for re-ammunitioning, there was a twenty-four-hour leave, so a single ticket to Havant, change to the London train, get off at Staines, get a bus to the station, to my office at Old Windsor, back to my home for a meal, train at Windsor station to Waterloo, then 2am paper train to Pompey, back on board by 0800 hours. What one does for love – and it lasted for sixty-five years, I am happy to say.

Dave Scratton: World War Two recollections

My naval training was served in two main places, HMS *Collingwood*, a shore base near Portsmouth, and HMS *Victory* barracks at Portsmouth.

All my seatime was spent aboard *Ramillies*. Built, with others of her 'Clan', the 'R'-class, prior to and during World War I, she was intended for service in the Atlantic Ocean, and North Sea areas, not for the tropics where much of her time was spent in World War II: places like the African coast, Mediterranean Sea, and the Indian Ocean. Conditions below decks could be extremely hot once she was in these regions of operation.

New recruit Dave Scratton.

On entering the Navy, I had applied for physical training instructor (PTI), having just completed two years' training at Loughborough College. I was interviewed, and informed that there were so many 'sportsmen' being called up for service – particularly professional soccer players – that I would be called on if required, but that if I were sent to sea, then I would not be recalled from that duty.

Rank, as such, never was or ever has been of interest to me, and that is not meant in any way as lack of respect for commissioned ranks, though some officers were distinctly more capable and likeable than others. I was conscripted into the Navy, although I had choice of the three Services, and chose Navy, mainly because of my great love for the sea, and I hoped, an opportunity, if I survived long enough, to see distant countries of which I had read so much as a boy. I remained a seaman throughout the war, and have never regretted it. It has enabled me to mix with all types of people, and I am sure it gave me the determination not only to see the Navy period through, but to achieve something so worthwhile in Holland, and New Zealand.

A seaman's duties included just about everything, and he was a foc's'leman, topman or quarterdeckman, responsible for the successful working of that part of the ship. This could include watch duties around the clock, both at sea or in harbour.

Wartime duties included repainting the ship's camouflage from waterline to spotting top, and the four huge 15in gun turrets. These guns were capable of firing shells weighing approximately one ton, a distance of fifteen to twenty miles! Emergency procedures were carried out even to the extent of 'weighing' anchor by manpower alone, ie, not power-assisted.

In harbour there was time to paint the ship. While in Mombasa, about ten of us were busily engaged in painting the funnel when the engines started up

S M Gibson and Dave Scratton at HMS *Collingwood*.

Dave Scratton with a crew member and local at Durban in 1942.

– they had forgotten about us! Suddenly it was very much hotter, and extremely dirty, with all the soot unleashed!

Sleeping was done in hammocks, slung up above mess decks and almost any other vacant place, and taken down and stowed away each morning – they were no help to good posture!

On the ship was the British middleweight weight-lifting champion, who had a small group of enthusiasts training. I joined them and got my introduction to weight-training. I also played water polo and boxed for the ship, the latter unfortunately without any training since my days at Loughborough, and was up against professionals as well as amateurs.

Action stations – my station was near the bowels of the ship – the HATS – high-angle transmitting station, for the 4.7in twin-barrelled anti-aircraft guns. To reach the upper deck from there in an emergency necessitated scrambling up through overhead decks, through manholes just large enough to squeeze through. I think it would take 7–10 minutes to reach the upper deck, with all watertight doors closed at action stations. If the ship was seriously endangered, this escape system could be closed off, so speed would have been essential in getting out! While at action stations we slept on the steel deck and cushioned our heads on inflated lifebelts.

Shore leave was given wherever and whenever possible. Usually a weekend in duration when home in Britain, or for longer periods if the ship was recommissioning or under repair, as in dry dock at Durban, after our return from being torpedoed in Madagascar. I was one of a small group sent to a sugar-cane plantation at Empangeni, Zululand, for about ten days' leave – marvellous! On D-Day, 6 June 1944, I was on *Ramillies*, and spent the total time of ten days below decks. No one could imagine the noise of the huge 15in guns firing shells as big as a man. The shells had exploding heads also!

On the last voyage of *Ramillies* back to Portsmouth, I was given the honour of 'heaving the lead' from the anchor platform, to report the depth of water to the bridge. We as crew had learned that the ship was to be scrapped ... I was released from service on 9 January 1946. My last few days aboard *Ramillies* were spent as part of one of the ship's motorboat crews, working ship to shore and return – it was a pleasant way to 'Farewell' the Great Ship.

CHAPTER 10

Royal Marines on *Ramillies*

John Taylor

In January 1943, I was drafted back to RMB Eastney, and immediately drafted to join the detachment of Royal Marines, for HMS *Ramillies*, a battleship of the *Royal Sovereign* class, which was at that time in Devonport, Plymouth. My opposite number, the second boy bugler, was one B/Bugler Weston, a name I shall never forget. The total number of the detachment (to the best of my memory), was in the region of 150 (including officers and NCOs), the O/C, Captain T K West, 2nd I/C Lieutenant Darby, and Lieutenant Miles. The sergeant major (appt) was Colour Sgt

John Taylor.

A Moore, who was of a height of 6ft 7½in. Below decks he could not stand fully upright, so most of his off-duty time he spent on the upper deck. If he spent too much time below decks, he either ended with a semi-permanent stoop, or would suffer repeated headaches, through stretching upwards too soon. Naturally, he was given the nickname of 'Lofty'.

From experience (looking back at my service time), I would say that in the Services one always finds there are times when we find a number of things that displease us to varying degrees, and in due course we tend to look back and compare life aboard each ship we served in. For me, without doubt the happiest ship for me was my first, *Ramillies*. That is not to say that I did not enjoy my subsequent commissions, for that I most certainly did, but I thoroughly enjoyed the comradeship of the *Ramillies* commission most of all.

My first ship

We left Eastney Barracks in late January '43 to travel by rail to Plymouth, via Waterloo, not to join the ship immediately, though. We were to go for what was called pre-embarkation training at an RM training camp across the River Tamar, into Cornwall to Blarrick Camp, just south of the village of Antony. The training was to last for three months, but I was sent aboard the ship early in April as the ship's bugler had been taken into hospital and I had to fill the vacancy. I have no regrets about that, except that I was just getting used to the new company of this detachment, when I had to start again with a new set of Marines, and a new environment, *Ramillies* – it was very disconcerting. The problem was not insurmountable, and not as traumatic as I had thought it would be, but what an introduction to my new home.

The ship was in dockyard hands, undergoing a refit, following damage sustained in Diego Suarez harbour in Madagascar following the invasion of the island in 1942. For anyone that has not seen a ship in dockyard hands, well, there is only one expression that suitably describes it, and that is, 'utter chaos'. The dockyard mateys must have gloried in taking over what at all other times was a completely tidy and well-ordered ship and in no time at all turning it into what would appear to be a ship, or the remnants of one, but resembling a thoroughly disorganised scrap yard (with honours for the most untidy). It just had to be seen to be believed.

Amongst all of this, I, the 'new boy', had to learn all about the ship's routine from the then ship's company, and the new one when they came aboard several weeks later. I did manage to get the general idea of what was expected of me, and a reasonable idea of how the ship's routine worked.

It was on 15 June that we left Plymouth for who knows where, but some days before that, suddenly (one could say, almost overnight), the chaos disappeared, along with all the dockyard mateys, leaving each one of us asking ourselves, were we dreaming, did all that mess exist at all? Somehow, miraculously, it had all gone, and *Ramillies* began to take on the appearance of an RN ship, just like I had once seen in Portsmouth as a boy.

There was a lot of work to be done before we could even consider leaving Plymouth. The ship had to be cleaned from top to bottom, and stem to stern.

After the time in dockyard hands, around twelve months (give or take a little), the dockyard men bring their tools and equipment aboard to do their tasks, whatever they may be, but they also bring a lot of rubbish of their own, and when they leave the ship, they take their tools and equipment, but leave everything else, rubbish mostly, for the ship's company to clear up. Apart from that, the ship needs to be stored (food and clothing, 'slops' to the Navy). Naval stores, fuelled, and she would need ammunition, which is a major task, and after that long in dockyard hands, all the exterior paintwork washed down (and in some cases painted), and many other jobs as well, the nature of which now escapes me, and it all takes a deal of time. Somehow or other it was managed and eventually, we did sail on time in June, but don't ask me how, and we did not know where we were headed.

Two days later, when at 4am I took my duty watch on the bridge (a bugler's place of duty at sea), I learned we were entering the Firth of Clyde, and at about 7am we anchored at the Tail of the Bank, a name given to the point on the River Clyde where it turns into a southerly direction close to

Greenock. Also in that area, on the west and north coast respectively, lie Gourock and Helensburgh.

This was quite an experience for me, a definite first. The furthest I had ever travelled from my home until then was London in one direction, Bournemouth to the west, and the Isle of Wight to the south. Add to that I was only then sixteen years old, a mere village boy, and on a battleship in time of war. Then it was quite something, but at that time, I did not have time to dwell on matters like that, everything that was happening was occurring so quickly, that there were moments when I thought I was living in a dream. Somebody barking an order at me would very soon bring me out of the dream world, and this brought me back to reality.

This experience was such a change of lifestyle, so strange, and I could not believe it was happening. Now, looking back, it was the making of the whole experience and of me. I feel I owe so much to all those who steered me in the right direction; who helped guide me on the right course for the rest of my life, and I am so grateful to them all.

Returning to life aboard *Ramillies* – from our arrival at Greenock, the next few weeks were spent on what was known as working-up trials, which involved putting to sea on an almost daily basis, to enable the whole crew to exercise in the daily running of the ship, in the various roles and duties which might be expected of her, and of the ship's company in war, as well as her role as a fighting ship. Some of these exercises were seen by some of the crew to be pretty boring and repetitive, but later on in our service aboard we all realised just how necessary it was, and that it was designed to make each of us appreciate how much we would come to rely on one another for our mutual safety.

During this period we left the Clyde, and went north to Scapa Flow, from where we again put to sea daily, committed to a whole series of exercises including gunnery practice.

Now for anyone who has not experienced naval gunnery at close range, I assure you it is not something that you would volunteer to undergo. It is an experience, which to say is deafening is an extremely mild description, and in particular, when the main armament of 15in guns were fired. Only on a few occasion were broadsides fired (that is, all eight 15in guns at the same time) and, believe me, you would not want to hear it. Invariably, it was salvoes, one gun at a time, or one or two turrets together. Even with salvoes, the whole ship would shudder, so just try to imagine how it would feel if a broadside were fired.

Arthur Smith, PO/X 4250: A life on the ocean wave and beyond

On reaching twenty years of age, I joined the Royal Marines, on a twelve-year engagement. From my home in Coventry, I travelled to the recruiting office in Birmingham, and then to Queen Anne's Mansions in London to be sworn in and given the King's shilling. After passing a medical inspection, I, with the others present at that time, proceeded to Deal in Kent to enter the Royal Marine Barracks, to be formed into 361 Squad for training under Colour Sergeant H L Ball. One month after our arrival at Deal, war was declared with Germany on 3 September 1939.

My initial training covered a period of six months, ending on 13 February 1940, when I was transferred to the Royal Marine Barracks, Eastney, in Portsmouth, for naval gunnery training. This encompassed a further three months, thus making my total training period nine months in all. On 19 May 1940, I found myself posted to HMS *Peregrine*, an airfield just outside Portsmouth, to guard bomb dumps within barbed wire enclosures in the middle of the field. We slept in tents. When off-duty we were permitted to fly on practice flights. I found one of these in which I took part, a mock raid on Fratton Park, to be a thrilling experience.

On 7 September 1940, I was drafted to Alexandria in Egypt to join the ship's company of *Ramillies*. From October 1940 to January 1941 we cruised the Mediterranean, the period when the Italians entered the war. They reported us sunk on many occasions. They must have been mortified when we entered the Atlantic to take up convoy duties between England and Canada in January 1941.

On our first trip after leaving the sunny Med, the ice froze on the gun barrels to a depth of 6in and shortly before arrival in Halifax, Nova Scotia, the ship's side was damaged in collision with the underwater part of an iceberg. We then had to proceed to St John, New Brunswick, for repairs in dry dock and so we had a respite of a few days. We continued to escort convoys on the same route, taking about three weeks for each crossing, as we had to accommodate the slower vessels. This meant that *Ramillies* was to some extent a sitting duck. Fortunately, we had destroyers patrolling the perimeter of the convoys, the latter usually consisting of one hundred vessels.

In October 1941, the German battleship *Scharnhorst* was reported sailing out into the Atlantic, whereupon we were called upon to make chase. However, before we could make contact, she had slipped into Brest for refuge. Following that incident, we proceeded to Reykjavik where the Prime Minister Winston Churchill came on board to give us his congratulations for the part we played in the Atlantic.

From Iceland we proceeded to Birkenhead to undergo some minor repairs, giving us the opportunity of some more leave. Following upon this much-enjoyed period of leave, we found ourselves bound for South Africa, via Sierra Leone, where we anchored in Freetown. On arrival in Cape Town, we immediately learnt of some trouble in Madagascar, and soon received orders to proceed to that area. On the voyage, a Royal Marines' landing party was formed, and upon arrival at the island, we fired a couple of broadsides and sent them in. The landing party met little resistance so we moved on to Diego Suarez, where the governor came aboard. After this, while lying at anchor in the harbour, we were hit in the bows by a torpedo. Immediately we raised anchor and, laying all the anchor chains on the quarterdeck, steamed stern first all the way back to Durban and dry dock.

While the repairs were being carried out, the whole ship's company was granted a fortnight's leave. We were given the choice of being in the country or a town. A Coventry shipmate, Bill Buckley, and I spent this leave on an orange farm just outside Pietermaritzburg. It was a quiet, but well-earned, refreshing break. Upon our return to the ship, we moved out into the Indian Ocean, calling at Colombo and Trincomalee, Ceylon. This was the time of the fall of Singapore to the Japanese. The vessel now set off on our homeward journey via the Red Sea, the Suez Canal, Gibraltar, and the Bay of Biscay, arriving back in Portsmouth on 10 October 1942. Here, the ship was paid off, the commission having been completed, and having been posted to Portsmouth, I was given three weeks' leave during which I was married, on 24 October 1942.

Joseph Smart (19??– 2009), Royal Marine PO/X 110857, HMS *Ramillies* 1943–46

We sailed down the Clyde on the afternoon of 4 June 1944. There was nothing secretive about it as we, the Royal Marines, stood to attention on the quarterdeck, and the band played military marches. As we passed down the Clyde, our escort, a destroyer manned by a Norwegian crew, the *Svenner*, played 'Colonel Bogey' on their loudhailer, which brought smiles all round. Unfortunately, they were sunk by a German E-boat in an attack off the Normandy beaches with a great loss of life. The *Ramillies*, of course, was their target, and we were very fortunate to escape, but *Ramillies* was always considered a lucky ship.

At dawn on 6 June, we opened fire with a full salvo from our 15in guns as we supported the landings on Sword Beach. My action station was below, in the cordite handling room; it took four cordite charges to fire one 15in shell. We were in action and closed up for two days and only had emergency food of Ovaltine tablets and barley sugar! On the evening of the second day, the cooks managed to dish up some lentil soup – it tasted magnificent and was much appreciated. When there was a lull in the bombardment, my action station was on the top of 'X' turret as crew of the four-barrelled pom-pom.

After three weeks of sporadic bombardment, we had emptied all our main armament magazines, some 250 tons of shells from each gun, so 1,000 tons in all (a 15in shell weighs one ton). We returned to Portsmouth where the dockyard mateys replaced all our 15in gun barrels. The ship's company had been given two days' leave meanwhile, and when we returned we were off to the South of France to support the American landings.

This was rather an anti-climax, as we only fired two salvos with our main armament at a German gun battery and they surrendered!

Above and right: Two photographs showing Royal Marines manning 20mm Oerlikon guns installed in protective tubs.

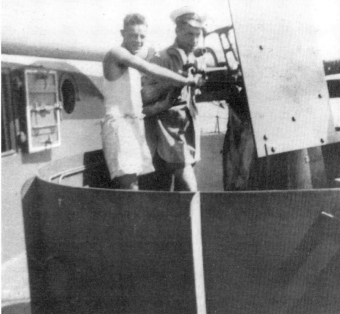

Photo Gallery: World War II

Crossing the Line ceremony on 13 December 1939.

Above: Larking about in the pool rigged on the quarterdeck.

Right: Someone getting a ducking.

Right: King Neptune and Queen Amphitrite!

Below: Having a shave whether you like it or not.

Left: The pulling power of a British battleship. Crowds waiting to board *Ramillies* in Wellington, New Zealand, January 1940.

Both photographs were captioned 'Mountaineering in the North Atlantic March 1941'.

Ramillies in dry dock at St John, New Brunswick, in March 1941.

Left: Reeving new signal halyards.

Below left: The rear of the fighting top viewed from the starfish on the mainmast.

Below right: looking over the forward 15in turrets and forecastle.

Ramillies at speed in this early war photograph. Note the unusual camouflage scheme.

The governor of Madagascar being welcomed aboard ship in 1942.

Two Jack Kettle drawings depicting aspects of life on board *Ramillies*.

The quarterdeck with 'Y' turret trained on the starboard beam.

Ramillies in Sydney Harbour in January 1940.

Astern of a County-class cruiser, *Ramillies* hoisting in a paravane.

Three Royal Marines posing by a cutter on the boat deck.

Ramillies about to enter French Bay, Diego Suarez, Madagascar, flying the flag of a rear admiral.

Passing through the Suez Canal.

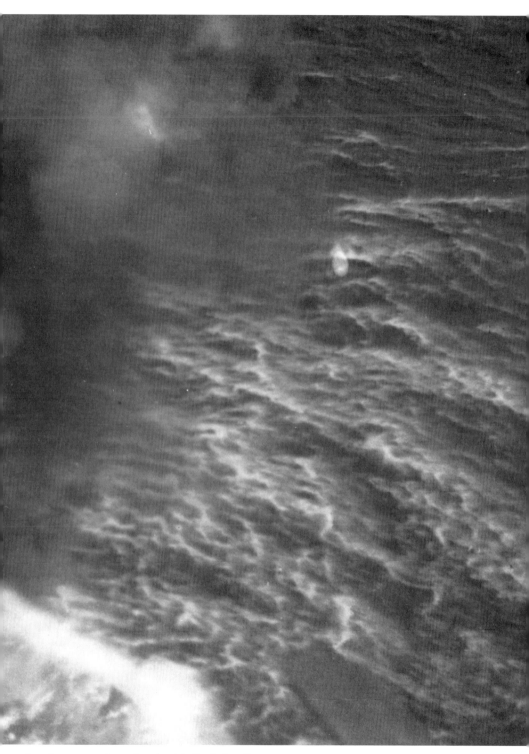

A main armament practice shoot in the Indian Ocean.

An early war photograph of *Ramillies* lying off Reykjavik.

Below: *Ramillies* in her final configuration. Note that she is flying battle ensigns.

Ramillies in disruptive camouflage in 1941. (Imperial War Museum)

Ramillies photographed in 1943. (Imperial War Museum)

Ramillies photographed in 1943. (Imperial War Museum)

Ramillies photographed in 1943. (Imperial War Museum)

CHAPTER 11

The Home Front

Mina Bennett, wife of Bob Bennett[43]

I was on an outing with my mother and we were the last to be picked up; there were only two seats left, and they were either side of the aisle. After we stopped for a coffee break, I went back to my seat and found a woman sitting in my seat nattering away to mum … I stood there waiting, but was stopping other people from getting onto the coach. The lady then said, 'Go and sit in my seat at the back of the bus,' so off I went and found the seat; there was my future husband, and we have seen each other every day since.

Mina Bennett.

He is so interested in the *Ramillies* as he had such fantastic friends. He was a stoker, and the two people that he mainly worked with he was very friendly with and kept in touch with them after. Unfortunately, they have both passed away now, but he has such good memories of them; he was the youngest, and the older of the three of them was the manager of the Co-op. He took my husband under his wing, so to speak, and he always respected him for it … I suppose if you come from a family of eight children you don't get that personal attention, but in the Navy he got it from these other two gentlemen, and it made him, I think. When he talks about the Navy, it's always these two chaps he is talking about.

When I was about seventeen I started wondering about what to do, as you would not get papers to call you up, and my father was in the Navy in the First World War, and I said that I would not mind going into the Wrens; my father said, 'No, you don't.'

I had always been very fond of animals, so eventually joined the Land Army, milking and general farming. It toughened me up. There were four of us girls, three from one farm, and one from the other. Not very comfortable billets, [but] there was a cottage on the farm with two up and two down, no running water, and outside toilet. We asked the farmer if we could take this over and he agreed and the powers that be provided us with camp beds, sheets and blankets, and we slept two in a bedroom. Heating was a fireplace with a side oven. For water, there was a pump in the field opposite, which was not drinkable, so every day we used to get a churn of water up from the farm, and we managed with that and cooked on the fire. We found old bits of furniture, and my parents provided us with a table, and we carried on and looked after ourselves. It made you appreciate things more.

We all had a pushbike each. In the summer it was Double Summer Time[44] and we had to work 6am till 11pm. When it was dark nights we used to ride from village to village on our bikes to dances. At the time there were Italian POW camps, and there was an American camp nearby. The POWs were allowed out to the dances, but if the Americans saw you dancing with an Italian, they would start fights. They were always causing trouble. We enjoyed it, though.

I come along with Bob to the Association meetings for the camaraderie. Everyone is so friendly. I sit and listen to everybody, listen to the men reminiscing. It's important to support Bob, as it was the most important time of his life. As I said, he came from a large family, but met real friends there on board the ship.

Anne Mycock, wife of Ernie Mycock[45]

I met him in the October, and two days before I was sixteen, he went in the Navy, and gave me this ring and he wrote to me from the *Ramillies* to ask me to get engaged. I was then about seventeen, and I said yes. He asked me to wear this ring as an engagement ring until he came home. We got married in 1947 and we had been married sixty-two years before he died. He has now been dead two years.

Anne Mycock.

My husband was the radar man. It wasn't hard him being away; because I loved him, I was true to him, I went dancing because I really loved dancing, but he was my only boyfriend. My mother was always reminding me, 'Only looking, as you have got him.' I never [had anyone] to bring me home or anything, I always used to go with the girls, that was it. When he came home he never liked dancing, so we never went again. We had two children, Margaret and Graham. Both have been good to me and seen me fair enough. Ernest had Parkinson's and osteoporosis, but for all he was like that, you talked to him about the Navy, and he remembered every little bit, and he remembered being on the *Petard*.

That was his story, he was on the *Petard* when it sank the German submarine, and three jumped off the ship, a galley boy, lieutenant and sailor, and went to board the submarine before it sank. They got there, but it was only the boy came back, the others got sucked in the tower. That was probably the best story that he told me.

He never told me much of what went on onboard the *Ramillies*. He did tell me about going to New Zealand. He told me about the *piupiu* skirt and things like that. It was very important for him to be part of the Association, and he had a full naval funeral. Standard bearers walked him in, it was really nice, and when he was going, they played 'Anchors Away'.

He was not from Portsmouth – he was from Compstall, Marplebridge, in the Stockport area. That was his wish to have his funeral there. He is now resting in St Paul's garden of remembrance, in the church near us where he was a choirboy, and where the children have been christened. He is near at hand, and we would have been married sixty-four years this 26 April. I will be eighty-five then. There will never be another man like him.

He pinched my hat when I first met him. He was in the ATC, and was a sergeant; he had been to a boxing match, and his coach pulled up in front of our cinema and I was going past the coach as he was getting off. I was wearing a white beret with Air Force wings, and he pinched it from my head and ran off with it … he ran all the way down to the station, and when I caught him up I said, 'Just for your cheek, you can walk me back,' and he did, and that was it from there on. My mum warned me off, saying he was too old for me, but he was eighteen in the September and I was sixteen in the April. He was a handsome guy.

Iris Bennison, wife of Jack Bennison[46]

Jack, my late husband, was a Royal Marine who loaded the guns on *Ramillies*; he was never harmed on *Ramillies*. He never talked about it very much at first and all this has come out since 1990, when people began to take an interest in what *Ramillies* did, when Eric and Dorothy Marks started it (the *Ramillies* Association). We joined and we all related to each other, what each had done, and that's how all this has come about which is lovely. I lost him in 2003.

Iris Bennison.

He was going to go onto the *Ark Royal* when *Ramillies* was decommissioned [but] he had got tinnitus through the guns going off, so they had to discharge him. He came out in 1946 and got a job in Hull where I met him.

The Association was very important to him – he loved it, loved coming to see everyone and that's why I keep on coming.

My own experience was that we spent most nights in the shelters (as a civilian in Hull) because of the air raids, and you would get three or four alerts during the night, but

Royal Marine Jack Bennison on board *Ramillies* in 1943.

we all still went to work at the right time during the day, buses were never late, and whatever was left of the city we tried to carry on … I worked in a large department store which was bombed out twice, and we moved to brand new premises, but we still traded. Like lots of things, you just accepted it and lived your life on. You never thought of folk getting killed. If you were in the pictures it would come on the screen, 'There is an air-raid warning,' and you were free to go, but if you went out and the guns were firing and the shrapnel, you could be killed, so I always used to stay in the cinemas. See, it never stopped us going to the cinemas!

Our house was damaged, but it wasn't ever bombed out, and bit by bit it was put back together again. I am thankful, because if it had been another fifty yards nearer to our house I would not be here. We were not in the shelter, it was early on, and we used to just go under the stairs, but later on when the doodlebugs came over, we only had a few, not like London. Then, of course, we dashed to the shelters. They had put some on the roads at the bottom of our street, because there was a big wide verge with trees, and there was room for all these shelters to go, so we all piled in there.

There is a Royal Marine in my life and a ship, and I am at the end, but I don't mind; it was lovely, and I think a lot about the *Ramillies*.

CHAPTER 12

Heroes Return: Normandy Revisited

Mick French

In 2005, the HMS *Ramillies* Association visited Normandy, the scene of battleship *Ramillies'* second-last action.

It was suggested at our 2003 Annual General Meeting that Association members should take part in the government-sponsored 'Heroes Return' programme, which enabled veterans of HM Armed Forces to return to one of the theatres of war in which they were involved, sponsored by government grant. It was decided more or less immediately that we should return to Normandy, where *Ramillies* took part in what would be one of her last actions.

The Pegasus Bridge which was raised as we visited the Café Gondrée.

Our trip was organised by our then Vice Chairman Bernard Mallion. Normandy had been chosen, because most of the members had been aboard *Ramillies* during the D-Day Normandy landings. After months of preparation, we came by coach from all parts of Britain to meet up at Dover. Literally hundreds of coaches from different veteran groups arrived, unloading their passengers, who were then organised on to other coaches according to their destinations, either the First World War or Second World War battle-fields.

Our coach, with fourteen of our members, proceeded to Folkestone, where we boarded a cross-channel train. On arrival in France, we had a five-hour journey to our hotel in Ouistreham, arriving there at 1930 hours. After an early

Association members John Taylor, Norman Burns, Vic Stamp and Alf Booker outside the Café Gondrée.

continental-style breakfast, our party turned out smartly with medals highly polished. Our coach was waiting to take us on the first of our many journeys throughout that week, which was to Pegasus Bridge, over the River Orne and the strategic Caen Canal where the first airborne landings were made by Major John Howard and the 6th Airborne Division at night in a flooded area with pinpoint accuracy. The original lifting

Jerusalem Cemetery.

bridge has been preserved and re-sited in a nearby museum, being replaced by a modern but very similar design. Hard to think that such a tranquil area was the scene of some very fierce fighting. The bridge is named after the shoulder flashes that the British airborne troops wear, a winged horse.

While visiting, we were lucky to see the bridge lifting to allow a yacht through on its way to Caen. Two of our members got stranded on the opposite bank, causing our tour guide some consternation. We made the most of the Café Gondrée which is also a souvenir shop owned by Mme Arlette Gondrée, who was a young girl at the time of the raid and whose family owned the same house – the first to be liberated on D-Day.

We then made the short journey to Ranville Cemetery, located next to a beautiful church. Here, many of the British fallen lie in beautifully laid-out, well-maintained peaceful surroundings. Every alternate grave seems to have a rose planted, so that each grave has the shadow of an English rose, signifying the flower of English youth. Everything so well-kept, and clean, and cared for. Returning to our hotel for our evening meal and sitting down to enjoying a 'sod's opera'[47] of sorts, a young German guest sent a bottle of champagne to our table with his congratulations. Of course, we wasted no time in toasting him!

On the following day we went to the Merville Battery, high above the town of Ouistreham overlooking Gold Beach and harbour. This gun battery was similar to the one a few miles away at Benerville that was a target for our 15in gunners aboard *Ramillies*, who knocked it out on D-Day. With each shell weighing a ton, there is not much that could stand up to the

The Cross of Sacrifice, Bayeux Cemetery.

pounding of a few broadsides! Looking at the damage caused by various means at Merville, one cannot imagine being on the receiving end of one of those massive shells. We then headed for Arromanches, with its reminders of the battle, the huge concrete caissons that had broken adrift in a storm on D-Day +3. Some are still there after sixty-five years and will act as a reminder for many more years to come. We then went to the D-Day Museum, which depicts scenes of that fateful day and the events that took place after. I had to search the exhibits before finding the *Ramillies* on a big photograph on the back wall. Her outline is very distinctive, but the amount of smoke from her funnel confirmed that this was indeed our *Rammy*! Again, our party was treated with great respect, with handshakes and welcomes offered from all ages and nationalities.

We then visited the area where the Pipeline Under The Ocean (PLUTO) came ashore. The pipeline was laid from Fawley to the Isle of Wight and then across the English Channel, a distance of almost three hundred miles to Port-en-Bessin. All along this stretch of coastline, we could not help but notice the amount of fortifications that were still there.

At Sainte-Mère-Eglise, we visited the museum and saw photographs of the devastated narrow streets in comparison to the present day; one wonders how they could have brought the little town back to as it was before the ravages of battle. Everywhere we went, there were Union Jacks hanging from the upper windows of houses as well as public buildings. Our party was touched by seeing the word *merci* everywhere, realising that it was not just for us, but for the thousands who had come back to visit the Normandy battlefields.

A visit was made to Jerusalem Cemetery, the smallest British cemetery in Normandy, and indeed the smallest cemetery of World War Two, containing just forty-nine graves, of which forty-seven are British, one Czech, and one unknown. It is so quiet and peaceful here. It is next to a group of farm buildings used as a field dressing station during the campaign. Of the soldiers laid to rest here, two are chaplains, and one soldier is just sixteen years of age. After the war, when the Commonwealth War Graves Commission wanted to move the fallen to a larger cemetery, the owner of the land said, 'They died here defending my land and my country. They have earned the right to lie in peace, and I gratefully give up this small area of land to enable them to stay here.' Such was the feelings involved that the small area in a little copse was indeed turned into an official war grave. Our party were visibly moved to see this tiny British outpost.

Back at the hotel, we were studying the evening menu, which had been roughly translated for us, the most popular translation being 'pig in sauce'. It tasted better than it sounded! During this meal we discovered that one of our party, Vic Stamp, was celebrating his eighty-sixth birthday so, needing no further excuse, we burst into a rendition of 'Happy Birthday to You'. This in turn led to a bit of a 'sod's opera' (general singsong for the uninitiated), led by our own 'Booker boys', Alf Booker and his shipmate Norman Burns. Some of the other guests of various nationalities joined in where they could. Norman was persuaded to tell a few of his jokes, and as he got well into his stride, his dear wife, Bronwen, not only glared at him, but also at me for egging him on in the first place, not that he needed it, mind! It was all in good fun, and we all thoroughly enjoyed it, at least I think the other guests did! On the

Glass sculpture with *Ramillies* depiction, British Garden of Remembrance, Mémorial de Caen.

following day, we visited Utah Beach where the American invasion forces had it comparatively easy compared to their countrymen on Omaha Beach.

Other places to be visited were Bayeux, with its distinct cathedral spire which somehow survived the bombardment, although the town suffered appalling damage. Bayeux is the largest Second World War cemetery of Commonwealth soldiers in France, containing almost 4,700 graves. This beautiful cemetery contains the Cross of Sacrifice, sometimes known as the War Cross; also in these grounds are some 360 German graves. The grounds were given for all time to the United Kingdom, in recognition of the sacrifices made by this country during the defence and liberation of France in the Second World War. Opposite the hallowed burial ground is the Bayeux memorial, which remembers and honours almost two thousand casualties of the Commonwealth forces who died in Normandy and have no known grave. There were a number of visits to other wartime sites, where significant battles or other incidents took place during the battle for Normandy, one common denominator being that the German armies always commanded the high ground, which gave them a great advantage over anything happening below

While most of our members went on a morning visit elsewhere, four of us decided we would like to visit Caen, to see the Mémorial de Caen, the Museum of Peace. We hired a taxi to take us from our hotel and for the return journey. Upon arrival we noted how impressive the building looked. It had been opened on 6 June 1988, the forty-fourth anniversary of D-Day, and so was still being added to. The museum itself is dedicated to all conflicts, but a great deal to Normandy in the Second World War. Our main interest was to find the British Garden, but we decided to have a quick look around, although being very short of time.

The American Garden, with its beautiful small lake and waterfall, with its arched wall of remembrance, was most impressive, and like so many of these memorials throughout Normandy, so wonderfully peaceful.

The Canadian Garden was much less ostentatious, with simple inscriptions, but even so instilled a lump in one's throat. Eventually we found the British Garden, with its pergola covered in roses, as yet not in bloom, but we could imagine the scent and the blaze of colour when the season was in full swing. There, at last, we found what we were looking for. A magnificent solid glass edifice, that stood a good 6ft high, and depicting various stages of the war. One of the etched and coloured items was the depiction of *Ramillies*, easily distinguished by the great plume of smoke from her funnel.

Our time was almost up, and as we made our way to the outside of the building, we saw that our taxi awaited us, ready to take us back to the hotel where we were to join up with the rest of our party for the afternoon tour. This was to the village of Villers-Bocage, the scene of a mighty tank battle led by German tank ace Michael Wittmann, which took place on 12 June against a British armoured division. Although this was nothing to do with anything naval, the story registered with our crew, who understood the ferocity of some of the land-based battles of the Normandy invasion. Our coach actually stopped on the crossroads where Wittmann's tank made its appearance with such devastating effect. As with other battle locations, you would never know what had happened here, at this very spot, as today it is so peaceful and serene.

Another coach trip took us to Pointe du Hoc, between the American Utah and Omaha Beaches. This was a 100ft sheer cliff-face that had to be climbed by the men of the US Ranger Battalion to disable the enemy casemates. The whole area has been preserved as a memorial to the Rangers. The blown-up casemates are still there. The most abiding memory for me was the size of the craters. Perhaps some of them were made by naval bombardment.

The road leading inland from the Pointe du Hoc is called Victory Road, and has names of the fallen on each quarter-mile post. The most poignant visit was made the following day. This was to the American cemetery at Colleville-sur-Mer. Our coach turned into a huge car park and we disembarked and followed the signs directing us to the vantage platform overlooking Omaha Beach.

There is much more vegetation now than in 1944, but one can observe the length of the battlefront and imagine the sound of machine-gun fire, and explosions going on below ... American troops coming ashore only to be mown down by the incessant hail of fire. The only cover was the anti-tank traps laid all over the beach, offering very little protection.

We followed the signs taking us across the top of the cliffs, to begin a very short gentle climb through pine trees. Opening up in front of us was the most awe-inspiring sight I have ever seen. Row upon row of white headstones stretching in straight lines almost as far as the eye can see. A lump came to my throat, a reaction that surely must affect those who come upon this awesome sight. Avenue after avenue, all facing in the same direction, some say for those interred that they are 'facing home'. You look at some of the inscriptions; 'Aged 18', 'Aged 20' – side by side are the two Nyland brothers, together forever. We walk among them; they are from all over the United States, resting here in peace, having given their lives for a country they did not know.

There are some nine thousand-plus graves here. A good many of those buried here had fallen on the first day. Gardeners are everywhere, keeping the grounds in a good condition, sowing new lawns, weeding, litter-picking. We saw in the distance, beyond a long memorial lake, a building with a gigantic statue and slowly headed toward it, past the Memorial Chapel with its ornate ceiling. The statue is made of bronze and stands some 35ft high. It is named the Spirit of American Youth

Looking at the faces of our Association members, I could see by their expressions that they had similar feelings to myself, amazed at the sheer number of graves and awed at the peacefulness and serenity of the area. Whatever our feelings, we realised once again how lovingly the whole cemetery area was maintained. Throughout the whole time we were there, many people came up to our party and engaged them in conversation. People of all ages, some in uniform. One very old gentleman wearing a Glengarry with a broad Scottish accent, others with medals gleaming, all taking a great interest in why we were here, I felt so proud and very humble to be in the presence of these men, who knows what horrors they had been through, and

A knocked-out gun emplacement at Omaha Beach.

to be in that beautiful place, to see for myself some of the sacrifices of our American Allies.

Beyond the statue is yet another breathtaking scene, the memorial known as the Wall of the Missing, set in a semi-circle in lovingly tended gardens. Mounted on the walls and covering a huge area are plaques that contain the names of some 1,500 missing men. It is now a place of peace and tranquillity and a fitting reminder to future generations of the sacrifices that were made by those who fought and lost their lives here.

Our final trip was to the area known as the Falaise Pocket. We started off in our coach to the high point of the area, Mont Ormel. In this area, which has a magnificent all-round view, fierce and bloody battles were fought against the Germans by Polish troops. Here there is a Polish Museum, tucked into the hillside with preserved vehicles, including a Polish tank, on display. Although heavily outnumbered and practically under siege from sustained attacks, the Polish troops held most of their positions until relieved some days later by Canadian troops. The German Panzer Division had forced their way through a small gap, their only way of escape from Normandy.

We boarded the coach once more, travelling down the mountainside past a preserved German 'Tiger' tank on route. As we got near the tiny village of Coudehard near Falaise, the approach lanes were so narrow our coach barely managed to pass through. As we slowly walked along the narrow lane, with its typical Normandy *bocage* hedges, the bushes seemed to be bearing blood-red berries. Our tour guide was trying to tell us of the sheer carnage that had taken place here all those years ago. The fleeing German army was literally being slaughtered in this tiny little village, which has largely remained unchanged all these years. We could see for ourselves some of the damage that had been inflicted on the few buildings that were here. The church tower, which had housed a German sniper, was badly marked by small-arms gunfire. The damage to some of the buildings could also be seen, as were the repairs that had been made to replace sections that had been blown away. The village was the scene of some very bitter fighting. It was while wandering around that we heard shouting in no uncertain terms. We looked around, and there was this little old lady, hobbling down a steep earthen path from her home, waving and gesticulating with one of her two walking sticks in our direction. We walked toward her to find she was shouting '*Merci, merci*,' and wanted to say thank you to our menfolk for liberating her and her country from the hardships they had suffered. She cuddled each of our men in turn giving them each a kiss. We had tears in our eyes, I can tell you! We found out later, she was well into her nineties, and made the effort to greet all veterans who visited the area.

The next morning we once again set off on our long journey home. Knowing that we would not find much to eat at the roadside café this particular tour operator used, we had stocked up with rations from our meagre breakfast, such as bread, ham, and yoghurt, some even managing to get hold of a boiled egg!

Vic Stamp, Norman Burns, Gordon Jenks and John Taylor
with the French lady who came forward to thank them.

Our memories of this trip, good and bad, sad and happy, have stayed in our minds, and we still often talk about it at our reunions. I for one am so glad I did it with our members, as it was a completely different experience being with them than it had been for me on a previous visit. I do think some of today's youth should be encouraged to make this trip to see for themselves what world war brings, in the hope that it instils in their minds that it must *never* happen again. *We will remember them.*

The *Ramillies* Sculpture

Clydebank artist Tom McKendrick had the idea of commemorating William Beardmore's shipyard at Dalmuir, where *Ramillies* was built between 1914 and 1917, by creating a sculpture of the ship.

On 9 September 2010, HMS *Ramillies* Association members visited the site to witness the provost of West Dunbartonshire council, Dennis Agnew, formally unveiling the sculpture. Of his work Tom McKendrick says, 'I was intrigued by a vision that has few parallels and many contradictions. An object to be feared, admired and perhaps even loved, and a ship that became the ultimate reality of our island's close relationship with the sea. The *Ramillies* with ease meets all of these descriptions as any acquainted with her history will know.'

The sculpture's base is constructed using components familiar to the shipbuilder and unseen by most. An inverted full-scale 'aft section frame' above the tip of the rudder forms the main arc. Within this arc, the shipbuilding components of 'camber', 'sheer' and 'frame spacing' are referenced. Heavy and robustly designed brackets that were used to support armoured decks are integrated into the tracery that forms the base, along with gently curved frames and a section of double bottom plating. Supported on four pillars high above is the interpretation of the *Ramillies*, launched from Beardmore's Dalmuir yard in 1916. The interpretation of the battleship addresses the 'distortions of the builder,' where working on an object of this scale introduces unusual perspectives. Towering above and viewed from below, the ship is elevated high on its stocks, held aloft as a monument to skill and endeavour. The great ship is a symbol of pride and purpose.

The sculpture is built from sheet steel and is approximately 11m wide by 11m high. The *Ramillies* is just over 6m long.

The *Ramillies* sculpture.

Notes

[1] Captain (later Admiral Sir) Edmund Percy Fenwick George Grant, KCVO, CB (1867–1952).

[2] Commander (later Vice Admiral) Charles Wolfran Round-Turner, CB, CMG (1879–1953).

[3] There were twelve old pennies or pence (d) to the shilling and twenty shillings (s) to the pound (£), thus one shilling is equal to 5p.

[4] Admiral Sir Frederic Wake-Walker, CB, CBE (1888–1945).

[5] Captain Geoffrey Meredyth Keble Keble-White (1895–1961).

[6] Commander (later Rear Admiral) George Verner Motley Dolphin, CB, DSO (1902–1979).

[7] Chaplain.

[8] *The Cruel Sea* (1951), by Nicholas Monsarrat, was a novel based on the events of the Second World War naval Battle of the Atlantic, also released in a film version (1953).

[9] 32°C.

[10] Captain (later Admiral) Gervase Boswell Middleton, CBE, CB (1893–1961).

[11] Clothes washing, from the Indian word *dhobi* (person who does laundry).

[12] Salvation Army club for service personnel.

[13] Now known as Maputo.

[14] *The Lost Weekend* (1944), novel by Charles R Jackson, and film (1945) of the same name, about an alcoholic binge-drinker.

[15] Drink of neat rum.

[16] Military police.

[17] Policemen.

[18] Dark blue raincoat.

[19] Commander (later Captain) Alan Fitzroy Campbell, OBE (1903–1956).

[20] Sick berth attendant – from 'tiffy' for 'artificer'.

[21] The following diary was written for members of the HMS *Ramillies* Association in 1994. Ken Williams called the piece 'Some Answers to "What's the Buzz, Bunts?", A Bunting's Sojourn in a Happy Ship'. Signalmen were referred to as 'Bunts' because of their association with flags and thus the term bunting.

[22] Captain (later Vice Admiral) Harold T Baillie-Grohman, CB, DSO, OBE (1888–1978).

[23] Captain (later Vice Admiral) Arthur Duncan Read, CB (1889–1976).

[24] Based on an interview held in the Royal Naval Club, Portsmouth, during the annual meeting of the *Ramillies* Association in April 2011.

[25] Slang for shilling.

[26] Navy, Army, and Air Force Institutes.

[27] Based on an interview held in the Royal Naval Club, Portsmouth, during the annual meeting of the *Ramillies* Association in April 2011.

[28] Transcribed and reproduced courtesy of Allana Bailey, granddaughter of George Louden, *WW2: People's War*.

[29] Based on an interview held in the Royal Naval Club, Portsmouth, during the annual meeting of the *Ramillies* Association in April 2011.

[30] Present-day Namibia.

[31] Sustain any damage.

[32] Based on an interview held in the Royal Naval Club, Portsmouth, during the annual meeting of the *Ramillies* Association in April 2011.

[33] Based on an interview held in the Royal Naval Club, Portsmouth, during the annual meeting of the *Ramillies* Association in April 2011.

[34] Based on an interview held in the Royal Naval Club, Portsmouth, during the annual meeting of the *Ramillies* Association in April 2011.

[35] 1cwt (hundredweight) is 112lbs, or 8 stone (around 45kg).

[36] Just under 60kg.

[37] 130°F, equivalent to 54°C.

[38] Punishment cells.

[39] Based on an interview held in the Royal Naval Club, Portsmouth, during the annual meeting of the *Ramillies* Association in April 2011.

[40] One pound weight (lb) is equal to 0.45kg.

[41] One gallon is approximately 4.5 litres. There are 8 imperial pints to an imperial gallon.

[42] Based on an interview held in the Royal Naval Club, Portsmouth, during the annual meeting of the *Ramillies* Association in April 2011.

[43] Based on an interview held in the Royal Naval Club, Portsmouth, during the annual meeting of the *Ramillies* Association in April 2011.

[44] GMT+2; ie, the clock time was two hours ahead of Greenwich Mean Time.

[45] Based on an interview held in the Royal Naval Club, Portsmouth, during the annual meeting of the *Ramillies* Association in April 2011.

[46] Based on an interview held in the Royal Naval Club, Portsmouth, during the annual meeting of the *Ramillies* Association in April 2011. Iris passed away in June 2011.

[47] Ship's concert or sing-song, after Ship's Opera and Dramatic Society, known as SODS.

Index

HMS *Ramillies*: Vital Statistics

1917

Length: 620.5ft
Beam: 101.5ft (bulged)
Draught: 33ft 7ins deep
Displacement: 33,570 tons deep
Armament: 8 x 15in; 14 x 6in; 2 x 3in AA; 4 x 3pdr;
   5 machine guns; 10 Lewis guns; 4 x 21in torpedo tubes
Armour: belt 13in; turrets 13in; decks 1–4in
Machinery: turbines driving 4 screws; 40,000shp for 23 knots;
   18 Babcock & Wilcox oil-fired boilers
Complement: 936
Cost: £3,295,810

From: R A Burt, *British Battleships of World War One*, Seaforth Publishing 2012

1945

Length: 620.5ft
Beam: 102.5ft
Draught: 33ft 7in deep
Displacement: 35,385 tons deep
Armament: 8 x 15in; 8 x 6in; 8 x 4in twin AA; 24 x 2pdr AA;
   23 x 20mm AA
Armour: belt 13in; turrets 13in; decks 1–4in
Machinery: turbines driving 4 screws; 40,000shp for 21 knots

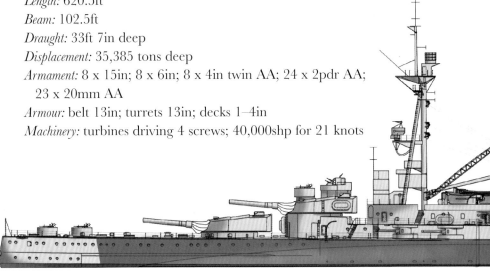